Morningstar

Morningstar

Growing Up with Books

ANN HOOD

W. W. NORTON & COMPANY

Independent Publishers Since 1923

New York | London

For information about permission to reproduce selections from this
book, write to Permissions, W. W. Norton & Company, Inc.,
500 Fifth Avenue, New York, NY 10110

For information about special discounts for bulk purchases, please
contact W. W. Norton Special Sales at specialsales@wwnorton.com or
800-233-4830

Manufacturing by Quad Graphics Fairfield
Book design by Chris Welch
Production manager: Lauren Abbate

ISBN: 978-0-393-25481-5

W. W. Norton & Company, Inc.
500 Fifth Avenue, New York, N.Y. 10110
www.wwnorton.com

W. W. Norton & Company Ltd.
15 Carlisle Street, London W1D 3BS

1 2 3 4 5 6 7 8 9 0

This book is for all the giants whose shoulders I stand on—

With thanks for letting me see farther

Contents

Morningstar

Introduction

WHEN I WAS FOUR YEARS OLD, FOR REASONS NO ONE in my family could explain, I picked up my older brother Skip's reading book and I read it. This was in 1959 or 1960, but I can still remember staring at that page and reading the words *Look! Look!* In that instant, all of my cells seemed to settle into place and I had one thought: *I want to live inside a book.*

I did not grow up in a family that owned books. My great-grandparents had immigrated from Italy in the late 1800s as part of the large exodus of southern Italian farm laborers who, burdened by heavy taxes, low pay, and harsh living conditions, came to the United States to work in the mills for higher wages and security. Their daughter, my grandmother Mama Rose, left school in third grade for a job in the big textile mill that loomed over the neighborhood. She never learned to read or write, except for her slow, careful, seemingly painful signature. Of her ten children, their education interrupted by the death of their father and the start of World War II, only three graduated from high school. The girls all went to work in various factories—making artificial flowers or luggage or soap; the boys became barbers or mechanics. Reading was not something for which they had time or inclination.

My father, a small-town Indiana boy from a family of nine, dropped out of high school to join the navy and see the world. He had a love for cheap paperbacks that he read at sea, Zane Grey and James Cain. But I never saw him read a book at home. In fact, I never saw *anyone* read a book at home.

Yet I did grow up with stories, stories told around the kitchen table on Saturday afternoons or after dinner during the week. Aunts and uncles, great-aunts and -uncles, cousins and second cousins and cousins twice removed, relatives with confusing family ties, all sat and drank black coffee and talked into the night. I learned early that you had to earn your place at that table. Your story had to start with a hook, include vivid details, have strong characters, and be full of tension or someone who talked louder and could tell her story better would overpower you. Truman Capote said that he learned how to write a story not from reading but from sitting on his aunts' front porch in Alabama and listening to them tell stories. This was my earliest education in the art of storytelling too.

But I yearned for another kind of story, the kind I found in books. When I was very young, each village in our town had its own library. These villages had all evolved around mills, and they had their own ethnic population: the French-Canadians and Irish and Italian and Portuguese and Polish, each a chapter in our town's own immigrant history. The Italians lived in Natick, and the Natick Library sat in a basement on a sad dead-end street on the banks of the Pawtuxet River, the river that led to all the mills being built in West Warwick and all the immigrants—like my great-grandparents—who flocked there for work. When I was a young child, the Pawtuxet River was brown and sluggish, topped by a yellowish foam. It flooded frequently. The books in that small library smelled of polluted water and mold and dank cellar air. I only got to go there a few times in first grade before it was shut down for good, but I remember picking up the books and bringing them to my nose, inhaling deeply. To me, that terrible smell was wonderful.

My small school at the bottom of the hill where our house was perched had no school library. Instead, each teacher had books on shelves in the back of the classroom—books we were not allowed to read until we'd finished all of our class work: the smudged blue mimeographed worksheets, the arithmetic written in pencil on small rectangular off-white paper, the connect-the-dots alphabet on yellow lined paper. I found it hard to concentrate on any of it. The books behind me seemed to whisper for me to come. I would glance over my shoulder, a fat pink eraser clutched in my hand, and read the titles, already trying to choose which one I'd read when I finally—finally!—finished my times tables.

It's hard to describe the magic that books held for me then. Even our class reading books brought me my happiest moments at school. I was an awkward, shy kid. Bad at sports and ignorant of playground etiquette, I usually sat alone on the blacktop and played jacks during recess, swiping up the shiny jacks and small red ball over and over so often that the side of my right hand was always scraped. But when Miss Dwyer or Mrs. McMahon announced it was time to get into our reading groups, I was always the first one to pick up my chair and sit in the circle, book immediately open in my lap. If my teacher had to go to the bathroom, she would order the class to take out their reading books and announce that Ann was going to read aloud until she got back. What pleasure I took in that, even though no one listened as I read. I didn't care. I was in the world of stories and words, a world I preferred to the classroom or playground.

But what is a child who loves books that much supposed to do when she has no access to them? Every week at home *Time* magazine arrived, and every month we got *Reader's Digest*. In the early evening, just before supper, the paperboy brought the evening newspaper. And so my earliest reading was "Milestones" in *Time*; "Life in These United States," "Humor in Uniform," "Drama in Real Life," and "How to Build Your Word Power" quizzes in *Reader's Digest*; "Dear Abby," horoscopes, and "Hints from Heloise" (save your old onion bags and use them for hairnets!) in the newspaper.

Until second grade. That's when I finally got a real book to read.

MY COUSIN GLORIA-JEAN—a year older, dark curly haired to my straight blond—went to Maisie E. Quinn, the new elementary school in town. Like us, our schools were physically opposites: hers a rambling one-story with lots of windows; mine, painted yellow with shiny wood floors and old enough that our grandmother and parents had gone there.

Maisie E. Quinn had a cafeteria; we ate our brown-bag lunches at our desks. And Maisie E. Quinn had a library.

That is where, I suppose, my cousin got a copy of and read *Little Women*, and passed it along to me. Until then, the only books I had access to were the ones in the Childhood of Famous Americans series that my second-grade teacher, Miss Virginia Nolan, kept in the back of the classroom. I was working my way through all of those orange-covered books. *John Philip Sousa, Marching Boy. Betsy Ross, Girl of Old Philadelphia. Eli Whitney, Boy Mechanic. Little Women* was something else. Fat, with small type and many chapters, it was a real book, the kind I glimpsed when my mother pulled me past the tiny Books department at Ann & Hope, the local discount store. The kind I imagined filled shelves in libraries.

From the first line—" *'Christmas won't be Christmas without any presents,' grumbled Jo, lying on the rug*"—I was hooked. With each detail—the introduction of the four March sisters, the utterance of that beloved nickname "Marmie" for their mother, the absent father away at war, the plays written and performed by the March sisters, the neighbor boy Laurie—I fell deeper and deeper into the story. All these years later I recognize how magical this experience truly was. I wanted to live inside a book, and this was the first time I really did.

"I'm going to call you Marmie," I told my mother, surely clutching *Little Women* because I did not put that book down.

"What? No. No, you're not," my no-nonsense mother said.

A day later: "May I carry a baked potato to keep my hands warm? And put it inside a muff?" I asked.

"No! Put on your mittens!" Then with a sigh: "Why are you so weird?"

She had dreamed of a beauty-queen daughter, a cheerleader, a popular girl. Instead she got me, a pageant dropout after just two trophies, too clumsy to be a cheerleader or playground star, quoting "Drama in Real Life" and wondering aloud about photosynthesis.

Little Women's pages brought me into a different world from my Italian immigrant one, which was large and loving, dramatic and loud. Our house was

ANN HOOD

always full of relatives, many of whom spoke very little English. We were taught to respect our elders, which meant to kiss them hello and goodbye. Even though this often earned me a few dollars from grateful relatives who pinched my cheek or stroked my blond banana curls, cooing, *Bella!*, I didn't like the way they smelled (I realize now that they smelled of food cooking, chopped onions and garlic, dirt and sun). I didn't like that we kids were required to give up our seats to them and crowd together on the sofa or floor, silent.

My great-grandmother, Nonna, was a strong, imposing woman, a *strega* who cured sciatica, migraines, and broken hearts through prayers and magic. People lined up on our block for her services, offering embroidered linens, homemade wine, and the best eggplants and squash from their gardens in lieu of money. Still, Nonna was afraid of two things: flush toilets because she believed they could flush you away, and furnaces because she thought at night they released toxic fumes. Luckily, we did have a toilet, though Nonna kept an outhouse in the backyard, a huge source of embarrassment for me. However she refused to get a furnace. Instead we had a coal stove in the kitchen until 1966. The coal man came every week, and Mama Rose and Nonna shoveled the coal into the coal bin in the dirt basement and started the fire in the kitchen stove early on cold winter mornings.

They also grew much of the food we ate. The community garden stretched far behind our house, and from it came the tomatoes and peppers and cucumbers and string beans; the cherries and pears and apples and figs; the zucchini and mint and basil and carrots. They raised chickens and rabbits too, and before I left for school I was sent into the backyard to kiss them goodbye, gagging at their blood-spattered aprons and the feathers and fur that lay on the ground at their feet.

Little Women took me away from all of this and transported me to the March household in Massachusetts during the Civil War. It was all I could think about at school: *What will Jo do when Amy burns her manuscript? Will Laurie join the sisters' club, the Pickwick Club? What will happen next?* As soon as I got home, Mama Rose would hand me a plate of bread covered in spaghetti sauce or a handful of figs, and I'd sit eating and reading until it was time to set the table for dinner. Some afternoons I would look up, surprised by the shift of light in the room. Surprised that I was actually still in the kitchen rocking chair at home in my little town, that my brother was at the table with his slide ruler and math book, that dinner was ready.

Then I reached chapter 36: "Beth's Secret." Beth is the most lovable, kindest March sister. Jo is confident and ambitious, Meg maternal and ordinary, Amy pretty and spoiled. But Beth! So sweet! So frail after an earlier illness. All fall she appeared to be melancholy, and now in chapter 36 she confesses to Jo that was because she knew she would die soon. Although Jo tries to convince her otherwise, Beth insists it's true. To my seven-year-old self, the idea that a beloved character might die was almost too much to bear. But the idea that we somehow know when we are going to die was downright terrifying. Had my mother's sister Ann—my namesake—known that when she went into the hospital to get her wisdom teeth pulled, she was going to die? Then why had she gone? Why didn't she cancel the operation and stay home? Had her brother, my uncle Brownie, known he'd have a fatal heart attack at a dance on Valentine's night? But why wouldn't he go straight to the hospital instead?

For several chapters, Beth goes virtually unmentioned, which lulled me into a false sense of security. See? She wasn't going to die! Would Amy and Laurie dance together in Nice if Louisa May Alcott intended to kill off Beth? Would Meg and John work so hard on their marriage if doom was around the corner? Would Jo throw herself into writing for the *Weekly Volcano* if her favorite sister were about to die? Would a writer dedicate so many chapters to illustrating the pros and cons of marriage—Meg and John's, yes, but also Jo's decision to say no to Laurie's proposal—if a main character was dying? I decided no. Beth would surely live.

As an adult, and a writer, I suspect that Beth *had* to die. Her role in the second half of the novel did not seem tenable. Elizabeth Lennox Keyser posits that Beth's quiet, old-fashioned character who clings to outdated values symbolizes the changing role of women and therefore had to die. Still, when I began chapter 40: "The Valley of the Shadow" at the breakfast table one morning and read about the family setting up a special room for Beth with her piano and Amy's drawings in it, an overwhelming dread filled me.

I tucked the book into my pile of textbooks and walked to school, that dread growing with each step. At school, I hung my red wool jacket with the toggle buttons on a hook in the hallway and took my seat in the back of the room, *Little Women* open in my lap. Meg was bringing the twins to visit Beth, almost like a farewell. I swallowed hard, afraid I might start to cry. I kept reading.

Our mornings began when Miss Nolan entered the classroom and all forty of us jumped to our feet.

"Good morning, class," Miss Nolan would say.

"Good morning, Miss Nolan," we'd reply.

We'd pivot to face the flag, bend our heads for a moment of silence, then place our hands over our hearts and recite the Pledge of Allegiance. After which Miss Nolan would announce the name of the patriotic song we'd sing—"America the Beautiful" or

"God Bless America" or, my favorite, "The Battle Hymn of the Republic." Miss Nolan would then make a downward motion with her hands and we'd sit.

But on the day Beth was dying, I didn't hear Miss Nolan enter the classroom. I wasn't aware of the class rising, or saying the Pledge of Allegiance, or singing a patriotic song. While all of that went on around me, Beth peacefully died. Just like that. When the class took their seats again, I looked up, stunned by grief.

Miss Nolan was looking right at me.

"Ann," she said, "you will stay in for morning recess because you refused to do the morning exercises."

It was the first time I'd ever had to stay in for recess, and if truth be told, that was almost a relief. I was terrible at kickball and jump rope, afraid of the monkey bars, and as a mostly friendless kid never really invited to be part of playground activities. When I wasn't playing jacks, I sat alone and made up stories in my head. It was also the first time I'd ever gotten into trouble, and I worried about what else it might mean. What if Miss Nolan made my mother leave work and come to school? What if she sent me home? I couldn't concentrate on anything but the big hand on the clock dropping into place at 10:10, when the bell would ring and send everyone, two by two, into the playground.

Finally, 10:10 came, the big hand on the clock clicking noisily into place. The bell rang. The class filed out. And Miss Nolan, sitting regally at her desk, beckoned me forward. Clutching *Little Women*, I made my slow way up the aisle to her. So terrified was I that I still remember that I was wearing a pink-and-white polka-dot dress that day, and that I held the heavy book to my chest.

Miss Nolan turned her rheumy blue eyes toward me.

"Why didn't you do the morning exercises?" she asked me. "What were you doing?"

I opened my mouth to answer, but I couldn't put into words the enormity of the effect this book had on me, how I could think of nothing else, how I reread sentences out loud just for the magic of them.

Finally, I held *Little Women* out in front of me and managed to sputter, "Beth *died*." Having said it out loud, I burst into tears and dropped to the ground with grief.

At first, Miss Nolan looked bewildered. But quickly she ordered me to get up.

"You're reading *Little Women*?" she asked, looking at the book in my hands.

Unable to muster any more words, I nodded.

"And you understand it?" she asked.

Again, I nodded.

Miss Nolan considered this for what seemed a very long time. Then she asked me to tell her what the book was about.

At this, I began to talk—about Marmie and the March sisters and the plays they put on, about Laurie next door and vain Amy and Jo who wanted to be a writer and how Beth died. I told her it was about family but also about war and dreams and writing and . . . "And," I said, "everything. It's about everything."

Now it was Miss Nolan who nodded. She paused, then pointed to the books—Childhood of Famous Americans—that lined the bookshelves in the back of the classroom.

"I don't want you to go out to recess anymore," she said. "I want you to stay inside and read all those books."

And I did. I read every one. Then Miss Nolan gave me all the third-grade books, and I read every one of them too. By the time I left her class, I'd finished half of the fourth-grade books as well.

How can I describe what reading gave to me? An escape from my lonely school days, where girls seemed to speak a language I didn't understand. A glimpse into the possibilities of words and stories. A curiosity about the world and about people—the young Amelia Earhart seeing her first airplane, Helen Keller's silent world, Nancy Drew solving mysteries, David Copperfield surviving the streets of Victorian London.

My parents learned about life from hardship. My mother lost her father when she was only sixteen. She had to drop out of high school, where she was the social committee chairman and a star softball player, and go to work in factories: bleaching linens, making artificial flowers, attaching snaps to American Tourister luggage. My father dropped out of school too, to escape poverty in rural Indiana. He joined the navy, and by traveling around the world learned how to eat in a restaurant, what kind of cocktail to order, how to tie a tie and polish his shoes. They married young—she was nineteen and he was twenty-one—and grew up together, learning how to raise babies and cook dinner and save money and build a home.

Me? I learned from books.

For as long as I can remember, I wanted something big, something I could not name. I did not know what it was, only what it wasn't. It wasn't in my small hometown. It wasn't nine-to-five, or ordinary, or anything I had ever seen before. I would sit on the landing at the top of the stairs at home and look out the little window at Aunt Julia and Uncle Joe's house across the street. *Someday I will go beyond there*, I would think. I'd look at the rooftop of Auntie Angie's house. *And beyond there*. Then I'd look at the hill where Auntie Rosie and Uncle Chuckie's houses sat. *And beyond there*. I'd focus on a distant point, and think: *Someday I'll even go beyond there*.

This was in the late '60s and early '70s. I'd grown

up with the Vietnam War playing out on television. My brother, Skip, had changed from a boy in raspberry shorts and a matching polo shirt to a long-haired, bearded, cutoff jeans–wearing hippie. Newspapers splashed pictures of student protests, and the Kent State shootings, and marijuana and LSD. The same radio station played the Carpenters' "Close to You" and Crosby, Stills, Nash & Young's "Ohio." In such an upside-down world, how would I get *beyond there*? What did I want? Why did I feel this way? What did I believe?

In 1967, when I was ten years old, our town finally got a library.

I went there twice a week, walking past the children's section and heading right for adult fiction.

I can still remember craning my neck to look at all those beautiful books. I whispered the writers' names. Evan Hunter, Victor Hugo, Harold Robbins, Herman Wouk, Fred Mustard Stewart, Dashiell Hammett, Edith Wharton, Dorothy Parker. So many books! At random I pulled one from the shelf. And then another. I filled my arms with books.

And I read.

I read about small-town gossip in *Peyton Place* and inner-city schools in *The Blackboard Jungle*; I read about Hollywood in *Valley of the Dolls* and a horrific crime in *In Cold Blood*. In that library I was handed a blueprint on how to live the mysterious, unnamable, big dream life I wanted. I was handed books. And through reading them, I grew up to find that very life.

Lesson 1: How to Dream

· *Marjorie Morningstar* BY HERMAN WOUK ·

WHEN *MARJORIE MORNINGSTAR* WAS PUBLISHED IN
1955, *Time* magazine referred to it as "an outmoded
adolescent cliché." *Kirkus Review* wrote: "It is the
kind of book women—just past the age of illusion—
will read with absorbed interest, occasional ironic
recognition, and ultimate critical detachment. But—
despite the ease with which the story can be crit-
icized, it will be read." And read it was. *Marjorie
Morningstar* sold more copies than *Gone with the
Wind*, and in 1958 it was made into a movie star-
ring Natalie Wood as Marjorie.

But as a teenager, I chose the books I read not by reviews or jacket copy or book sales. No, I chose by heft. I loved nothing more than the weight of a heavy book in my arms as I moved through the school hallways. In study hall, my homework finished, I fell into a fat novel that seemed to never end. That I didn't want to end. Halfway through a seven-hundred-page book, hundreds of pages still waited for me. *Doctor Zhivago*. *Les Misérables*. James Michener's *Hawaii*. Anything by Harold Robbins. I read indiscriminately. Highbrow. Lowbrow. Without any guidance from the librarians in my small mill town in Rhode Island. Their job seemed to be just to stamp due dates in the back of the books, not to recommend them. It was with this lack of direction, this love of novels the weight of cement, that I came upon *Marjorie Morningstar*.

I first read Herman Wouk's novel in 1972, when I was fifteen years old. And I have reread it almost every year since. As an adult, I saw the similarities between the Morgensterns and my own family. Marjorie's father had come to the United States at the age of fifteen, *"a fleck of foam on the great wave of immigra-*

tion from Eastern Europe." I lived with a dizzying array of Italian immigrant relatives. In the novel, Mr. Morgenstern owned the Arnold Importing Company, *"a well-known dealer in feathers, straws, and other materials for ladies' hats."* Like my own father, who commuted several hours every day to his job in Government Center in Boston so that we could rise above our blue-collar immigrant roots, Wouk writes of Mr. Morgenstern: *"Every year since his marriage he had spent every dollar he earned on the comfort of his family and the improvement of their station in life."* And like Marjorie, who understood her father's sacrifices— *"her parents had done much to make up for their immigrant origin. She was grateful to them for this, and proud of them."*—I too took pride in how my parents, two high-school dropouts who'd married before they were old enough to vote, had bought our family a slice of the American Dream: two cars, family vacations, T-bone steaks on the grill, and Tanqueray and Johnnie Walker in the liquor cabinet.

But at fifteen, that first time I read the novel, I thought that Herman Wouk had somehow climbed into my brain and emerged with my story. *I* was Marjorie Morningstar. Slightly spoiled. Boy crazy. Curious about sex. Terrified of sex. Raised by prudish, old-school parents. Although we lived far from Manhattan and an apartment on Central Park West, my life seemed a mirror image of Marjorie's. West Warwick, Rhode Island, my small hometown, was once famous for Fruit of the Loom manufacturing and a bustling main street with two fancy women's clothing stores and a men's shop that sold expensive suits. But by the time I was a teenager, the shops and mills were mostly boarded up and the Pawtuxet River, which had helped those factories run, was polluted. The one factory that still operated made soap, and that was the smell that filled the air on hot afternoons. At Christmas, they opened their doors and sold Jade East soap on a rope at discount prices.

My immigrant great-grandparents left Italy in the late 1800s to work in the great Natick Mill, buying a house right up the hill from it. The Natick Mill burned down in 1941, the summer before my mother turned ten. But her family stayed put, working in factories around the state. I grew up in the house my great-grandparents bought when they arrived in the

United States, where my grandmother married and had ten children, where my mother at the age of eighty-five still lives. The house is small, just three bedrooms with sloping ceilings upstairs and one bathroom downstairs.

As I've said, as a teenager I would sit at the top of the stairs, staring out the tiny window there. I could see the rooftops of three of my aunts' houses. I could see a distant water tank. On a clear day I could see all the way to the next town. *Someday*, I would think, *I'll even go beyond there.* Just thinking this would thrill me. Deep inside, I had a gnawing, a yearning, for something I could not name. All I knew was that I wouldn't find it in West Warwick, or even in Rhode Island. It was *beyond there*. Despite my parents' warnings, I threw myself into the path of everything that might take me *beyond there*. At fourteen, I became a Marsha Jordan Girl, one of eight teen models for Jordan Marsh, the fancy Boston department store that had opened a branch at our new mall. That job took me all over New England. My friend Beth and I went by bus and train alone to modeling jobs, landing spots in fashion shows for

Brides magazine and *Mademoiselle*. With the money I earned, I took vacations to Bermuda and the Bahamas before I finished high school.

But that wasn't enough for me. As a junior I tried out for and won the coveted role as teen editor from Rhode Island for *Seventeen* magazine. I wrote dispatches from Rhode Island on fashion, pop culture, and trends. At the end of my yearlong tenure, I won a Best Teen Editor Award, which gave me another year at *Seventeen* and a heavy silver charm with their logo on it. All of these things were somehow going to get me wherever it was I was trying to go. And this yearning I felt was the same one that Herman Wouk expressed so perfectly in the character of Marjorie Morningstar.

Marjorie defies her parents by taking a job as an actress in a summer stock company in the Catskills. And then she defies them even more when she falls in love with and begins a sexual relationship with the director, Noel Airman. What is evident to everyone—her fellow drama club friends at Hunter College, the other summer stock actors, and Marjorie herself—is that she is special, talented, destined for great things. Before she meets Noel, Marjorie dates many boys, all of them worthy suitors. She enjoys teasing them, flirting, kissing. But her traditional Jewish parents warn her about the dangers of sex, warnings that she holds dear until the summer she's nineteen.

Marjorie falls for Noel the summer before, but he is involved with another actress. That winter, she goes downtown to Bank Street to stand "*across the street from the shabby red brick house where he lived, staring at the windows, while snow caked her beaver coat and caught in her eyelashes.*" I read this as if I'd made a great discovery. I sighed. I read the passage again, out loud. I remember where I was—on my bed with its yellow-and-white checked bedspread— and what I wore—my faded Levi's and red peasant blouse. In my doorway hung long strands of colorful beads that I'd spent months stringing; taped to one wall was a Jules Feiffer dancer cartoon; on the stereo Simon and Garfunkel sang "The Dangling Conversation." That song spoke to my yearning too, to my desire for a love in which "*you read your Emily Dickinson, and I my Robert Frost . . .*"

Why did Marjorie standing on a snowy street staring at the apartment where the man she loved lived so affect me? Perhaps because sometimes at night I sat in my parents' Chevy in front of Peter Hayhurst's house—he who had broken my tender heart—hoping for a glimpse of him? Perhaps because as she longed for Noel, Marjorie let Wally Wronken court her, just as I let boys take me to the movies and kiss me in their convertibles while I longed for Peter Hayhurst? Perhaps because Marjorie's romanticism, bravery, idealism, and foolishness were just like mine? Marjorie Morningstar knew me. She *was* me, and I was her.

The light outside had dimmed as I sat reading, and I leaned over to turn on the light by my bed. In the very next chapter, Marjorie goes on dates with dull boys and walks alone on Riverside Drive, mooning for Noel. "*The soft April air blowing across the blue river, the smell of the blossoming cherry and crab-apple trees, the swaying of their bunched pink branches, filled her with bittersweet melancholy. Often she would slip a book of poetry in her pocket, and would drop on a bench, after walking far, to read Byron or Shelley or Keats.*" I remember having to put the book down. I remember crying, filled with my own teenage bittersweet melancholy. Like Marjorie, I dated dull boys who tried hard to impress me, buying me steaks at Valle's Steak House or taking me dancing at the Ocean View by the beach. I too took long solo walks—not on a city street, but on the beach—and sat in the salty air to read Emily Dickinson and Robert Frost, Allen Ginsberg and Rod McKuen.

When I composed myself, I picked up the book again. Wally Wronken appears at the Morgensterns' apartment to invite Marjorie to accompany him to the Cloisters in a rainstorm. After the rain stops, he leads her "*around a corner of thick bushes into a curving shadowy path filled with a curious lavender light.*" He has led her onto an avenue "*solidly arched and walled with blooming lilacs.*" With water dripping on her upturned face, Marjorie takes Wally's hand. "*She was not sure what was rain and what was tears on her face. She wanted to look up at lilacs and rolling white clouds and patchy blue sky forever . . .*" *Yes!* my brain, my heart shouted. *That's what I want too!* So moved by this is Marjorie that she looks at ugly, young, pathetic Wally and kisses him on the mouth. "*They were holding each other's hands, and raindrops were dripping on them from the lilacs.*" "*I'm going to plant lilac lanes all over town,*" Wally tells her in a hoarse voice. But Marjorie is already done with him. "*It's fading,*" she tells Wally. "*It's becoming just a lane of lilacs.*" Still, she promises him there will be another kiss only when they find such lilacs again.

Somehow, that yearning I felt was taking shape as I read *Marjorie Morningstar.* I wanted a man like Noel Airman. I wanted to move away from home and defy my prudish Catholic parents and have sex with a man I loved. But I wanted the kiss under the lilacs too. That kiss and those lilacs seemed enormously important to me, even though less than a hundred pages later, when Wally and Marjorie see each other at South Wind the next summer, she doesn't remember them.

What I understood when I read *Marjorie Morningstar* as an adult is that of course Noel Airman will break Marjorie's heart and destroy her dreams. "*I eat little girls like you,*" he tells her. Then he does just that. But as a young girl, I held my breath as I followed every twist and turn of their affair. I felt the sharp pangs of heartbreak along with her, recalling how Peter Hayhurst broke my own fragile heart.

But it is the final nine pages of the novel, written in the form of Wally Wronken's diary, that truly break my heart every time. Marjorie gave up on her acting career, married a lawyer, and moved to Westchester. Marjorie Morningstar became Marjorie Schwartz, suburban wife and mother. Critics argue that Wouk is suggesting that Marjorie is lucky: she has had sex with another man, yet still marries a nice Jewish doctor. Perhaps, some critics contend, Wouk is telling readers that sex and rebellion and striving aren't as great as young women hope they will be.

As a young woman back then and today as a middle-aged woman, those last nine pages slay me because Marjorie has let me down. *"And if she wasn't the bright angel I thought, she was a lovely girl,"* Wally tells us. *"And where is that girl now? She doesn't even remember herself as she was."* Wally acknowledges his own loss in Marjorie Morningstar becoming Marjorie Schwartz: he will never have that second kiss under the lilacs. *"Yet how beautiful she was! She rises up before me as I write . . . her face wet with rain, nine-teen years old, in my arms and yet maddeningly beyond my reach . . ."*

What I know now looking back at that girl on the bed with the yellow-and-white checked bedspread in the sad mill town, is that *Marjorie Morningstar* moved her so much not just because she saw herself in Marjorie and her family in the Morgensterns. No, *Marjorie Morningstar* gave her—me—the passion to never forget the bright angel who wanted every-thing, all of it, to go *out there*, wherever that might be. What I decided, what I knew in the deepest parts of me as I read those final pages through tears that wouldn't stop, was that I would, in the final analysis, not be anything like Marjorie at all.

Maybe that's why I reread it every year. Maybe, as time beats me up and grief or loneliness or a new kind of bittersweet melancholy take hold, I need to remind myself to keep going, keep reaching, to not forget the girl who believed she could have every-thing and anything at all. Maybe even now I am still waiting for that metaphorical kiss under the lilacs. Maybe I always will.

Lesson 2: How to Become a Writer

·   *The Bell Jar* BY SYLVIA PLATH   ·

IT WAS THE SUMMER I SPENT STRINGING YARDS OF beads to make that curtain for the doorway to my bedroom. I did other things that summer, of course. I rode the waves at East Beach and Scarborough, slathered Coppertone on my long skinny body, lay under the hot sun with lemon juice in my hair and sand in my bikini bottom. I learned to play Frisbee. The boy who taught me was a college boy, nineteen years old, a friend of my brother Skip's. I was only fourteen, and to sit beside that older boy in his white VW Bug was one of my greatest pleasures. That summer, he took me to movies I didn't fully understand. *Getting Straight* with Elliott Gould and *Carnal Knowledge* with—surprisingly to me—Art Garfunkel, whose angelic voice sang some of my favorite songs from my record player—"The Sound of Silence" and "April Come She Will" and "Kathy's Song" and "Bridge over Troubled Water."

Those beads.

Where did I get them, that summer of 1971? Too young to drive, stuck in a town with a main street of boarded-up stores and an X-rated movie theater and dark bars, somehow I acquired enough beads to fill a doorway. I remember the oblong garnet ones, the round amber and the clear teardrops, the midnight blue and cobalt blue, the tiny silver. Although I remember them as glass—the way they sparkled as I strung them in my backyard under the sun!—surely they must have been made of plastic. So many beads! I kept them on a cookie sheet (though in my household cookie sheets were called pizza pans) so that I could better see them, the sizes and shapes and colors, and decide in what order I should string them.

My bedroom was girlish—white furniture trimmed in gold, yellow-and-white gingham bedspread with matching curtains, a frilly bedside lamp—and I suppose that beaded doorway was meant to show who I really was, or who I was trying to become. A girl who didn't match, someone exotic and mysterious and deep. I would lie on that gingham-covered bed and play "The Dangling Conversation" and I would yearn for a boy who knew who Frost and Dickinson were, who would read beside me, who would understand this peculiar person I was. I would play "I Am a Rock" and I would cry as Simon and Garfunkel sang: *I have my books, and my poetry to protect me . . .*

I had nothing at all to be depressed about, or even to cry about. My parents adored me. Skip—five years older than me—had finally stopped farting in my face and turning his eyelids inside out to scare me; and after years as a lonely, alienated child, adolescence had brought me friends and slumber parties and all the giggling and inside jokes I needed. Still, a rock of sadness settled in my gut, immovable and heavy. When my ninth-grade English teacher taught us about haikus and then set us free to write our own, I wrote: *Waves wash away sand / Just as He washes away / The life we cherish.* "Is Ann depressed?" the teacher asked my mother in an emergency conference. "No," my mother said, "she's just weird."

That weirdness seemed to grow stronger with puberty. Insomnia hit, and at night beneath my gingham bedspread I'd watch Johnny Carson and then Tom Snyder on my tiny portable black-and-white television. After Snyder, TV ended, and I would read until my eyes drooped. But once I turned off the light and got on my side, panic gripped me. My heart raced and I'd sit up, turning the light back on, almost certain I would find something there. What that something might be, I can't say. We were a family that believed in ghosts, and often at breakfast we reported sightings: mysterious bruises on my father's arms came from a ghost pinching him; the dip of the bed beside my mother was a ghost sitting next to her; the soft breeze my grandmother felt even though the windows were closed tight meant a ghost had kissed her. Perhaps I was expecting to find my dead great-grandmother or aunt in the room, but the fear felt bigger than even ghosts.

When my mother called out to me and asked what

was wrong, I could never name it. "Nothing!" I would say. *Everything*, I would think. Many nights she got dressed and drove me to the Dunkin' Donuts down the street, where we'd sit in a booth and drink coffee and eat glazed doughnuts until I'd calmed down. It didn't occur to me until I was an adult how difficult those forays into the night must have been for her— she had to be at work at the candy factory by seven the next morning. By the time I emerged from my grateful sleep for school, she was long gone.

THE SUMMER OF the beads, I read *The Bell Jar*. I remember the cover. A pink so pale it almost looked white. The black letters with their curlicued *T* and *B* and *J*. The red rose stretched across the edge. Unaware as I was of things like book reviews, I didn't know that the book I'd plucked from the library shelf was a new one, just published in the United States. I didn't even know—though surely this was in the author's bio—that Sylvia Plath had committed suicide on February 11, 1963, just a few weeks after *The Bell Jar* had been published by

Harper & Row in Britain under the pseudonym Victoria Lucas. After her death, her estranged husband, poet Ted Hughes, promised her mother, Aurelia Plath, that the novel wouldn't be published in the United States during her lifetime. But the wild success of Sylvia Plath's poetry collection *Ariel* and the rumors that Victoria Lucas was indeed Plath, made the demand for *The Bell Jar* in the United States huge. Bookstores in New York City sold bootleg British copies of the novel, but it wasn't until an editor at Random House learned that it was no longer eligible for copyright protection, thereby forcing Harper's hand, that *The Bell Jar* was finally published here, despite Hughes's promise.

An immediate bestseller, Plath's story of beautiful, brilliant Esther Greenwood's breakdown spoke to my generation. The minds of women were just being discussed openly as feminism soared. Questions of career, sex, marriage, and finding yourself were, I suspect, what kept me up at night. In my small town, only a handful of graduating seniors went on to college. People who were born in West Warwick tended to stay in West Warwick. But I wanted to leave. For what I cannot say, nor could I say then.

I wanted to be a writer—in fact, *was* a writer in many ways, filling purple notebooks with poems and stories and short plays—and imagined a writer's life, perhaps in Greenwich Village or Paris. Certainly there were no writers in my town, or as far as I knew, in all of Rhode Island. When my ninth-grade guidance counselor asked me what I wanted to do with my life, I told him I wanted to be a writer. Mr. Stone, in his brown corduroy suit and tinted aviator glasses, shook his head sadly. "Ann," he said, "people don't do that."

My eyes drifted to the shelves against the wall. "Then how do we get all these books?" I asked him.

Mr. Stone glanced at the books for a moment, then told me "All those writers are dead."

He was right, of course. This was, after all, 1969 or '70 and we only read the dead white guys. Would I write in anonymity, I wondered, and have my stories published only after I died?

By then, our library had opened at last. I read every book I could get my hands on. And I had just read a paperback called *How to Become an Airline Stewardess* by Kathryn Cason. *For that special breed of young women with their eyes on the stars—and their hearts set on a jet-paced career with wings!* the cover proclaimed. Inside were promises of breakfast in New York, lunch in Bermuda, dinner in Rome, and boyfriends in every city in the world.

"Then I'd like to be an airline stewardess," I told Mr. Stone.

He shook his head again. "Ann, smart girls do not become airline stewardesses. You should be a teacher or a secretary or make your life nice and easy and get married."

I don't know how I replied to his suggestions, but I know that I dismissed them. I didn't want to be any of those things—teacher, secretary, wife. But unable to name this yearning I had for something different, all I knew was that I wanted to get out of West Warwick. Writers, I thought, needed adventures. Airline stewardesses had adventures. If my ticket out was on a jet, then I would take it. Those adventures would give me ideas for the novels I would write. The next time I went to the library, I checked out *How to*

Become an Airline Stewardess again, and dutifully recorded the qualifications (height! weight!) and the interview tips (don't wear a turtleneck!) in one of my purple notebooks. I would see the world, I decided. I would run with the bulls and jump naked in fountains in Paris. And then someday, somehow, I would be a writer.

THE BELL JAR seemed to be written just for me. Esther Greenwood wanted to be a writer too. She had won a fashion magazine contest that sent her and eleven other girls to New York City for a month with all their expenses paid and *"piles and piles of free bonuses, like ballet tickets and passes to fashion shows and hair stylings at a famous salon . . ."* Esther had the same doubts I had. *"How could I write about life when I'd never had a love affair or a baby or even seen anybody die?"* Esther wonders. She remembers a girl who won a prize for a short story about pygmies in Africa and asks: *How could I compete with that sort of thing?*

Despite the perfect boyfriend, Buddy, who wants to marry her, Esther doesn't want to get married.

She's curious about sex, but doubtful about matrimony. She worries that once someone liked her, he would "*sink into ordinariness*," that she would find fault after fault with him like she did with Buddy. Esther Greenwood was the first character I met who expressed the very things I worried over as "I Am a Rock" played again and again on my record player. I worried over ordinariness—mine in particular. I worried over the idea of getting married and staying in my hometown forever. I worried over that thing I wanted that no one could help me name or find. No one except Esther. "*The last thing I wanted was infinite security and to be the place an arrow shoots off from,*" she says to explain why she doesn't want to get married. "*I wanted change and excitement and to shoot off in all directions myself, like the colored arrows from a Fourth of July rocket.*"

Around me, my older cousins got married at our church, Sacred Heart. The brides wore flowing white gowns embellished with tiny pearls and lace, long veils, bouquets of lilies; the grooms wore tuxedos and shiny shoes, boutonnieres and clean-shaven faces. There were bridesmaids, in mauve velvet or pale yellow jersey knit and dyed-to-match shoes, clutching chrysanthemums or daisies; groomsmen in too-tight rented tuxedos, their shirts the color of those dresses. At the reception at the Club 400, whiskey sours flowed from fountains, the Champagne toast was pink and sweet, and we ate ziti, chicken stuffed with rice, green beans amandine, and iceberg lettuce topped with a wedge of tomato.

The couple moved into an apartment, then bought a small house. They had a baby, then another baby. On Sundays they came to our house and visited Mama Rose and ate lasagna and threw barbs at each other. He complained that she never let him have fun. She complained that he didn't talk to her enough. They stared out at us blankly, their faces as bland as bologna. I remembered Buddy Willard telling Esther that after she had children she wouldn't want to write poems anymore. Esther compared being married to being brainwashed: "*afterward you went about numb as a slave in some private totalitarian state*," she said. I watched my cousins and knew Esther was, once again, right.

And then, there was madness itself. Didn't I

sometimes feel out of control? And other times par-
alyzed? Like Esther, I worked hard all my life to get
A's, worried over each test and research paper, studied and studied and studied. But wasn't that need to
get those A's part of what drove her mad? Esther
obsessed about the Rosenbergs; I obsessed about
Charlie Manson and Richard Speck. If Esther
Greenwood with her scholarship to a good college,
her adoring boyfriend, her good grades and writing
talent, could go mad, then couldn't anybody?
Couldn't I?

AS THAT SUMMER came to an end, I hung those beads
in my doorway. My parents, ever practical, ever
befuddled by my strange desires, refused to remove
the door to my room, so I pushed it open and held it
that way with a heavy iron doorstop. The beads made
a glistening curtain that whispered when I walked
through it. They looked exotic, sophisticated,
important.

As we always did before school started, my cousin
and I took the bus from the bottom of the hill to

downtown Providence. Downcity, it was called. The bus cost thirty-five cents and made one stop: at the state mental hospital. Maybe reading *The Bell Jar* added to my fascination with that place, which looked almost like a college campus with its curving walkways, large leafy trees, and small groupings of brick buildings—except the windows in those buildings had bars on them. I didn't know then that the hospital where Esther Greenwood went was a private one, surely more lovely than the one I saw outside the bus window. I didn't know such differences even existed. Onto the bus stepped a handful of patients: a man who mumbled to himself, a blank-eyed woman led by a nurse, a woman with an angry face who periodically shouted obscenities, and—most fascinating to me—a woman with her hair dyed bright red, her lips smeared with hot-pink lipstick, her entire eyelids painted baby blue, her cheeks overly powdered and rouged. She wore multiple shiny necklaces and a Kelly-green dress. I thought she looked like human neon. Someone behind me whispered, "Crazy," as the woman regally walked down the aisle to an empty seat. I thought of Esther sitting in the Boston Public Garden reading a scandal sheet of stories about murders and robberies and suicides, or sitting all day on a beach in a skirt and high heels fingering a box of razor blades. I thought of myself sobbing over "The Dangling Conversation," or pacing in the middle of the night, how things felt so enormous to me, so vital. What was the difference between Esther and me? This woman and me?

In Providence, at the department stores Shepard's and Gladdings, my cousin and I tried on clothes in front of triple mirrors that multiplied our reflections over and over, a strange effect that always fascinated me. We went to Alexander's for lunch, a restaurant with white tablecloths and Salisbury steak. We felt so grown-up with our shopping bags crowded into the red booth eating our fancy food. In one of those bags was my first-day-of-school outfit: mauve hot pants with a matching vest that came below my knees and a flowered puckered shirt.

Weeks later, in that very outfit, I was walking through Jordan Marsh into the mall when a woman sitting at a table at the entrance stopped me. "Have you ever thought about modeling?" she asked me. I said yes, though I hadn't thought about it at all. She invited me to sit down with her so she could explain about Marsha Jordan Girls. Marsha Jordan Girls were ambassadors for Jordan Marsh, she said. They modeled the clothes in the Juniors department, worked at VIP events here and in Boston (Boston! The very idea gave me shivers!), and represented the store in dozens of ways throughout the year.

"I want to be a Marsha Jordan Girl," I said. It felt like my world had just been blown open, like I was handed a new life, not unlike the one of my vague, big dreams. The woman was explaining that Bonne Bell Cosmetics would come and teach us how to put on makeup, and that we would get special uniforms— she slid a glossy photo of a girl in a gray-and-white pinstriped pantsuit toward me—and have our pictures hanging in the Juniors department. I thought of Esther in New York City, getting hairstyles and clothes, going to fancy lunches. Being a Marsha Jordan Girl sounded similar.

Apparently, lots of girls wanted to be Marsha Jordan Girls, but they only needed eight. I filled out the application eagerly, already imagining a picture of me in that pinstriped suit hanging in the Juniors department. I didn't know that girls had been coming to the store all day to apply, or that I had just had an interview. I only knew that I wanted to be a Marsha Jordan Girl more than anything in the world.

How I longed to *know* things, to be sophisticated and worldly. My father had traveled the globe when he was in the navy, and his stories inspired me to do the same. He told me about eating stuffed dog in Africa and hundred-year eggs in China; he explained communism and Castro, having lived in both Peking and Guantánamo; he told me to always order name liquor—Heineken, Tanqueray, Johnnie Walker; steak, my father, told me, should always be eaten rare. Yet even all of this advice did not tell me everything I needed to know to leave my working-class upbringing behind.

In *The Bell Jar*, Esther makes social blunders too. When she first arrives at the Amazon hotel in Manhattan, a bellhop carries her suitcase up to her room, then doesn't leave. Instead, he shows her the hot and cold water, how to use the radio, what stations are on the dial, before he finally leaves, slamming the door behind him. *"You ninny,"* her friend Doreen explains later, *"he wanted a tip."* At least a quarter, Doreen continues. Esther can't believe it: *"Now I could have carried that suitcase to my room perfectly well by myself, only the bell hop seemed so eager to do it that I let him. I thought that kind of service came along with what you paid for your hotel room."* When my family traveled, we stayed at motels with swimming pools and ice machines and Magic Fingers on the beds: for a dime the bed shimmied beneath you for a full minute. But I intended someday to stay at fancy hotels in big cities, and then I would tip bellhops, and cabdrivers (Esther quickly learns that they get 15 percent of the fare).

When I got home from the mall that afternoon, the phone was already ringing. I was one of sixteen finalists. On Saturday I was to go to the store for a tea. That day was a blur of brownie sundaes, Jordan Marsh executives, and fifteen other smiling girls. Those brownie sundaes were worrisome: a big square brownie, topped with vanilla ice cream, hot fudge, whipped cream, and a cherry, served in a frosty silver goblet. As we ate, the executives and the woman I'd spoken to the other day asked us questions about fashion trends, our favorite subjects in school, and our dreams for the future.

"I want to be a journalist like Barbara Walters," I said, trying not to smear hot fudge on my face or dribble ice cream down my shirt. How could I not think of the scene in which Esther has lunch with her benefactress, Mrs. Guinea, and saw her first fingerbowl? *"The water had some cherry blossoms floating in it, and I thought it must be some clear sort of Japanese after-dinner soup and ate every bit of it, including the crisp little blossoms."* Mrs. Guinea never says anything to Esther, and she muses how it was only later *"when I told a debutante I knew at college about the dinner, that I learned what I had done."* What were the rules for eating a brownie sundae? Should I leave the cherry? To be safe, I did.

In fact, I did not want to be a journalist like Barbara Walters; I wanted to write stories. I have no idea why I said that, except perhaps that teachers and guidance counselors and relatives always laughed when I said I wanted to be a *writer*, to make up stories and publish books. A journalist like Barbara Walters seemed more practical somehow. And the man looked impressed.

By dinnertime the phone rang again. I was a Marsha Jordan Girl.

ALL THESE YEARS later, I spend a good amount of my time knitting. I do it to calm myself, to soothe my confused and broken heart, to keep sadness at bay. I do it so that I won't lose my mind. That long-ago summer, when I felt like I was a giant nerve ending exposed to the harsh world, I didn't realize that stringing those long strands of beads in my hot backyard was accomplishing the same thing. That, and reading *The Bell Jar*. The novel was a warning. A possibility. An alternate version of the self I might become. It made me understand that young women did go to New York City and write. It made me glimpse a world of stylish clothes and new hairstyles and independence. It also made me tremble as I glimpsed the other side of a creative soul. How scary our talents and desires can be! How close to the edge we actually live.

Lesson 3: How to Ask Why

· *Johnny Got His Gun* BY DALTON TRUMBO ·

"TODAY IN THE WAR," WALTER CRONKITE SAID TO ME every evening from our black-and-white Zenith. Behind him, a map of Southeast Asia, Vietnam divided into north and south, Cambodia and Laos snuggled into it. I barely looked at that map, or the images of soldiers that followed Cronkite's introduction. I played with my favorite doll, Little Miss No Name, an orphan in a burlap patched dress, scraggly blond hair, and one big plastic teardrop on her cheek. Or I cut paper dolls or drew intricate series of stairs on my Etch A Sketch. By junior high, I talked on our heavy black telephone, sitting in front of the television as Cronkite announced the number of dead that day. Artillery fire flashed across the scene. I did my homework, dunked chocolate-covered graham crackers into a glass of milk, wrote haiku in purple ink in my poetry notebook. It had silhouettes of a boy and girl holding hands on a beach. Walter Cronkite said, "Tet Offensive." He said, "Viet Cong. Saigon. Hanoi."

I didn't know why we were fighting in Vietnam. In fact, it was many years later that I learned it all began in 1949, when Mao and communism came to power in China (where my father as a young man in the navy was sent). I knew only the simplest things: Ho Chi Minh was bad, Hanoi was north and Saigon was south, and we had been sending soldiers to fight over there . . . well, to me, forever. The shifting allegiances of the United States, Russia, and France were unknown to me, as was the fact that France had ruled Vietnam—Indochina—and was driven out in 1949. Although I knew that north and Hanoi was communist, I didn't know that the Geneva Accords had established the Seventeenth Parallel as the boundary between Vietnam's Communist north and non-Communist south in 1954, or that the Hanoi regime then resumed war by means of infiltration and southern insurgents. Even though I'm sure Walter Cronkite told me about the assassination of South Vietnam's dictator, Ngo Dinh Diem, in 1963 that led to the bombings and large-scale ground forces under President Johnson, I don't remember these historical details. I just remember watching it: the bombings, the soldiers fighting, the war.

The war ended in 1975, the year after I graduated from high school. I had no childhood without the Vietnam War in it. The draft loomed over everyone's head. At first, there were college deferments. Even so, around the kitchen table my aunts and uncles talked about writing to congressmen or someone—anyone—important. Our family did not know anyone important. But my father had a certain amount of cachet in our relatives' eyes. He had worked for Admiral Rickover at the Pentagon, though only as his driver and assistant. When he retired from the navy after twenty years, he took a job at a company called RMK that shipped goods to Vietnam. The job had required a high security clearance. His boss, Mr. Carothers, adored him. Surely he knew *somebody* who could keep my cousins Stephen, Michael, David, Alfred, and Chip out of the army, out of Vietnam, home and safe.

Stephen enlisted before he could get drafted and spent his time in the army in Walla Walla, Washington. Michael and Alfred got college deferments. But David got drafted and was shipped to Vietnam almost immediately, leaving his fiancée Claudette behind to plan their wedding alone. In my house, Mama Rose lit candles at the feet of statues of saints in the small shrines she kept around—the Virgin Mary, Saint Anthony, Saint Christopher. Novenas were made. I watched the war on TV, emotionless, not once thinking of Cousin David or any of the boys fighting on the screen right in front of me. This was my generation: immune to the horrors of war because it had been playing out in our living room our entire lives. One day our dog barked and growled like crazy outside and we all ran to see what was the matter. Cousin David was making his way up the sidewalk, home again.

Had one year passed? Or two? I have no idea. But the wedding was waiting for him. The bridesmaids had their shoes dyed to match their gowns. The groomsmen rented tuxedos with shirts the same color. At the bridal shower David and Claudette received electric knives and electric can openers and electric toothbrushes. As a girl, I loved weddings, and although I don't remember where this one was to be held, to me then weddings meant those fancy whiskey-sour fountains and string beans amandine and the hard, pale candies the women wrapped in tulle and tied with a ribbon. But just like that, the wedding was called off. David couldn't go through with it. And it seemed to have something to do with what happened in Vietnam. At night great debates roared around the kitchen table. Did they have to return the wedding presents? Did she have to return the engagement ring? Were they breaking up? Or just postponing the wedding?

That was the first indication I had that this war was not a two-dimensional image on my television screen. That gunfire was real. Those bodies falling were people. People dying. A person could go to war in love and return unable to go through with the wedding. Of course, I knew this was true of World War II. All of our fathers, except mine, who was just young enough to miss it, had been in the War. There were lingering bad feelings toward Japan and Germany. We celebrated V-J Day every August—Victory over Japan. We knew who Hitler was (though not the atrocities, not yet), and we knew what had happened on Omaha Beach and Iwo Jima. My cousin's neighbor Frenchie had one arm, the other lost at Iwo Jima. In the eponymous movie about the battle there was a character named Frenchie: him. He was one of the men in the famous statue of soldiers raising the flag. To me—maybe to all of us my age—that was the War. This thing on television was more like the show *Combat!* on Monday nights, Vic Morrow crawling toward the camera in his camouflage, clutching his gun.

The other war—World War I—seemed to have happened a million years earlier. It wasn't until high school that I even learned what had started it, Gavrilo Princip jumping out in front of Archduke Ferdinand in Sarajevo and shooting him and his wife. My father used to tell me about a teacher he had in grade school back in Indiana who was "shell-shocked from the war." If a child tapped his pencil or foot, the teacher would start to shake and run to the closet to hide. I never bothered to ask which war he'd fought in; it wasn't until many years later that I understood it was World War I. In front of the high school in our town stood a statue of a World War I soldier called Jerry, but to me the statue seemed to be there not to commemorate a war but rather to get spray-painted red and white by the Coventry Oakers, our football rivals on Thanksgiving weekend every year. When I watched *All Quiet on the Western Front* on *Saturday Night at the Movies* with Skip and Mama Rose (our parents out playing cards with my aunts and uncles as they did every Saturday night), I didn't even realize the movie was about World War I. World War II was the war that still haunted us, that in many ways seemed more real than the one we were actually fighting at the time.

ALTHOUGH I CAN'T say for certain, I must have gotten a copy of Dalton Trumbo's *Johnny Got His Gun* from one of my brother's friends. They often gave me books to read, most of which I didn't really understand. *The Tin Drum. Siddhartha. The Painted Bird. The Teachings of Don Juan.* But unlike those books, *Johnny Got His Gun* had a profound and lasting impact on me. Originally published in 1939, it is the story of Joe Bonham, an ordinary young man, in love with his sweetheart back home, who loses his arms, legs, face, ears—after a bomb dropped on him during World War I.

The book I read was a small paperback, and had a black cover with a large white hand forming a peace sign on it. Inside the palm of the hand stands the silhouette of a soldier in the iconic doughboy helmet of World War I, pointing a rifle. It was the edition I read a few years after it was released, dog-eared and wrinkled from so many readings by so many young men facing the draft. *"This was no war for you. This thing wasn't any of your business. What do you care about making the world safe for democracy? All you wanted to do Joe was live."* The little I knew about the Vietnam War sounded eerily similar. The United States was over there fighting for democracy, weren't they? North Vietnam was Communist. Communism was spreading. If they took over South Vietnam, no one was safe from it, were we? *"Oh why the hell did you ever get into this mess anyway? Because it wasn't your fight Joe. You never really knew what the fight was all about."*

Wait, I thought as I read, this was what my brother and his friends were saying in our backyard, on the beach, and sitting around our kitchen table. This wasn't our fight. This wasn't any of our business.

Sometimes I tried to imagine Skip or one of his friends in a uniform, holding a gun, standing in a jungle. I tried to imagine their faces on the soldiers who fought on my television screen every night on the news. But it was too frightening—in the war I watched on TV, the soldiers got shot. They died. I saw coffins draped in American flags, dead boys inside, waiting to come home. It sounds foolish to say this now, but it wasn't until that summer that I realized the war I saw on television was real. Now when Walter Cronkite announced the day's death toll, I listened.

They knew what was important. . . . They died with
only one thought in their minds and that was I want
to live I want to live I want to live.

SKIP AND HIS friends had college deferments. But
still the draft loomed over them. They drank beers
and ate Mama Rose's meatballs and sausage and
pepper sandwiches and talked about going to Canada
or Sweden for amnesty. Although there was something thrilling about that idea—sneaking over a bor-
der at night on foot; living among fjords and the
Northern Lights—I knew that if you did that you were
never allowed home to the United States again.
Surely Skip wouldn't opt for that, would he?

They discussed the viability of filing as a conscientious objector. A well-told story in our household
was that my mother had dated a conscientious objector during World War II. He was a Quaker and Quak-
ers were against war. (Of course, I had no idea what
a Quaker was, except that one peered out at me from
our container of oatmeal and that William Penn,

founder of Pennsylvania, had been one too.) Was it too late for Skip to convert and become a Quaker? I wondered. After all, our father had converted to Catholicism in order to marry our mother and he always said it was really nothing. "You believe what you believe anyway," he'd say.

All of these conversations made me unsettled in a way I couldn't explain. Suddenly, the war itself made me unsettled. I grew up in a mostly traditional family, surrounded by dozens of relatives who were Democrats, went to town hall meetings, and voted in every election. Two of my uncles had fought in WWII. The other had a bad heart and the army wouldn't take him, but he tried to enlist because you fought for your country. In other words, I was raised a proud American. My father was even born on the Fourth of July. He loved that his birthday was the same day as Independence Day. He'd blast John Philip Sousa music from the minute he woke up, and often at night the men who had come to his party, all of them WWII veterans, picked up broomsticks and mops and marched around the yard with tears in their eyes.

But after I read *Johnny Got His Gun*, I started to

question the things I'd been raised to believe. What were we fighting for in Vietnam anyway? Did Americans have the right to tell other countries how to live? What did it even mean to be an American? I started watching the news more carefully, and reading the newspaper reports about the war that I'd been ignoring. I sat in the backyard with Skip and his friends and listened to what they thought, what they believed. They discussed how Johnson had escalated the war, how we'd killed four hundred civilians at My Lai, how we'd secretly bombed Laos and Cambodia. No one could be trusted, not our president or any of the authority figures in charge.

Johnny thinks of himself as lying like a side of beef for the rest of his life. And for what? "*It was a kind of duty you owed yourself that when anybody said come on son do this or do that you should stand up and say look mister why should I do this for whom am I doing it and what am I going to get out of it in the end?*"

Around me, most of my cousins stayed on the path our parents had set us on. My father used to joke that we just followed our town's main street: baptized at

Sacred Heart, wedding at the Club 400, funeral at Prata's Funeral Home. As a child, I had found comfort in our church with its smell of wax and incense, the sounds of shoes walking on marble, the brilliance of its stained-glass windows. I'd loved those weddings at the Club 400 too, the specialness of that whiskey-sour fountain bubbling forth cocktails the adults caught in special half-moon-shaped glasses.

But asking "Why should I do this?" wasn't just about the war. It was about everything I thought I believed and knew. I'd always had this yearning for something I couldn't name, that no one could help me name. Maybe that yearning was a big question: why?

SOMETHING NEW STARTED taking up airtime on the news. Or maybe it had been happening before I began questioning, became *aware*. But it seemed to me that suddenly college students were protesting the war. They appeared in front of college buildings and on college greens, dozens and dozens of them, long hair and earnest faces, carrying signs: MAKE

LOVE NOT WAR and HELL NO WE WON'T GO. They were angry and passionate as they stood shoulder to shoulder, shouting and singing protest songs by Bob Dylan and Peter, Paul, and Mary like "Blowin' in the Wind" and "Where Have All the Flowers Gone?" I wanted to be one of them, to be a person who cared that much about something, a person who made a difference.

Once again, my world had been cracked open by a book. But this time, the world that was shifting around me—my own small one and the one outside it—and the book itself crashed together in such a way that I felt like I was suddenly awake. Around me, my classmates still seemed unaffected by the war, the demonstrations, all of it. Vietnam had become the backdrop of our childhoods and it was easy to keep it that way, in the background. But I'd had a summer of college boys sitting in my backyard discussing the war. I'd heard them debate my father at our kitchen table and for the first time in my young life I disagreed with him. I'd read *Johnny Got His Gun*, perhaps the greatest antiwar book ever written, a book of which Trumbo himself wrote: "Johnny held a different meaning for three different wars. Its present meaning is what each reader conceives it to be, and each reader is gloriously different from every other reader, and each is also changing. I've let it remain as it was to see what it is."

AT SCHOOL I was labeled a hippie. Even one of my favorite teachers took to calling me Hippie Ann. I wasn't offended; I was proud. To me, being a hippie meant that you cared about the world, that you wanted to help stop the war in Vietnam. With my gypsy skirts and John Lennon round wire-frame glasses, I dressed the part too. Except I wasn't acting; I was a girl too young to really do anything except try to be heard. In 1970, when the Ohio National Guard shot and killed four students at Kent State, I wore a black armband to school for a week. When I watched students on TV protesting the war, I used to think, *Wait for me. Wait for me to grow up enough to join you.*

Of course, the world didn't wait for me to grow up. By the time I went to college, the Vietnam War was finally ending and protests were a thing of the past. The hippies who were still on campus were burnouts who had smoked too much pot or dropped too much acid to do anything meaningful. Those socially minded students had been replaced by boys in white leisure suits and girls practicing the Hustle in their dorm rooms and playing the soundtrack from *Saturday Night Fever*. There were discos instead of sit-ins, high heels instead of sandals. In other words, nothing was how I'd hoped it would be when I arrived at college.

But the events I'd watched take place around me as an adolescent left me someone who leans further left than even my Democratic parents; who still protests and resists war. Although the war of my youth was fought in Vietnam, *Johnny Got His Gun* took place half a century earlier. Reading it didn't just make me take notice of what was happening around me; it showed me the horrors of all wars, of all the dead boys and misguided politicians. It made me ask why then, and it makes me still ask why now.

Lesson 4: How to Buy Books

· *Love Story* BY ERICH SEGAL ·

EVERY WEEK MY MOTHER TOOK ME ALONG WITH HER
to the local discount store, Ann & Hope, where she
bought curtains, bath mats, and tablecloths on the
cheap. Much to her disapproval, I brought my
allowance so that I could buy a Nancy Drew book.
The entire series was lined up, yellow spines out, the
numbers and titles in order, beginning with *The
Secret of the Old Clock* and ending with *The Spider
Sapphire Mystery*. I had no sisters, just a mathemati-

cally obsessed brother who solved problems on a slide ruler for fun. But my cousin Gloria-Jean, a year older than me, shared my passion for reading and she also used her allowance to buy a Nancy Drew book every week. Our plan was to read every one of them, trading our newest ones after we'd finished.

At the cash register, my mother shook her head and sighed. "I cannot believe you are wasting your money on a book. A book! Of all things!"

I didn't care. I held that yellow book close to my chest, and happily handed over my two dollars, the bills damp and creased.

Along the river of my small town, mills that had produced textiles in the nineteenth century now stood empty, leaving most of the town unemployed. A Champlin Grant to build a library led to breaking ground behind Main Street, where the movie theater showed XXX movies; Newberry's, the five-and-dime, was boarded up; and sleazy bars replaced what had once been fine clothing stores. To avid readers like Gloria-Jean and me, the progress on the library seemed practically glacial. By the time it finally opened, we had read every Nancy Drew book and were ready to move on.

Move on we did. Agatha Christie and Charles Dickens; Harold Robbins and Herman Wouk; Victor Hugo and Evan Hunter. We read indiscriminately. We read everything. Three, four, five books a week we read. "A waste of time!" my mother would say when I hung up with Gloria-Jean after chatting about our latest reads. "Put the book down and go outside and play!" In family pictures during this time, I am always holding a book in my lap, my finger holding my place.

Then, in 1970, something almost more miraculous than a library came to town. The Warwick Mall opened, just a mile from my house, an easy walk on a Saturday morning. Boston department stores Jordan Marsh and Filene's anchored each end of the mall. And on the path from one to the other stood the first bookstore I had ever seen. Waldenbooks was a small rectangle tucked between a fast-food steak house and a Spencer's Gifts. Although the lure of a

$3.99 steak and a lava lamp were great, nothing called to me more than that bookstore.

At the front, a wooden display showed hardcover bestsellers, face-out. Beside it, a spinning rack held paperbacks, more than I ever imagined existed. Sometimes, I went there and touched every single book, the smell of incense and French fries from the neighboring stores filling my nose, all of it intoxicating.

On one of those visits, the novel *Love Story* caught my eye. The book was slender, white, with the title in big red, blue, and green letters. I still remember how Erich Segal's name sat beneath it in red, and how the words "*Love means never having to say you're sorry*" seemed more profound than anything I had ever read. That spring and into fall, *Love Story* remained on the bestseller list, securing its spot on the front display of Waldenbooks. Although I cannot remember how much the book sold for in 1970, I do remember that the price seemed—no, *was*—astronomical to an eighth grader in West Warwick, Rhode Island. If my mother thought spending $1.99

on a Nancy Drew book was a waste of money, what would she say if I brought home this beautiful, expensive hardcover book? I was not a kid who got in trouble, but I could imagine my mother's wrath at such a purchase.

One day, as I stood fondling the book and pondering how love meant never having to say you're sorry, it occurred to me that giving a book to Gloria-Jean would be the most wonderful present anyone had ever given her. Even though we already owned those Nancy Drew books, this book, *Love Story*, was a real book. A hardcover! A bestseller! Imagine owning such a thing! I remember that the cold weather had arrived, and I was wearing my pale blue winter jacket. Yet I shivered at the thought of it.

I saved my allowance until the December day I could go into Waldenbooks and buy *Love Story*, the first real book I'd ever bought, and the first book I would give as a gift. Could the shaggy-haired, green-eyed boy who rang up the purchase understand how important this moment was for me? I don't think so. After all, he stood behind that cash register all day selling books, as if it were nothing special. Muzak

Christmas carols filled the air. Lights twinkled from every storefront. I had never felt the Christmas spirit as much as I did at that moment. But when he asked me if I wanted the book gift-wrapped, I hesitated and shook my head, even though the wrapping paper there was much more beautiful than the kind we had at home from Ann & Hope.

Instead, I tucked the slim book in its Waldenbooks paper bag inside my jacket, and walked home along the snowy streets, past the dilapidated mill houses with their flashing blue Christmas lights, over the bridge that crossed the sluggish Pawtuxet River, past the three churches, and up the big slippery hill. Once inside and warm, I pulled my treasure from the bag. Then I carefully opened the book the tiniest bit, and read it from beginning to end without cracking the spine. I think I began to cry at the first line: *"What can you say about a twenty-five-year-old girl who died?"* By the end, when Jenny dies of leukemia and her young husband, Oliver, delivers that iconic line— *"Love means not ever having to say you're sorry"*—to his wealthy father, I was sobbing.

Certainly I was sobbing because Jenny died, and

because Mr. Barrett had acted so mean to her and Oliver, and because the father and son were together again. But looking back on it now, I think too that this story of a blue-collar girl from Rhode Island falling in love with a rich Harvard jock made me— perhaps for the first time—aware of deep class differences. In my town, though there were a few wealthy families with lawyer or businessman fathers, most of us were varying degrees of middle class. We were used to the kids, many of them, on welfare; we barely took notice of the kids who couldn't afford rain or snow boots and came to school with Wonder Bread bags tied around their shoes with rubber bands. Jenny and Ollie, I realized, came from two different worlds. And those worlds didn't easily accept each other. What would my place be in this big world I wanted so desperately to see? Through teary eyes, I closed the book and wrapped it in the flimsy Ann & Hope Christmas paper, topping it with a big silver bow.

Since that long-ago day, I have given more books than I can count as Christmas presents. But none have meant as much to me. That first one showed me something I already knew—that owning books is not a waste of money, not at all. But I now realize that it was my first step toward a kind of independence, entering into that world of books and language that was so foreign to my family. But not to me—no, I understood that I would always buy books, that I was a reader and a writer and that to be surrounded by books would always bring me comfort.

THIS SUMMER, I FOUND myself in the throes of upheaval. Newly divorced, I was leaving my home of almost twenty years, a cozy red Colonial built in 1792, and moving across town with my twelve-year-old daughter Annabelle to a big bright loft in a renovated factory. Of course the week I had to pack and move was the hottest one of the summer, with temperatures and humidity in the nineties, and that old house had no air-conditioning and windows that stuck shut when they swelled. In those hot, airless rooms I packed up my married life—the carefully saved art my kids had made, my enormous stash of yarn, the Fiestaware and Italian pottery I'd collected. My final task: the rows and rows of books that lined three walls of one room.

Back when I moved into that house, on another summer day, I'd happily alphabetized the books, separating them into categories: fiction, memoir, biography, poetry, drama, reference. How happy I'd been that day as slowly the books took their places, as my daughter Grace twirled around the empty dining room (we couldn't yet afford a table and chairs for it) in her sparkly tutu and my son, Sam, sang "Wonder of Wonders" from *Fiddler on the Roof*. And what a contrast this moving day was, this taking down of all those books and putting them into boxes—FICTION A–C, FICTION M. Sam grown and living in Brooklyn, Grace dead fourteen years, my heart, once so full, now broken again.

I cried as I packed my books. And I screamed. But I smiled too, a lot. As I held each book, deciding if I really needed to take it with me, I could remember reading—and sometimes rereading—it. Here were all my Alice Adams short story collections, a writer hardly known anymore but whose stories I still quote when I teach; my small paperback of Raymond

Carver's *What We Talk About When We Talk About Love*, read on a New York City subway; *Bright Lights, Big City*, which I bought at the Spring Street Bookstore the day it came out; my dog-eared copies of *The Collected Stories of F. Scott Fitzgerald* and *So Long, See You Tomorrow*; three copies of C. S. Lewis's *A Grief Observed*, all given to me after Grace died to help soothe my grief, which it did ("*Her absence is like the sky*," Lewis wrote, "*it covers everything*"). So many books, each of them returning a piece of myself to me—starry-eyed optimist, new writer, single Manhattan young woman, grief-stricken mother.

My new home had no built-in bookshelves, so my books stayed in the dozens and dozens of boxes until the new IKEA shelves were built; the older, smaller shelves found places in the loft; and still more bookshelves were bought and assembled. Until one day I looked up and the boxes were gone, the books—alphabetized and by genre—lined up again. *What is this life?* I ask myself almost every day as I look around at my new home, so big and open and sunny. I have two cats, Hermia and Gertrude, who sleep on my feet and lap. I've bought a turntable so that I can play my albums again, those songs of my youth also returned to me. And the lines that had so moved me as a teenager, that played even as I sat on my bed and read *Love Story*, move me still, perhaps even more true all these years later: *I have my books, and my poetry to protect me . . .*

Lesson 5: How to Write a Book

· *The Grapes of Wrath* BY JOHN STEINBECK ·

IF ONE BOOK CARRIED MAGIC, IMAGINE WHAT FOUR books could do. Four books nestled together in a box wrapped in red-and-green striped paper, topped with an extravagantly large bow, like a red dahlia had perched there, sitting under the Christmas tree with a tag bearing my name. Those four books were all by John Steinbeck, a writer most kids today have read by ninth grade when they were assigned *Of Mice and Men*. In my junior high, however, we weren't assigned novels. We read the short stories in our English literature textbook: "The Lottery" by Shirley Jackson; "Bartleby the Scrivener" by Herman Melville; "The Celebrated Jumping Frog of Calaveras County" by Mark Twain. And I loved those stories, loved taking essay tests on them and discussing them in class, loved reading them and thinking about them. Why did Bartleby *prefer not to*? What would I do if I was the one chosen in "The Lottery"? Could I have sat through Simon Wheeler's long story about Jim Smiley and his jumping frog?

But oh! A novel! And that Christmas of 1973, four novels!

"He's really good," my brother Skip said as I held that boxed set of Steinbeck in my hands. I wonder now if he saw that his gift made me cry? Somehow, he knew the real me; knew that I was someone who wanted nothing more than to read books; knew that, as C. S. Lewis said, "You can never get a book long enough to suit me." Two of those Steinbeck books were big, fat ones, the kind I loved to read most: *The Grapes of Wrath* and *East of Eden*. The other two were slender: *Of Mice and Men* and *Travels with Charley*.

Skip was telling me how Steinbeck had won both

the Pulitzer Prize and the Nobel Prize for Literature. But I had no idea of the import of those prizes, or even what the distinction between them was. I managed to say thank you and to give him a quick kiss on his bearded cheek before I slipped away. Alone, with the twenty-four hours of Christmas music playing on the radio downstairs and the smell of Mama Rose's baking lasagna wafting up to me, I tore off the plastic and let the books drop from the box into my lap. I touched each cover in turn, held each book in my hand, opened to random pages. *"Charley is a mind-reading dog. There have been many trips in his lifetime . . ." "I remember about the rabbits, George . . ." "All great and precious things are lonely . . ."* And then this: *"To the red country and part of the gray of Oklahoma, the last rains came gently, and they did not cut the scarred earth."*

I read that first line of *The Grapes of Wrath*, and I couldn't stop.

THE GRAPES OF WRATH was published on April 14, 1939. Steinbeck wrote it in just four months, from June to October of 1938, when he was thirty-six years old. He put himself on a writing schedule to complete the novel in 100 days, averaging 2,000 words a day. Though some days, when the pressures of his life intruded (houseguests, buying and renovating a ranch) he only wrote 800 words, other days he wrote as many as 2,200. On October 26, he wrote the final 775 words and beneath them, in inch-and-a-half-high letters: "END."

Steinbeck had that ending in mind from the start, an image that he wrote toward, something the writer John Irving does too. "I have last chapters in my mind before I see first chapters," Irving told *The Paris Review* in 1986. "I usually begin with endings, with a sense of aftermath, of dust settling, of epilogue. I love plot, and how can you plot a novel if you don't know the ending first?"

When I finished reading *The Grapes of Wrath*, so many things about writing a novel became clear to me. Plot. Character. Conflict. Escalating stakes. Metaphor. *The Grapes of Wrath* begins with a drought and ends with a flood. Years later I would hear a lecture by a writer on this very device, which she called the rules of polarity. In my own novel *The Knitting*

Circle, the protagonist, Mary, is empty-handed, both literally and emotionally, at the beginning; the final image is of abundance, Mary holding so much yarn that her arms are overflowing. When the Joads are in a rain-soaked barn at the end, I understood the impact of such a polarity.

In that barn they encounter a starving man and his son, whom the father had given their last bit of food. The dying man needs soup or milk to survive. The eldest Joad daughter, Rose of Sharon, has had a stillborn child. Ma Joad and Rose of Sharon "*looked deep into each other*," and Rose of Sharon says, "*Yes.*" Ma smiles: "*I knowed you would. I knowed.*"

> *For a minute Rose of Sharon sat still in the whis-*
> *pering barn. Then she hoisted her tired body up and*
> *drew the comfort around her. She moved slowly to*
> *the corner and stood looking down at the wasted*
> *face, into the wide, frightened eyes. Then slowly she*
> *lay down beside him. He shook his head slowly*
> *from side to side. Rose of Sharon loosened one side*
> *of the blanket and bared her breast. "You got to,"*
> *she said. She squirmed closer and pulled his head*
> *close. "There!" she said. "There." Her hand moved*

behind his head and supported it. Her fingers
moved gently in his hair. She looked up and across
the barn, and her lips came together and smiled
mysteriously.

I had never read an ending that affected me like
this one of Rose of Sharon giving her milk to the
dying stranger. Speechless, I read the final scene
again and again, its power never lessening. Even as
a teenager, I understood the symbolism and power
inherent in Rose of Sharon's selfless act. In *A Life in
Letters*, Steinbeck said that he had "tried to make the
reader participate in the actuality, what he [the
reader] takes from it will be scaled entirely on his
own depth or hollowness." Referring to there being
five layers in the book, he added that "a reader will
find as many as he can and he won't find more than
he has in himself." It may seem hyperbolic, but I
believe understanding this not only shaped me as a
writer but also led me to become an English major
when I went to college. I wanted more symbolism,
more of those layers in literature. I wanted to find as
many as I could, in both my reading and my writing life.

·

FOR YEARS MY math whiz brother was a mysterious blur in my life. Five years older than me, he mostly kept his distance from his bookworm little sister. I was, in the way of all little sisters, a nuisance. I cried if he sat too close to me in the backseat of the car. I cried when he got control of the television and forced me to sit through *Combat!* or *The Three Stooges.* I snooped on him and his first girlfriend, a tough-looking blonde with plum-colored suede boots and a leather miniskirt. I snooped on him and his buddies when they whispered together in his room, the air thick with exotic, musty, sweaty smells. He sat across from me at the dinner table, reigning over the bowl of mashed potatoes, getting extra pieces of steak from our grandmother, always the slide ruler nearby. "Does your face hurt?" he'd ask me. "'Cause it's killing me!"

Then he was gone, off to college in his raspberry Bermuda shorts and matching polo shirt. I barely noticed. By then, I was entering junior high and my world became slumber parties and crushes on boys. I never even thought about Skip. Until he returned home that summer, now long-haired and wearing ripped jeans and pocket T-shirts, driving a lime-green VW Bug. He brought boys with him. And not just any boys, but *college* boys. Loads of them, each in their own VW Bug. Once again, he seemed to reign, this time over the picnic table in the backyard with a cooler of beer beside it. He worked that summer as a stock boy at Zayre, a local discount store, and there he acquired a cool, aloof, freckle-faced girlfriend who wore brown suede moccasins and a hard stare.

I kept a diary back then, mostly documenting how boring my life was. The one glimmer of emotion came in March of that year when I heard that Paul McCartney had gotten married. *Oh God*, I wrote, *please don't let it be true*. The next day's entry: *Bored*.

But when my brother's new girlfriend arrived, hanging back by the front door, glaring, clutching his hand, I began to write about her. And them. If I had been a more mature twelve-year-old, I might have recognized the sexual tension between them, understood that her constant desire to "go *now*" was sexual desire. Instead, they seemed oddly

mysterious, with their whispering and disappear-
ances. I became the Nancy Drew of romance, mis-
taking that sexual energy for what, I believed, must
be love.

This, of course, made me even more of a nuisance.
No, I couldn't go with them to the mall. Or for ice
cream. Or on a walk. Or to the beach. Or anywhere.
Still, I persisted in asking, and reported to my
mother every time I was rebuked. My mother knew
exactly what was going on, and she didn't like it,
didn't like this brown-moccasined girl who kept my
brother out late, made him miss dinner with the
family, and wouldn't join a game of cards with us.
Take your sister, she'd insist, and sometimes he would
relent. I'd sit squeezed into the backseat of the Bug,
watching his girlfriend's hand rub his thigh.

By Skip's junior year, they'd moved in together
and he hardly came home at all that summer. And
then, as his college graduation approached and he
got a job with a chemical company in Connecticut,
they announced they were getting married. Reluctantly, his fiancée asked me to be a bridesmaid, and
she and her friends mostly ignored me through the

endless bridal showers and gown fittings that ensued. The May day they got married I stood holding a bouquet of daisies, dressed in a pale yellow chiana gown, as "Sunrise, Sunset" played. But I was insignificant—to the wedding, and to my brother.

Or so I thought.

When he returned from his honeymoon in Europe later that summer, he brought me a gift—a cork box shaped like a windmill from Portugal. Perhaps he knew I was already chasing after windmills? We sat at the picnic table in the backyard together, his new gold wedding band glinting in the hot sun.

I asked him about his travels, and he told me that there was a shortage of cork trees and someday wine would all have twist-off caps. That was the thing about my brother, the thing I didn't realize until after he died nine years later. He was a visionary, always predicting technological advances and changes in the world as we knew it. Years later he would buy one of the first Betamaxes, showing me the miracle of taping television shows and watching them whenever you wanted to, zipping past the commercials. And a few years after that, he was one of the first people in the United States to get corrective eye surgery, restoring his bad eyesight to twenty-twenty vision and eliminating the need to wear glasses. So long ago was this that the surgery, performed by a Russian ophthalmologist, was done with scalpels instead of lasers.

That afternoon in our backyard, Skip asked me about myself, as if I were someone he'd just met. "What do you *do*?" he asked me. The answer was that I did a lot. I listed my activities: Marsha Jordan Girl, traveling back and forth to Boston to do fashion shows and mother-daughter teas, a floater at Jordan Marsh covering people's breaks and vacations in the Linens or Misses department. As I told him all this, he cocked his head and looked at me as if for the first time. He grinned. My brother had the most charming grin

"Mostly," I said, "I read."

BEFORE SKIP GAVE me that boxed set of Steinbeck, no one had ever given me a book as a gift. But the gift was even bigger than he'd imagined. When I read the first line of *The Grapes of Wrath*—"*To the red country and part of the gray of Oklahoma, the last rains came gently, and they did not cut the scarred earth*"—some writerly thing broke loose in me. "Spread a page with shining," Steinbeck once advised writers, and I could see that shine as I read. I understood it. I had read big, fat novels before, losing myself in Victor Hugo's *Les Misérables* and Boris Pasternak's *Doctor Zhivago*. Those sweeping stories, tragedies and triumphs spanning years and years, had captivated me for their otherness. But *The Grapes of Wrath* was so American, and the Joads so familiar somehow, and the language so lyrical, and the setting so real, that by reading it I saw what writers could do. And it dazzled me.

For years I had asked English teachers and guidance counselors how to become a writer. No one could tell me. John Steinbeck could though. *Write like this*, he seemed to be saying. *Tell our story. Tell your story.* Steinbeck intentionally wrote *The Grapes of Wrath* in five layers, intending to "rip the reader's nerves to rags by making him participate in its actuality." By writing the novel this way, Steinbeck ensured it would have an impact on all kinds of readers, and that impact might be personal, historical, sociological, or political. Grace Paley said: "No story is ever one story, it's always at least two. The one on the surface and the one bubbling beneath." I understood this somehow when I read *The Grapes of Wrath*, those layers slowly revealing themselves to me, showing me how a novel can have such breadth and touch anyone.

I only wish my brother had lived to see my first novel in a bookstore window. But he died on June 30, 1982, in his bathtub in Pittsburgh, when he slipped and fell, drowning in less than an inch of water. My first novel, *Somewhere Off the Coast of Maine*, was published five years later. For years I had been writing a dreadful first novel called *The Betrayal of Sam Pepper*, about a woman in her mid twenties living in Marblehead, Massachusetts, and feuding with a neighbor who has betrayed her boyfriend—in other words, a woman very much like me. How I toiled over that mess, staying up late at night to revise the pages I'd written in hotels on layovers as a TWA flight attendant. Some chapters sounded very much like imita-

tion Hemingway, some like imitation Fitzgerald—
which is exactly what they were. The plot meandered
and grew preposterous, the dialogue was stilted,
characters appeared and then vanished from the
story, forgotten. Hundreds of handwritten pages.

The summer that my brother died, I moved home
to be with my parents, until one day in August my
mother told me to leave, to "go and live your life."
What a gift that was, to free me from their grief. A
few weeks later, I boarded an Amtrak train to New
York City, my clothes and manuscript in a Hefty
trash bag, $1,000 in my front jeans pocket. I moved
into a tiny sublet on Sullivan Street in Greenwich
Village, with a door topped with a piece of foam on
a sawhorse for a bed. I had never lived alone and
wasn't actually sure what to do. So I did what I
always did—I wrote. Except after what had happened
to me that summer, *The Betrayal of Sam Pepper*
seemed banal and facile and dull—which it was. I
gathered all those hundreds of pages and threw
them in the dumpster in front of my building. Then
I sat down at my newly acquired electric typewriter
and typed: "*To Sparrow her father was a man standing*

in front of a lime green VW van . . ." The first line of my first published novel, *Somewhere Off the Coast of Maine.*

I began writing it the September after Skip died, trying, I see now, to understand what happened to him, to my family. I once heard an interview with the writer Kaye Gibbons in which she said all of her novels are about the death of her mother. Confused, the interviewer notes that none of her novels are about that. Gibbons said, "Oh, yes they are. Every one." Nowhere in that novel does a character resembling my brother appear, yet to me he is on every page.

Like many first novels, *Somewhere Off the Coast of Maine* tackled a lot of themes and topics: grief, friendship, love (romantic, parental, first love), cancer, the upheaval of the 1960s, the materialism of the 1980s, and even more. Overly ambitious perhaps, but I wanted those five layers that Steinbeck wrote about. All those years ago, on that Christmas when I sat on my yellow-and-white gingham bedspread and read *The Grapes of Wrath*, I understood viscerally and intellectually how good books illuminate so much more than the story on the surface, as Paley

would say. True, the Joads are "*a people in flight*," and
the plot follows that flight from Oklahoma to California. But Steinbeck is also writing about the post-
Depression urge for mobility and striving, political
protests, the American Dream, desperate misery
and suffering, disillusionment, and somehow hope.
How I knew this as a sixteen-year-old reader, with
no one with whom to share my ideas about literature,
I cannot say. But I did know it, and I knew too that
all I had to do to make my own dream of becoming a
writer come true was to write every day, and to read
every book I could get my hands on, to spread pages
with shining.

Lesson 6: How to Fall in Love with Language

· *Stanyan Street & Other Sorrows* BY ROD MCKUEN ·

"ONOMATOPOEIA," MY EIGHTH-GRADE ENGLISH TEACHER said. Then she wrote the strange word on the board. "A word that imitates the natural sound of the thing," she continued.

I copied the word into my notebook, my mind already excited by this new thing, this word with too many vowels.

"Whoosh," she was saying. "Cock-a-doodle-doo. Splash. Bang."

Wait. There was a word for that? This was my first introduction to the world of literary devices, and I felt like a door had just opened into a kingdom where I belonged.

The teacher told us to write down examples of onomatopoeia, and once I began, I couldn't stop.

Rat-a-tat-tat. Plop. Slap. Rustle. Cuckoo.

I filled one lined page and began another. Buzz! Boom! Onomatopoeia!

That year, I was trying not to be the kid who always raised her hand with the right answer, the kid who kept asking questions long after the lesson had ended. My endless curiosity for learning, my hunger to discuss everything with anyone, even sometimes exhausted my teachers. It definitely irritated my classmates. I had vowed to stop. But when the teacher asked for some examples of onomatopoeia, I couldn't control myself. I stood and read my forty-two examples, so thrilled by the sounds of those words and the fact that there was actually a name for them that when I'd read all the ones I'd written down, I kept talking because more examples of this lovely thing were still popping into my head.

"Snap, crackle, pop!" I said, delighted.

My classmates either glared at me or turned their glazed eyes toward the window, where autumn had just started to announce itself with a spattering of red and yellow leaves.

The teacher thanked me, then asked me to sit down, please.

The class clown said, "Belch," and everyone laughed. Except me. I was too busy to join in.

I GREW UP in a family that spoke Italian. In fact, most of the people in my neighborhood spoke Italian—black-clad women toting handmade baskets full of eggplants and tomatoes they'd grown, mustachioed men sitting at card tables on the sidewalk playing cards and smoking stogies. Our houses held two or three generations, our yards were gardens and orchards and chicken coops (no swing sets or tree houses), shrines to the Virgin Mary sat at the front door, and Italian filled the air. My great-grandmother spoke only Italian, no English. My grandmother spoke broken English.

My mother and her siblings moved back and forth between the two languages, even when they were sitting around the kitchen table playing cards or gossiping. Usually they slipped into Italian when they didn't want us kids to understand what they were saying, perhaps about scoundrel uncles or loose women.

We were forbidden from learning Italian because these three generations had suffered so much cruelty and prejudice for being immigrants. They were made fun of for the lunches they brought to school, the smell of garlic and onions that emanated from their kitchens, their olive skin and large noses and larger families. They were called "wops" and "guineas"; they were told they were greasy and dirty. No, the older generations decided, we were going to be spared all that. We were going to be American. So Italian floated around me like a pleasant fog, a kind of poetry, I realize now. The older cousins mastered the swearwords, and taught those to us. They felt delicious on my tongue, those foreign dirty words, forbidden.

Auntie Angie used to sit with me when I was little

and read the stories I'd written. There were seven girls and three boys in my mother's family, and Auntie Angie was the one who never had a daughter. Her son Stephen was the oldest of all the cousins, exactly ten years older than me, so that by the time I was in school he was off to college and then onto his life. Auntie Angie loved all her nieces, exotic birds in ruffled dresses.

One afternoon, when I was seven or eight, as I sat beside her at the enamel-topped kitchen table, she produced from the depths of her handbag a neatly folded newspaper clipping. She smoothed it out and told me to read it out loud.

" 'I never saw a Purple Cow,' " I read. " 'I never hope to see one. But I can tell you, anyhow, I'd rather see than be one!' "

Auntie Angie hooted with laughter. "This guy, Ogden Nash, he makes the best rhymes!"

Why this poem was in the newspaper, or how Auntie Angie had heard of Ogden Nash, I cannot say. What I do know is that reading that nonsense poem out loud, feeling the rhymes slide off my tongue, reaching the delightful ending—*I'd rather see than be one!*—was an experience that I still can't describe, like the first time you ride your bike without training wheels or watch television in color instead of black and white. A world opened up.

Perhaps seeing my surprised expression, Auntie Angie said, "It's a *poem*. It *rhymes*."

Poem. Rhyme. Still a wonderful mystery even as I read it over and over, with Auntie Angie explaining that "cow" and "anyhow" rhyme.

Finally she went back into that bottomless handbag and retrieved a small lined notebook and Bic pen. "Here," she said, "you write down some rhymes."

I stared at the blank paper until Auntie Angie, muttering, "Jesus, let me start," made columns with words at the top: "Hair." "Car." "Dog." Not unlike the day years later when I understood onomatopoeia, I began to write, slowly at first and then with wild abandon. Words tumbled from my brain. I was rhyming!

Auntie Angie lit a fresh Pall Mall and checked my list from time to time, but mostly went back to talking with her sisters. Before she left, she turned to a fresh page in the notebook and said, "When I

come back, find a rhyme for this word." And in perfect block letters, she wrote: PURPLE.

For several agonizing days, I struggled unsuc-
cessfully to find a word that rhymed with "purple."
Maybe she would forget, I hoped. Maybe she wouldn't
come back. Neither of these possibilities were even
remotely likely to happen. Auntie Angie never forgot
anything. And, like all of my aunts and uncles, she
came to visit three or four or even five times a week.
Sure enough, one afternoon I came home from
school and there she was, Pall Mall dangling between
her red-lipsticked lips.

"Well?" she asked almost immediately.

I swallowed hard and reluctantly admitted, "No
word rhymes with purple."

"Ha! That's not what our friend Ogden Nash says!"

Years later I would learn that Ogden Nash hadn't
invented that nonsense rhyme. But at that moment,
I hated him. And maybe even Auntie Angie.

"Maple surple rhymes with purple!" Auntie Angie
said, and laughed good and hard.

I frowned. Maple surple wasn't a thing or a word.
But slowly I understood. Words and rhymes were

fun. You could play with them, mix them up, turn them around, rearrange letters, make things up. Grinning, I climbed onto Auntie Angie's lap. She dug into that giant handbag again, pulled out the notebook and pen, and told me to do some rhyming. Yes, I was back in love with Auntie Angie, but I was in love with something else too, something big and strange and thrilling: language.

FIRST THERE WAS onomatopoeia, and then there was simile—*as blue as the sky, as blue as denim, blue like the morning*, I wrote—and then metaphor and haiku and sonnets. Suddenly my world of prose was broken up and all I wanted to do was write poetry. We read "Annabel Lee" and "The Raven" and "Richard Cory" and "The Road Not Taken." We got extra credit for memorizing Oliver Goldsmith's "The Deserted Village." How I loved sitting alone in my room, saying that poem aloud: *Sweet Auburn, loveliest village of the plain, / Where health and plenty cheered the laboring swain . . .*

It did not occur to me that somewhere in the

library sat volumes of poetry. It seemed to me a precious thing, a poem, and I could not begin to imagine where poems resided. But one night as I played my favorite album, Simon and Garfunkel's *Sounds of Silence*, it struck me that its eponymous song was actually a poem. Wasn't *darkness, my old friend* personification? And *words like silent raindrops fell* a simile? *The neon God* a metaphor? I played the song over and over, a notebook in hand, teasing out its meaning. Then I turned my attention to *I am a rock*—metaphor! *I am an island*! When we had to write a paper on our favorite poet, my classmate Nancy wrote hers on Robert Frost and Steven wrote his on Edgar Allan Poe. But me, I wrote mine on Paul Simon.

ONE SATURDAY WHEN I was in tenth grade, as I made my circuit around the Warwick Mall, a book caught my eye in the window at Waldenbooks. Slim, with an electric-blue cover and yellow and white letters that reminded me of a Peter Max poster, it read *Stanyan Street & Other Sorrows* in yellow, and above it, in white, the name Rod McKuen. Beside it was another Rod

McKuen book, *Lonesome Cities*. Also slim, with a moody gray cover of clouds and, in the same psychedelic typeface, the title in hot pink. I went inside the bookstore, and picked up *Stanyan Street & Other Sorrows*.

"The words within these pages are for music," the inside flap read. "They sing of love lost and found and lost again. They are hymns to the dying, sonnets to the summer and verses of the joy of being wanted—even for a night." All of the poems were written by Rod McKuen, the flap said, one of the finest chansonniers in the country. Later, of course, back at home, I went directly to my Reader's Digest dictionary and looked up the word "chansonnier": a poet-songwriter, solitary singer, who sang his or her own songs. But standing there with that book in my hand, it only mattered that I was holding a book of poetry, a book that spoke of dying and summer and loneliness, the very things that I paced my room worrying about at night.

The poems themselves were slight, most just two or three short stanzas. But they were so profound, I thought. They weren't like the few we'd read in school, which though I'd loved their rhythm and rhyme were formal and complicated. These poems

ANN HOOD

by Rod McKuen seemed to speak directly to me, perhaps directly to every teenager in 1970. *"Sometimes I think people were meant to be strangers . . ."* Why at the tender age of fourteen I felt so lonely and alienated I cannot say. But when Paul Simon sang, *"I am a rock, I am an island,"* my heart screamed, "I am too!" And when Rod McKuen wrote about not getting close to others to avoid damaging your heart, it sounded like he had read what was in *my* heart.

I knew nothing of love, having only kissed a boy once at the Rocky Point amusement park the summer before. But I believed what Rod McKuen wrote: *"I know that love is worth all the time it takes to find." "Think of that,"* he said, *"when all the world seems made of . . . empty pockets."* I too would be *"content to live on the sound your stomach makes,"* content to eat *"marmalade and oysters for breakfast." "If you keep the empty heart alive a little longer / love will come. / It always does . . ."* he wrote in "Some Thoughts for Benson Green on His 27th Birthday." Yes! I thought as I read. I could keep my empty heart alive!

In "Spring Song" he asked: *"Where were you when I was growing up and needed somebody?"* Standing in that Waldenbooks, I began to weep when I read that line. As much as I'd loved to carefully write the rhyme patterns on poems at school and to ponder their meanings, Rod McKuen's free-form poems made me feel like he was whispering secrets to me. I memorized the simile that ended "State Beach"— *"the rain comes down like tears"*—and wrote it in my purple lined notebook with all the other snippets of songs and sentences I collected there.

I don't remember how much the book cost, surely no more than six or seven dollars, but whatever it cost was too expensive for me. Instead, every Saturday when I went to the mall, I stood memorizing the poems in *Stanyan Street & Other Sorrows*, and later in *Listen to the Warm* and *Lonesome Cities*. Even now, long after I've learned better poems, long after I've fallen in love with E. E. Cummings and Emily Dickinson and Elizabeth Bishop, I can still recite Rod McKuen's poem "Ellen's Eyes": *"All the space is taken up / remembering Ellen's eyes."*

FROM THE DISTANCE of so many decades, I understand the appeal to a yearning, dreamy young girl of a chansonnier who wrote about the beach and the rain, both of which remain important to me. I even understand how all that loneliness spoke to me, a girl who felt alone in the world in which she lived. But I see too how those poems reflected my yearning to leave my familiar world. And in 1970, when teenagers left home, they went to San Francisco. The Summer of Love had been just the year before, and magazines and newspapers printed photographs of hippies every day, long-haired girls with flowers in their hair and blue-jeaned barefoot boys in Haight-Ashbury. Even a group as seemingly benign as the Cowsills sang about loving the flower girl, who sits smiling in the rain with flowers in her hair—*Flowers everywhere!*

Part of what seduced me on that long-ago Saturday afternoon at the Warwick Mall was the poetry of Kearny Street and Sausalito, of hills and fog, of San Francisco. Years later, when I went to San Francisco for the first time, I got a map from the hotel concierge and had him point out Stanyan Street to me. Then I made my way there, to Haight-Ashbury and that street lined with Victorian houses. All of the girls who wore flowers in their hair were long gone by then, and Stanyan Street looked very different from what I'd imagined. Yet when I looked up at the street sign with its name on it, I remembered the poem of that name: "*I have total recall of you / and Stanyan Street / because I know it will be important later . . .*"

How could I know all those years ago how important these words and Paul Simon's and Ogden Nash's and that afternoon when the world broke open and I learned about onomatopoeia would be? How all of these things, these poems, turned me into a lover of language and its infinite joys. Pop! Boom! In that moment on Stanyan Street, I saw that girl standing in that bookstore in that mall, clutching a slim neon-blue volume of poems that promised someday she would fall in love, be loved, and find herself in San Francisco. Even that young girl knew that such is the power of poetry, a gift that stayed with her the rest of her life.

Lesson 7: How to Be Curious

· *A Stone for Danny Fisher* BY HAROLD ROBBINS ·

AS A TEENAGER I READ INDISCRIMINATELY. AT THE library, as I've said, I usually chose books by their size—the fatter the better. Although that meant that I discovered Victor Hugo and Tolstoy and Dickens by the time I was fifteen, it also meant that I read— and, I admit, loved—Irving Wallace, Jacqueline Susann, and Harold Robbins with equal fervor. In one week I might read *Anna Karenina* and *Hawaii*, the next *Les Misérables* and *Valley of the Dolls*. I devoured Evan Hunter's *Paper Lions* with as much intensity as I did *Great Expectations*. Doris Lessing could have been talking about me and my reading habits when she said, "With a library you are free . . . it is the most democratic of institutions because no one—but no one at all—can tell you what to read and when and how."

When I look back on the books that shaped me, the ones that taught me how to think and live and dream, a surprising one keeps coming into my mind: *A Stone for Danny Fisher* by Harold Robbins. The cover screams bodice ripper. A raven-haired beauty half reclines on a bed, wearing a silky black slip and stockings held up by garters. Below, a glistening shirtless Danny Fisher stares down at a man he has just knocked out in a boxing ring. When I began to reread it again a half century later I could hear the advice I give writing students: don't overuse the action of looking; don't repeat words; don't use ellipses; stay in the point of view; avoid sentimentality and melodrama—all of which Robbins employs on every page. The plot revolves around Danny, a young Jewish boy who at eight years old moves with his family to a home he loves in Brooklyn. He acquires a dog and friends in short order and soon even learns that the older teenage girl across the street likes to leave her shades up so he can watch her undress, something that makes him feel filthy. Danny punishes himself by taking showers so cold they hurt.

There's lots of sex in *A Stone for Danny Fisher*, though often I couldn't tell if he had just kissed someone, actually had sex with her, or just felt her breasts. More than once I had to reread scenes, confused by Danny's feelings of guilt after being with a girl. But second and even third reads left me just as confused. Perhaps these vague sex scenes were just right for my naïve teenage self—enough to titillate but not enough to terrify me.

One night, Danny's parents and sister go to the movies, leaving him home alone. Mimi, the girl who sexually taunts him from across the street, comes to his house and tries to seduce him in one of the strangest seduction scenes I've ever read. Of course, as a fifteen-year-old, confused by sex myself, it must have seemed sexually charged and exciting to read. Mimi holds a tumbler of cold water, then puts her cold hands on Danny's face. He doesn't move or respond. So she presses her lips against his and bends him backward across the sink, at which point Danny grabs her by the shoulders and squeezes so hard that she gasps in pain, which makes him laugh. *"Don't fight with me, Danny,"* Mimi tells him. *"I like you. And I can tell you like me!"* They hear a car in the driveway and Mimi leaves. So why is Danny racked with guilt? What did they even do that made him feel *"soiled and dirty"*? Not only does Danny take one of those frigid showers, he also slaps himself so hard that he doubles over in pain. Often these scenes are followed by such cruelty toward the girl that Danny seems almost insane. When Danny sees Mimi again the next day, he stares at her coldly and then tells her, *"I hate your guts."*

Surely, I thought after I read this scene as an adult, I had read this book over and over as pure escapism. Although I didn't have very discerning taste as a fifteen-year-old, I could see this book for what it was. Even now I like to sometimes indulge in the guilty pleasure of reading a book that literary snobs would never consider reading. And I enjoy them, those paperbacks I don't mind leaving behind on an airplane. They make long flights pass pleasantly. I don't have to marvel at the use of language or metaphor or puzzle over how the author pulled off such a mind-bogglingly intricate plot. I just read it and forget it, perhaps a habit I learned back in high school when I read any book I could get my hands on.

But then why did *A Stone for Danny Fisher* come to mind immediately when thinking of books that shaped me, right beside *The Grapes of Wrath* and *Rabbit, Run*? I cannot say with honesty that when I read it back in 1971 or '72 that I recognized it as a lesser literary achievement. In fact, I remember loving it, every word. I remember how hard I sobbed when Danny's dog dies, and when he visits the Brooklyn home his family was forced to leave, when he dies at the end, and at the book's final line: "*To live in the hearts we leave behind is not to die.*" I also remember that after reading it several times, I took out other Harold Robbins books and couldn't even finish them. I didn't like them at all. No, *this* novel spoke to me.

As I reread *A Stone for Danny Fisher* this past summer, slowly I understood. I believe that magically the book we are supposed to read somehow appears in our hands at just the right time. This happened for me when I struggled to manage multiple points of view as I wrote my first novel, *Somewhere Off the Coast of Maine*. Perhaps out of fear of writing an entire novel, I'd considered the book as interconnected short stories. But here I was, trying to make those stories a novel. Pages covered my living room floor in my Bleecker Street apartment. What was I thinking, trying to use so many points of view? Convinced I would never figure out how to make it work, and that I would have to give back my advance, I decided to take a long walk. I ended up at the Spring Street Bookstore in Soho, where I picked up a book by a writer I'd never heard of before—Anne Tyler. The book was *Dinner at the Homesick Restaurant*, and it was written in multiple points of view, a detail I didn't know when I bought it. Back at my apartment, I ignored all the pages on my floor and flopped, dejected, onto the couch. I read that novel straight through—enchanted, yes, but also, I know now, learning from it how to manage the narrative style. Recently I read that Tyler had originally written *Din-*

ner at the Homesick Restaurant as interconnected stories too. That book landed in my hands at just the
right time. And now I realize so did *A Stone for Danny
Fisher.*

IN THE SUMMER of 1970, my brother, Skip, brought
home a new girlfriend. His high-school girlfriend,
Weezie, had been a freckle-faced, big-toothed girl
whom I loved. She treated me like a kid sister and
happily gave me extra scoops of ice cream when I
went to the Newport Creamery at the mall, where she
worked. But Weezie broke Skip's heart, and the summer after his freshman year at college, at his job at
Zayre, he met the girl he would eventually marry, the
one who appeared in our kitchen one hot, muggy
night, wearing torn jeans and moccasins, a type of
shoe my mother believed only "bad girls" wore.
Where she got such an idea I don't know, but she also
believed—and still does—that "bad girls" drink soda
straight out of a bottle instead of using a straw. To
this day I have never seen my mother lift a bottle of
soda to her lips. She sips from a straw.

The moccasins were the least of the problem, however. The girl was Jewish, which did not bother my parents (though my Italian grandmother didn't much like it), but infuriated *her* parents. So much so that they forbade Skip from dating their daughter or even calling her. *That* infuriated my mother, who didn't like anybody who did anything against her kids. Barring Skip from their house was an insult to her, to all of us, and so a kind of war between the two families began. When the girl's father called my father and insisted my parents keep Skip away from his daughter, my mother took the phone and gave him a piece of her mind. Who the hell did he think he was anyway? I listened, afraid and excited in equal measure. Somehow we were in a feud—the Hatfields and McCoys, the Capulets and Montagues. It all seemed terribly romantic to me.

Although my family was Catholic, we were not really churchgoers. My father, who had converted from Baptist to Catholic back in 1950 in order to marry my mother, liked the folk masses at Sacred Heart Church and happily went once or twice a month to sing "Day by Day" and "Michael, Row Your

Boat Ashore" while the young priest strummed the guitar. When he first met my mother, her family didn't like him—he was a sailor, he wasn't Catholic, and worst of all, he wasn't Italian. His Midwestern family viewed my mother as some kind of exotic creature because she was Italian and Catholic. Their nicknames for her—unbelievable now were "wop" and "fish eater," the latter because Catholics didn't eat meat on Fridays. When she offered to make them spaghetti and meatballs during a visit to Indiana, she was shocked that she couldn't find some of the ingredients—parmesan cheese, fresh parsley, garlic. Still, even without these key things, they marveled at the meal. They'd never tasted anything like it.

But all of that was twenty years earlier, and in time my grandmother fell in love with my father. The two of them fried the crispelles and baked the sweet bread at Easter, and cleaned the eel and calamari for the Feast of the Seven Fishes on Christmas Eve. Religious differences seemed old-fashioned and trivial by 1970. We knew exactly one Jewish person: Jean Goldstein, a friend of my auntie Emma. She arrived at our house a few times a year, always heavily tanned and shiny with gold and diamond jewelry. Jean Goldstein became an emblem of our family's openness in this war. "Jean Goldstein sits right at this table and eats sausage and peppers!" my mother would remind us after another call from Phil, the girl's angry father. "I would never tell Jean Goldstein she wasn't welcome in my house. Who does he think he is?"

My family had no understanding of the Jewish religion or of Jewish history. Mama Rose believed the Jews had killed Jesus, so she didn't trust them. Surely my parents knew about the Holocaust, but to what degree I cannot say. And as terrible as it sounds, religion just didn't matter to them and therefore they couldn't accept it as such a big deal— big enough to cause all this trouble. That summer, and into the fall and winter, we got calls that the girl had run off to be with my brother at college; calls insisting that we had to do something, make Skip leave her alone. The calls often came late at night, and I would hear my father's weary voice say, "The more you try to stop them, the more they'll want to be together. If you let them see each other, this thing will blow over."

It didn't. Instead, at the tender age of twenty, my brother announced they were getting married. My parents had married at nineteen and twenty-one, so they weren't bothered that Skip was so young. But he also announced that he was converting to Judaism, which did not go over very well. Mama Rose cried, claiming he was breaking Jesus's heart and that he wouldn't be able to get into heaven. "What about Christmas?" my mother said, and she was crying too. Even though we were only nominally Catholic in many ways, my mother held on to certain aspects of the faith. She considered saying something against Catholicism blasphemous. "Jesus cries," she'd tell us if we questioned a tenet or told a joke that involved a priest. She says her prayers—Hail Mary, the Lord's Prayer, and the Act of Contrition— every night. She loves the Virgin Mary and all the saints, especially Saint Anthony. How would having a Jewish son fit into this construct of her faith? My father, on the other hand, didn't really care. "It's just words," he said. "What matters is who you are, not what you are."

With the announcement of the conversion, the girl's parents were suddenly our best friends. Phil brought my father cigars and Eileen went shopping for mother-of-the-bride and mother-of-the-groom dresses with my mother. They came over for Christmas Eve, happily eating shrimp cocktail and drinking my father's special punch: Hawaiian Punch, rum, strawberries, and rainbow sherbet. As the wedding neared, we saw them more than we saw almost anyone else. There were decisions to be made on color schemes and tablecloths and yarmulkes. My isolated world of Catholic immigrants was all at once steeped in Judaism. And at the same time, in that magical way books have, I slid *A Stone for Danny Fisher* off the library shelf. Attracted by its size—494 pages!—and perhaps by that sexy cover, I inadvertently picked a book at least nominally about Judaism.

JUST ABOUT EVERYONE in my hometown was Catholic. In second grade the class showed up on the playground one spring morning with our foreheads smudged with ashes. This happened every Ash Wednesday. Before school we went to church and got our ashes. But that year I noticed one girl with a clean, shiny forehead. Her name was Sandra Goldsmith, and I approached her that morning with a great deal of curiosity. Maybe she was going to get her ashes after school, I thought. Ash Wednesday marked the first day of Lent, and the talk on the playground that morning was about what everyone was giving up for Lent—candy, soda, television.

"What are you giving up for Lent?" I asked Sandra.

She kicked at the pavement with the toe of her scuffed brown shoe and shrugged.

"I'm giving up candy," I offered, already missing the flying saucers filled with tiny beads of sugary candy that I preferred.

Sandra remained silent.

I still remember the moment so clearly, remember the bewilderment I felt at her behavior. Even though I went to a public school, playground conversation often involved discussions about Pope Paul VI and when the secrets of Fátima would be revealed.

We were kids or grandkids of immigrants, French Canadians and Italians and Portuguese and Polish Catholics who had come to work in the textile mills that still lined the river that cut through town. That there were people in the world who were not Catholic never occurred to me.

"When are you getting your ashes?" I asked, not meaning to bully.

Sandra finally looked up, her cheeks red and wet with tears. "I'm not Catholic!" she blurted.

Before I could ask her what that meant—what were you if not Catholic?—Sandra ran out of the playground gate, down the sidewalk toward home.

Ten years later, I had a Jewish brother.

DURING SKIP'S CONVERSION I learned about the Jewish High Holy Days, the stories of Passover and Chanukah; I learned what it meant to keep kosher and what a family did on the Sabbath; I learned that some Jews wouldn't use elevators or turn off lights from sunset Friday to sunset Saturday. To me, it sounded mysterious and exotic. Then I read *A Stone for Danny*

Fisher and, coincidentally, was cast as Tzeitel in my high school's production of *Fiddler on the Roof.*

I had learned how to live through reading a lot of books, with a smattering of pop culture thrown in. And that year I learned about the pogroms in Russia, why Jews covered their heads and wore prayer shawls, and the importance of keeping their faith—all through a Broadway musical. With kerchiefs on our heads and aprons over our dresses, we sang "Matchmaker, Matchmaker," and we danced with brooms and clasped our hands together as we twirled to "Tradition." During my marriage to the tailor Motel Kamzoil, the cast picked me up as I sat on a chair and danced, holding me aloft. Two months later I watched this happen at my brother's wedding, shortly after he and his bride took their vows to "Sunrise, Sunset."

A Stone for Danny Fisher opens at Mount Zion Cemetery a week before the High Holy Days. *"For this is the week that Lord God Jehovah calls His angels about Him and opens before them the Book of Life. And your name is inscribed on one of those pages. Written on that page will be your fate for the coming days,"* it begins, and then continues to explain that the book remains open for six days, during which you devote yourself to acts of charity, such as visiting the dead. To make sure you get credit for your visit, *"you will pick up a small stone from the earth beneath your feet and place it on the monument so the Recording Angel will see it when he comes through the cemetery each night."*

Although much of the novel deviates from an exploration of Judaism, Danny's Jewishness is established from the start. In the first chapter, two boys corner Danny in his new neighborhood and demand to know which church he will attend. When he tells them, *"I'm a Jew and I go to shul,"* one of the boys snarls, *"Why did you kill Christ?"* Reading this, surely I remembered my own interrogation of Sandra Goldsmith on the playground and my grandmother telling Skip that the Jews killed Christ. In the next chapter, Danny has his bar mitzvah, the scene rich with details of the synagogue and the ceremony. After school I was watching the boys in the cast of *Fiddler* practice singing "To Life" and in my bed at night I was reading about Danny's parents shouting it to him at his bar mitzvah. Robbins

describes the white silk tallith emblazoned with a
blue Star of David and the white silk yarmulke that
Danny wears; a few months later I sat in a synagogue
at my brother's wedding looking out at a sea of men
wearing yellow yarmulkes to match the couple's
color theme.

I don't remember the confluence of these events—
my brother's conversion and marriage, reading *A
Stone for Danny Fisher*, and performing in *Fiddler on
the Roof*—striking me then as important. But from
the distance of years I see how a bestselling book and
a popular musical helped me navigate the changes
in my family, how they showed me through songs
and stories a glimpse into a world I had been, until
then, unaware of.

In all the years that have followed, I have visited
dozens of countries and witnessed countless tradi
tions and cultures. I've attended a voodoo ceremony
in Brazil and visited a witch doctor in Uganda. I've
been splattered with paint during the festival of Holi
in India and heard the muezzin call Muslims to
prayer in Egypt; I've seen single women wear their

hair in braids by law in Turkmenistan and pilgrims approach temples on their knees in Tibet. All of these things, and so many more, I've watched with curiosity and an open heart. Thanks in no small part to Harold Robbins, Joseph Stein, Jerry Bock, and Sheldon Harnick, who showed me a glimpse of a world and a belief different from my own.

Lesson 8: How to Have Sex

· *The Harrad Experiment* BY ROBERT H. RIMMER ·

I HAD EXACTLY TWO LESSONS IN SEX EDUCATION. THE first came from my ninth-grade, gray-haired, bespectacled home economics teacher. Mrs. Follett taught the cooking half of home ec, but one day she led all of us girls (the boys were busy building bookends in shop class in the basement) to the gym and showed us an antiquated-looking film on menstruation. We sat on the bleachers, horrified at the dancing cartoon ovaries and fallopian tubes and giggling as the bobby-soxed girls asked an offscreen interviewer why they suffered with pimples, cramps, and moodiness.

After the movie, Mrs. Follett brought us back into the home ec room with its stoves and mixing bowls and deep sinks, stood in front of us wearing a serious expression, and said, "Girls, there's a difference between necking and petting. Necking is above the pearls, and petting is below the pearls. Necking is okay. Petting is not."

She nodded solemnly, then handed out recipe cards for fudgies.

I'm sure I wasn't the only one in this classroom full of daughters of immigrants—Italian and Portuguese and Irish, our mothers at work in mills or diners or industrial cafeterias—who felt confused. Pearls? Who in this town wore pearls? And what was *above* them? I thought of pictures I'd seen of flappers with their long strands of pearls skimming the hems of their short dresses. I thought of the movies I watched on television on Sunday afternoons with Doris Day or Grace Kelly in cocktail dresses, a necklace of pearls at their collarbones. Where, then, was the line between necking and petting? I needed specifics, clarity, my own set of pearls that fell to the perfect safe length.

Marie Mattias, my cooking partner, had already donned her apron and was collecting the ingredients for our fudgies. It was rumored that she had already kissed a boy, so perhaps this necking/petting thing made sense to her. I watched her place sugar and milk, butter and cocoa powder, rolled oats and peanut butter on our workstation. Beside us, my friend Jane was frowning—not at the recipe but at everything that had happened that afternoon, the dancing ovaries, the discussion of pimples, the pearls.

I lined a baking sheet with wax paper and joined Marie in dumping all the ingredients into a saucepan. We didn't have to bake the cookies, just drop them by the tablespoonful onto the wax paper and put them in the refrigerator for thirty minutes. When they had cooled and hardened, we would place them onto a silver serving tray and bring them to the boys in shop class. It smelled good down there, musty and woodsy at the same time. When we walked in, the boys lifted their goggles onto their heads and devoured our cookies while we watched.

Later—not that day or even the next, but weeks later—I went home after school with Marie. We were on double sessions: the seventh and eighth graders went to school from seven to noon; we ninth graders went from twelve thirty to five thirty. Marie lived up the street from the school, in one half of a mill house. It was almost dark by the time school ended, and the autumn air smelled of leaves burning and the sharp scent of winter approaching. At her house, her brother lazed on the sofa. He wore blue jeans and a pocket T-shirt, and although he was barefoot he had drawn what looked like the straps of sandals across the arches of his feet, ending in a pointed V between his big toe and the one beside it. This, Marie explained, allowed him to enter restaurants and stores barefoot, as clerks and waitresses thought he had on sandals. The Mattiases had a dog named Frog, and Marie and her brother liked to give him a tablespoon of peanut butter and then watch him try to swallow it. We made fudgies, and while we waited for them to cool we gave Frog peanut butter and watched him smack it loudly on his tongue.

When the cookies were ready, Marie pulled out a Ouija board.

"Ask it anything," she said.

I looked at her curly hair and black-lined eyes.

"What's a French kiss?" I asked.

We placed our hands on the planchette and waited. Slowly, haltingly, it moved across the board, spelling out: KISSING WITH TONGUE. Grossed out, I lifted my hands suddenly from the planchette, just as Marie nudged it toward S. Our eyes met briefly. I stood and said I had to go home. *Kissing with tongues?*

MY SECOND SEX education lesson came, in a way, from my mother. As a Catholic, I was told that a girl saved herself for marriage long before I understood what exactly I was saving. "You don't buy the cow if the milk is free," my mother would tell me, another thing I did not understand. What were girls giving away? And why, if boys wanted it, did they not want the girl? If I prodded my mother for answers, she did not respond. The last thing my prudish mother wanted to do was talk about sex. "Let me just say," she told me once, eyes averted, cheeks red, "you have to *really* love a man to do that with him." What was *that*? I wondered. And why was it so mysterious, so valuable, yet so disgusting?

My mother and my aunts had a terrible term for promiscuous women, one that disturbed me then and disturbs me even more so now. "She's a pig," they'd say about the divorcée who dated lots of men or the teenager who got pregnant. Today, I ask my mother not to use that word to describe any woman. But as a girl I just cringed. One thing I knew for certain was that I never wanted to be called that. I had no concept of how girls got pregnant, or even of how sex worked. Once I heard Joan Rivers on *The Merv Griffin Show* say that she'd read *The Joy of Sex* and took its advice by wrapping her naked body in Saran Wrap and greeting her husband, Edgar, at the door like that. The audience laughed but I only felt confused. The next time I went to Waldenbooks at the mall, I found *The Joy of Sex* and flipped through it. The illustrations of naked men and women, pubic hair drawn in squiggly lines, arms and legs thrust in every direction, looked disgusting. "You *really* have to love a man to do that."

I was twelve when I got my first period, an event I only anticipated or knew about because my cousin, a year older, got hers the year before. For months I hoped I'd find blood on my underwear, but when nothing happened I forgot about it. Then I went to a birthday party for a girl with the magical name of Staria (at some point it lost its magic when I learned her mother had plucked it from a book about a horse with that name). Staria lived in a new development and had many wonderfully exotic things to marvel at—her family ate at a kitchen table that had benches instead of chairs, for one thing. And her basement was not dirt-floored like mine, or a second kitchen like the ones so many people I knew had, but rather was bright and large with indoor/outdoor carpeting and a door that led outside into the yard. At the party there was a long table with all kinds of mayonnaise-y food—tuna salad and egg salad—something I'd never seen before. We didn't even have a jar of mayonnaise at home.

"It's time for lunch," Staria's mother announced.

I wore a hot-pink minidress with a scalloped hem and white go-go boots, an outfit bought just for the occasion. As soon as her mother told us it was time for lunch, I stood and went to the buffet table (though of course I didn't know that's what it was called, having never heard the word "buffet" before), peering at those finger sandwiches, taking the least offensive-looking one and piling chips onto my plate. There was a hot tray of tiny meatballs in red currant jelly. I took two on their cellophane-tipped toothpicks just to be polite. Where I came from, meatballs were large and covered in red sauce. When I looked up, I saw that I was the first one getting food. Everyone else had formed a line and was waiting. Everyone except a soft-spoken girl named Nancy, who still sat primly perched at the edge of her chair.

"Ann," Staria said, "since you went first, you can't be Miss Peanut."

Miss Peanut? Clearly I had done something wrong, but I had no idea what it was. Hadn't Staria's mother told us it was time to eat? My stomach cramped. The smell of mayonnaise, unfamiliar and sweet (perhaps it was actually Miracle Whip?), wafted upward and I had to swallow a wave of nausea.

"Miss Peanut is polite," Staria continued, "and lets others go first."

Now my stomach was really hurting, and something strange began—I had my first headache, a pounding that was thunderous and painful. I thought I might have to go to the bathroom—there was one down there! In the basement! Staria's mother had pointed it out to us when we arrived.

"Today," Staria announced, "Miss Peanut is Nancy!"

Nancy blushed a deep red. Staria grinned at her, and as she went to bring Nancy a large prize of some kind, my stomachache got so bad that I ran to the bathroom. I'm sure that the other kids thought I'd left out of embarrassment for being the antithesis of Miss Peanut. Crammed into the tiny bathroom— her mother had called it a "half-bath"—I yanked down my underwear and there it was: two smears of dark red blood.

That afternoon, after I snuck upstairs and called my mother on Staria's fake old-fashioned crank telephone that hung on the kitchen wall, trying not to cry; after my mother picked me up and I left the party without saying goodbye or thank you; after my mother silently handed me a strange belt and a box of sanitary napkins; after she showed me how to attach the napkins to the belt; she handed me a slender, mustard-colored paperback, almost more of a pamphlet, with a silhouette of a young woman's face and some vague title about mothers and daughters. "Read this," she told me, and I dutifully did, a hot water bottle on my aching stomach, a bulge of Kotex between my legs. The book told me this would happen every twenty-eight days, that I could get pregnant on day fourteen of my cycle, that boys had a penis that resembled a mushroom and a sack below it that contained two balls the size of plums.

Was it any surprise, then, that when someone showed up in ninth grade with a book called *The Harrad Experiment*, a novel about fictional Harrad College and its experiment to have men and women live together and feel free to have sex, argue about politics and philosophy, change partners, and think and act "freely," I eagerly read it? And reread it, especially the dog-eared pages 160–167, which describe the act of sex and orgasms in graphic detail? So, I thought, this is what all the fuss is about.

The Harrad Experiment was published in hardcover

in 1966, and in paperback a year later. The copy that
was surreptitiously passed around my ninth-grade
classroom was that original paperback, with a naked
college-age boy draping a sheet around a naked girl's
shoulders. They are both tanned and blond, he looking down at her, she looking directly at the reader. It
was racy and titillating, that cover. Reading the book
as I did in 1970, when teenagers were moving in
droves to Haight-Ashbury in search of free love and
just a few years earlier *Time* magazine had featured
the Pill on its cover, it seemed to me to be a poster for
just that. Initially, Sherbourne Press printed 10,000
mail-order copies sold through an ad in *Playboy*
magazine because the novel was too racy for bookstores. But Bantam promoted the paperback edition
that I read with sexy billboards and advertisements.
It sold 300,000 copies within a month. Eventually,
more than 3 million copies were sold, with reviews
posted on Amazon as recently as February 2016.

ONE OF THE rules at Harrad College is that all sports,
exercise, and swimming in the pool had to be done

in the nude, an idea that I found impossible to imagine. That year, in ninth grade, we had to change out of our clothes and into our gym uniform in tiny shared dressing rooms connected to smelly, moldy showers. My dressing room partner was a girl named Joanne, who, out of embarrassment or perhaps out of bravery, would hustle into our small space, whip off her clothes, and pull on the one-piece pale blue gym uniform, seemingly in one motion. I caught a flash of her flesh, pink and still baby chubby, and then she was snapping up the front snaps while I tried to strategically drape my towel in a way that would hide as much as possible. The thought of climbing the rope, or bouncing on the trampoline, or doing calisthenics naked as Danny Kaye sang *"Go, you chicken fat, go!"* from the record player, horrified me. What was this place called Harrad? Did people ever really feel comfortable enough to swim naked? In front of other people? Did people ever feel comfortable enough to be naked at all?

Yet the character Harry writes: *"Every day when I go to Physical Education, there they are . . . girls . . . naked, swimming in the pool, playing volleyball . . . yell-*

ing, screaming, soprano-joyous." One day, his classmate Sheila plops down beside him at the edge of the
pool, water dripping from her breasts, and tells him:
"*You know just two weeks ago when I first came here and
had to walk out in front of everyone naked, I thought I'd
die of embarrassment. Now it seems the only way to be . . .
naked.*" Really? I thought when I read that. Someday
I might feel comfortable walking around naked? The
idea seemed both impossible and exciting. And very,
very far away.

A COUPLE OF years before I read *The Harrad Experiment*, a boy approached me on the stretch of asphalt
that served as our playground, and said, "You want
to go out with me?" "Going out" meant that you wore
his ID bracelet, stood by the fence with him every
morning before school and again after lunch, and
maybe met him at the mall on Saturdays. My parents
would absolutely kill me if I went out with a boy, even
in this benign fashion. Yet the idea that a boy liked
me made me consider the offer. This boy was tall and
broad-shouldered, dark-haired and strong-jawed.

He was also several years older than anyone else in our grade, having stayed back a rumored three times. He wore a leather jacket, short black Beatles boots, tight jeans, and a scowl that was almost frightening. And *he* liked *me*? The girl who raised her hand too much in class, wore glasses, and carried around books the size of bricks?

Before I could answer "Okay!" he said, "If you go out with me, you gotta stop using so many big words. No one likes a girl who uses so many big words."

My vocabulary, honed by taking the monthly *Reader's Digest* "How to Improve Your Word Power" test and reading books far beyond my ken, was one of the things of which I was most proud. To not use it seemed almost a punishment. I guess I took too long to think about his offer because he looked at me in disgust and said, "Ah, forget it. You just like big words, not me."

When I read Ruth's observation to Stanley in *The Harrad Experiment*, *"Anyway, darned few men want to marry a brainy woman. They want somebody to tell them they are wonderful, and be ready to cuddle with them or baby them,"* I thought of that boy. Was it true that all boys were like him? Stanley does suggest to Ruth that perhaps a girl could be cuddly and intelligent, but Ruth responds, "*Sure, intelligent. She can read the bestsellers and take on little civic problems in her women's club . . . but let her really get her own interests . . . let her not be completely children and house oriented . . . then watch out, she's in for trouble.*" Later in the novel, Beth describes love like this: "*Love is something else . . . Something more dynamic, all consuming. Something that makes you want to kneel down before somebody, humble yourself to him. Give yourself irrevocably.*" These debates, which continue throughout the novel, articulated my own confusion about sex and love. What was the difference? How did I know if the feelings I had were sexual ones or real love? Was it really okay to have many sexual partners and someday think, as Valerie does, "*Sometimes I wake up in the night and for a sleepy moment I may forget whether I am with Stanley, Jack or Harry, and then I feel warm and bubbly.*"

Yes, *The Harrad Experiment* helped me, a sexually naïve, even prudish fourteen-year-old girl, to put words to all I was wondering about in the shifting values of the 1970s. But arguably more important, it told me how sex worked, what actually went on between a man and a woman when they made love, what went where and how it felt. The pages that I read over and over—pages 160 to 167—were exactly what I needed to understand. Reading them made me blush and squirm uncomfortably, but they also empowered me. Finally I understood.

The scene involves two characters who are practicing a method of sexual intercourse called sexual communion, a concept based on Hindu Tantric literature. Before Sheila and Stanley try sexual communion, Rimmer introduces philosophical and historical information about it. The basic idea is for a couple to delay orgasm—a word whose meaning I had to run to the dictionary to find. "A climax of sexual excitement, characterized by feelings of pleasure centered in the genitals and (in men) experienced as an accompaniment to ejaculation." *What?* I thought when I read that. *Pleasure in the genitals?* I remember slamming the fat dictionary shut, sitting on my bed, and trying to absorb what I'd just read.

But this scene between Sheila and Stanley made it all seem less scary, less confusing, and even exciting. Stanley enters her and they lie side by side reading to each other. At one point, Sheila tells him she's about to explode, at which point I realized that women get to enjoy this too. For seven pages, they read out loud and touch each other and shift positions, until finally, on page 167, they can't take it anymore. The book falls to the floor with a thud, and Stanley tells Sheila he's past the point of no return. To my surprise and delight, it's Sheila who kisses him wildly and shouts, "*Oh, God! Darling . . . darling . . . so have I. So have I!*"

Like so many of the 1950s values and ideas on which I'd been raised, sex had been challenged in this changing world I was living in, *The Harrad Experiment* brought me headfirst into understanding—and almost ready to join—the sexual revolution of the 1970s. A fear of pregnancy, the wrath of my mother, disappointing Jesus, and a general "good girl" hang-up kept me safely innocent and relatively pure through high school. It was years before I felt comfortable being naked, years before I had my first sexual relationship, years before I fell in love. Yet it was a book that taught me about sex and love and how to not confuse the two, a book that told me what even my sex ed teacher and my mother could not.

Lesson 9: How to See the World

· *Doctor Zhivago* BY BORIS PASTERNAK ·

I GREW UP LISTENING TO MY FATHER'S STORIES OF his days in the navy. He described Lombard Street in San Francisco—*the crookedest street in the world!*—and how in the tropics it would rain on only one side of the street. He told me again and again his stories about how in Morocco he once ate dog for dinner—*they starved the dog for a week, then fed it rice, and then killed it and cooked it, and the rice was the stuffing, right inside the dog!*—and in China he ate "hundred-year" eggs, which were buried and preserved and smelled and tasted rancid—*they made me gag but I had to eat them. You can't insult your hosts.* He skied in Greece; he stood at the railing of a ship and threw pennies into the Caribbean off the coast of Haiti for children to dive for and collect; when he lived in Naples he drove a Fiat Topolino, which was the smallest car in the world; in China he saw people die in the street from starvation. And I, the little girl on his big lap, tracing the tattoo of an eagle in front of a setting sun on his forearm, wanted to do all of those things and more. California and Morocco and Greece and Italy and China . . . "Where else?" I used to ask him. He smelled of Old Spice and Vitalis and Ivory soap and cigarettes. "In Cuba I was bit by a mongoose," he told me, "and I had to go into the hospital and get rabies shots right in my stomach."

Where else? There was always, always somewhere else.

But mostly we stayed put.

My mother did not like to travel. She did not like to leave her own mother, who had a vague heart ailment and always seemed close to death, though she lived until she was eighty or eighty-two or eighty-

three (no one really knew, because they'd changed
her birth date so she could go to work in the mills
sooner). Every other summer we four—Mom, Dad,
my brother Skip, and me—got into our green Chevy
station wagon and drove to Indiana to visit my
father's family. To make it exciting each time we
stopped at a different attraction—Niagara Falls; Her-
shey, Pennsylvania; Amish country; Montreal. I
thought it was exciting anyway, leaving Rhode Island
and driving through six other states, sleeping in
motels with pools that reeked of chlorine and beds
that shook if you put a dime in them. My mother
packed a cooler with fried chicken and sodas and
kept Underwood deviled ham and potato chips in a
bag at her feet. But the night we stopped at the motel
we ate out, maybe at a Howard Johnson's or Cracker
Barrel, and we got to order anything we wanted.
Once, in Montreal, we ate at a steakhouse and Skip,
who had just started to learn French in school,
ordered *petits pois* and *bifteck*, impressing us all; in
Niagara Falls we ate in a restaurant at the top of a
building that slowly rotated, a feat of engineering
that dazzled me.

I carefully wrote down all the license plates I saw, wishing I lived in New Mexico for its yellow-and-red one with LAND OF ENCHANTMENT on it, or Colorado with its green license plate and white snowcapped mountains at the bottom. After one trip, I wrote to the governor of Rhode Island and suggested we change from our dull black-and-white plate to a blue one with whitecapped waves. He never wrote back. But that was how great my desire for somewhere special was, I would design a new license plate just to make my little state stand out somehow.

My hometown of West Warwick had once been special, long before I was born. In 1809, the Lippitt Mill was built there, and it holds the distinction of being the second-oldest mill in the state, and one of the oldest textile mills in America. And Fruit of the Loom was born in my town in 1865, eventually having more than one thousand looms at work in its mill. But when I was a kid, the biggest mill had long since burned down, and many of the other mills that lined the polluted Pawtucket River had closed. We had a main street, with a square stone town hall and a square stone post office and a square stone bank that stayed open late on Friday evenings. There were two women's shops and one men's—Maxine's, Seena's, and St. Onge; a Newberry's five-and-dime with a lunch counter, cages of parakeets, and bins of notions; Irene's, a hat shop, where my mother got the hats she wore to church (this was her standard Mother's Day gift until Irene's closed); and the Palace Theatre, where for thirty-five cents my cousins and I saw double-feature matinees like *A Hard Day's Night* and *Up the Down Staircase*. There was a New York System too, a Rhode Island oddity that sells special small hot dogs—*hot wieners*—in steamed buns with a secret meat sauce, chopped onions, mustard, and celery salt on top. Usually a person would eat three hot wieners, except my brother and father who ate six or even nine.

But by the time I was in ninth grade, although the square stone buildings and the New York System remained, everything else was gone, the buildings boarded up, the XXX movie theater replacing my beloved Palace Theatre. St. Onge had moved to the new mall, the other stores had simply vanished. Even though my father still went to the bank on Friday evenings, he came right home. No more window-shopping or ducking into Newberry's for shiny buttons or artificial flowers for my mother to arrange as a centerpiece. Living in what I saw as a dead-end town, I wanted, even more than ever, to *go*. I wanted to eat dog stuffed with rice in Morocco and go skiing in Greece.

Then I found the perfect novel sitting on the library shelf: *Doctor Zhivago* by Boris Pasternak. At 1,059 pages, it didn't so much sit on the shelf as dominate it. And the title—the mysterious combination of *Zh* . . . I tried to imagine how to pronounce it. Like *Shh*? Like *Za*? The writer's name too: *Boris*. I lived in a world of Michaels and Stevens and Johns; Vinnys and Tonys and Joes. The only Boris I'd ever heard of was Boris Badenov from *Rocky and Bullwinkle*. So I knew that this writer was Russian. Somehow even then, as a thirteen-year-old girl who knew almost nothing, I did know the magic of books. I understood as I held that hefty book in my hands, staring at the unusual cover—a drawing of a small house in a snowy field with a horse-drawn carriage approaching, all of it covered with what looked like a child's crayoned lines in mustard, mauve, and teal—that this Russian novel would transport me from my own little town to Russia, a place about which I knew nothing except that they had nuclear bombs pointed at us, they were Communists, and just the summer before they had invaded Czechoslovakia—Mama Rose and I had watched on television as the tanks rolled down the streets of Prague.

THERE HAD BEEN a movie of *Doctor Zhivago* five years earlier, with Omar Sharif and Julie Christie. My parents had walked out halfway through—too slow, too boring, too long, too much snow. But the novel—the novel!—was none of these things. At least, not to me. It was confusing, jumping in time and point of view. Vladimir Nabokov called *Doctor Zhivago* "a sorry thing, clumsy, trite and melodramatic, with stock situations, voluptuous lawyers, unbelievable girls, romantic robbers, and trite coincidences." Reviewers described it as "having no real plot, confused chronology, oddly effaced main characters, and contrived coincidences." All of which is true, even though Boris Pasternak won the 1958 Nobel Prize for Literature shortly after *Doctor Zhivago* was published.

I admit that I loved those coincidences that Nabokov and many critics hated. I loved how Yuri could end up in the same town as Lara and wander into the library and see her there, or how Yuri gets wounded and is a patient, and later a doctor, in the military hospital where Lara is a nurse. I believed, or wanted to believe, in chance encounters, true love, and romance. I was confused by the characters, all of whom had three names and even nicknames, almost impossible to keep straight. But that didn't really matter to me because all I cared about was Lara and Yuri, their unrequited love. How he looked at her in wonder and amazement! How he vowed to try not to love her! But love is stronger than that, Pasternak told me. Yuri couldn't resist. And ever so briefly, Lara is his.

In his introduction to a reissue of the novel, John Bayley wrote: "The best way to understand *Doctor Zhivago* is to see it in terms of this great Russian literary tradition, as a fairy tale." Except in *this* fairy tale, no one lives happily ever after. Yuri Zhivago dies

alone in Moscow; Lara dies in a gulag during Joseph
Stalin's Great Purge; their daughter, Tanya, aban-
doned in the Urals by her mother when she was a
child, is a laundress.

Perhaps ultimately *Doctor Zhivago* was what it
never intended to be, as Richard Pevear wrote in his
introduction: "a moving love story set against the
grim realities of twentieth-century Russian history." The novel opens in 1903 at the funeral of Yuri's
mother and moves from there to the Russian Revolution of 1905, the civil war, World War I, and World
War II, with uprisings and protests and skirmishes
and Cossacks and the White Army and Tsarists and
more throughout. So many historical events and
facts that I had never heard of that I made a list while
reading: *Nikitsky Gate, The Presma, Bourgeoisie, Faust,
Komuch, Tolstoyan, Pushkin* , , , And I spent long
afternoons looking up all of these things and more.

In school, we had studied American history and,
that year, ancient Rome. But to me, Russia was a
mysterious place with nuclear missiles pointed at us,
a country I knew virtually nothing about. Until *Doctor Zhivago*. I read Pasternak's descriptions of the six-

mile-long Kologrivov estate with sheaves of wheat and a river gleaming beyond "fields following fields" until they were lost in the distance. *"These vast expanses gave him [Yuri] a feeling of freedom and elation. They made him think and dream of the future."* Wasn't I too seeking that feeling of freedom? My town offered only the opposite; the mills and polluted river seemed to conspire to prevent elation.

We had no grand houses really; the town had streets lined with old mill houses and the triple-deckers the immigrants eventually bought. Even the newer developments, though neat and tree-lined, offered only small split ranches or colonials. To read about the Gromekos' house, with its top floor of bedrooms and studies and a boudoir—*Boudoir!* Another word I had to look up!—was intoxicating. My own house was typical of the 1960s makeovers: Formica and paneling, artificial flowers and fruit, avocado and harvest-gold accents. The Gromekos' curtains were pistachio colored, their upholstery olive green, and their potted plants resembled seaweed *"like a green, sleepily swaying seabed."*

The Gromekos hosted chamber music with piano

trios, string quartets, and violin sonatas. So unlike the Johnny Cash music my parents played on our stereo, or the folk records I played alone in my room! Even the food Pasternak described, the supper table *"white and long as a winter road," "the frosted bottles of red rowanberry cordial"* and *"crystal cruets in silver stands"* transported me to a different world, a place completely unlike my home, with the tablecloth covered with plastic and the red sauce and meatballs and sausage—delicious and comforting and plentiful, certainly, but served on mismatched platters and bowls. No *"picturesque arrangements of game and zakuski* [yet another word to look up]" or *"baskets of mauve cineraria* [and another!] *smelling of almonds."* All of it—the golden domes of churches and the girls in white dresses on Whitsun Eve, the green birch saplings hung over the church railings, the potatoes covered with old blankets and hay in the cellar, even the Proclamations posted on doors describing the various rules and punishments under the Red Army—whetted my already big appetite for travel and adventure, for some other place, pointed my compass outward.

But *Doctor Zhivago* pointed me inward too, toward other Russian novels, like *Anna Karenina* and *War and Peace* by Leo Tolstoy; nonfiction books about Russia, like *The Gulag Archipelago* by Aleksandr Solzhenitsyn and *Nicholas and Alexandra* by Robert K. Massie; and toward epic novels in general. After I had devoured all of the Russians, I discovered Victor Hugo's *Les Misérables* and began the same obsession with French literature.

Like *Doctor Zhivago*, *Les Misérables* has its critics. At 1,232 pages (arguably the longest novel in European literature), it is described by *The Guardian* as a novel of "gargantuan length and exaggerated coincidences," in which "everything seems utterly improbable and every plot twist operates through coincidences: a father doesn't recognize his son, a criminal doesn't recognize a man he has pursued for years . . ." Even Hugo himself called *Les Misérables* "formidable, gigantic, colossal, monstrous." But these were the very things I loved about epic novels, which by definition center upon a hero and great events narrated in an elevated style. I loved nothing more than to lose myself in these gargantuan novels with their pages and pages of characters and stories and settings and drama.

By the time I read *Les Misérables*, as a sophomore or junior in high school, I had also fallen in love with American literature of the 1920s (How? I cannot really say except once again I serendipitously discovered Fitzgerald and Hemingway on the library shelves), in particular with Zelda Fitzgerald (I read and reread the Nancy Milford biography that came out the following year) and her life in Paris. Hugo's novel was described by scholar Kathryn Grossman as "in many ways, a love affair with Paris." While Hugo was in exile in Britain, Baron Haussmann razed the old Paris that Hugo loved, and that is the setting for *Les Misérables*; a Paris of narrow streets and alleys and hidden neighborhoods that had existed since medieval times but was replaced with the broad avenues and open plazas we associate with the city today—a plan meant to eliminate the congestion that fostered diseases and to prevent the building of the very revolutionary barricades that Hugo describes.

Of course, *Les Misérables* led to my reading *The*

Hunchback of Notre-Dame and *The Count of Monte Cristo* and to fall in love, as I had with Moscow and the Urals, with Paris, where in the Luxembourg Gardens *"the air was warm, the garden was inundated with light and shade . . . the sparrows were giving vent to little twitters in the chestnut trees"* and where, at the Saint-Paul-Saint-Louis church in the Marais, *"people halted on the Rue Saint-Antoine to gaze through the windows at the orange flowers quivering on Cosette's head."* Hugo once said, "He who contemplates the depths of Paris is seized with vertigo. Nothing is more fantastic. Nothing is more sublime." His novel, written more than a century before a teenager in a small town in a small state read it, did just that for me.

During my high-school years, I read my way across oceans and mountains, through history and politics and cultures, into epic tales of love and sorrow and bravery and passion. These stories opened doors that led me out and ultimately away from home, fueled by the hope of glimpsing golden domes and rose windows of cathedrals; labyrinth streets and fields of wheat; of glimpsing this big, beautiful world that I began to imagine on my father's knee, and then began to almost grasp with a book in my hands.

"*He who sees Paris*," Victor Hugo wrote in *Les Misérables*, "*seems to see all history through with the sky and constellations in the intervals*." How similar to what Yuri says in *Doctor Zhivago*: "*The roof over the whole of Russia has been torn off, and we and all the people find ourselves under the open sky*." The sky. Endless and full of possibilities, the door to the past and to the future. Somehow I understood this as I read. And all these years later, if my father were still here beside me, I could tell him, "Look, Daddy, I have seen Paris and Beijing and Istanbul. I have gazed at the Great Pyramid and the Himalayas and Machu Picchu. I have eaten yak and horse and deep-fried crickets. Thank you for showing me the world that books helped me imagine." If only he and Hugo and Pasternak and everyone who pointed me toward the sky could know I am still looking upward.

Lesson 10: How to Run Away

· *Rabbit, Run* BY JOHN UPDIKE ·

HERE I AM, THE GIRL WHO USED TO SIT ON THE SMALL landing at the top of the stairs that led to our bedrooms and stare out the window there. When I look back at that girl, I picture her there. I could see rooftops of houses, including my uncle Joe's across the street; when the trees were bare I could see all the way to the mall; on clear days I could see the community college buildings and vague roofs in the next town. I played a game: *Someday, I will go beyond all of these buildings.* Beyond Providence, which was ten miles away. Beyond Boston, which was fifty miles away. *Someday, I will go farther than I can even imagine.* Farther than anyone can imagine. I meant that both literally—I would leave this small town, this small state, New England, maybe even the United States—and figuratively. How far I wanted to go!

As I watched cousins getting married in heavy white beaded wedding gowns, I vowed to wear champagne or even pink. Their husbands were all nice guys from town who ran delis or worked at Electric Boat or as electricians or plumbers. I would find a poet, I decided, maybe even someone from England or France. We would name our children Summer or Sage, live by the beach or in a loft. We, *I*, would be different.

Much of this thinking I attribute to growing up in the 1960s. Around me, the world changed while I watched. Men still wore hats; teenagers grew their hair long. My mother wiggled herself into a girdle every morning; other women burned their bras. People bucked the system, lived on the land, had sex before marriage, hitchhiked, bought Eurail passes and backpacks while fathers still pulled their Chevys into their driveways at five o'clock and walked into a home they'd bought with a wife making dinner and two kids watching television. We Shake 'n Baked our pork chops, made Hamburger Helper, and ate TV dinners, but health food stores were opening and there were suddenly granola and yogurt and lentil burgers. All of it confused me. Where did I fit into this shifting landscape?

This question haunted me for many years. I considered marriage young, but opted to move away and live alone in a city. I considered going to graduate school, but instead went to work for TWA as a flight attendant. Always a push and pull, never certain I'd chosen the right way, which most times was the unconventional one. Recently I heard Gloria Steinem interviewed by Terry Gross on *Fresh Air*, and she described the cause of her mother's depression as patriarchal tyranny. I wished I could point to something like that for what I'd always felt, but nothing fit. That yearning I could not name, the same one that kept me looking out that window as a teenager, never left me.

To me, one movie and one novel captured what I felt, and I turned to them again and again for validation and even solace that I wasn't alone with this feeling. *The Graduate* came out in 1967, and while I'm certain I didn't see it when I was only ten years old (even though my parents never restricted what movies I saw or what books I read, I doubt even they would have let me go see *The Graduate*), I know I did see it young, at thirteen or fourteen, perhaps at the Midland Cinema. Oddly, our mall had a small movie theater that showed foreign and independent films. I loved going there, loved how what I saw often confused or embarrassed me, how the movies there made me think in ways that only books did. I saw *Women in Love* and *Le Genou de Claire* and, I think, a rerelease of *The Graduate* in 1970 or '71. From the moment Dustin Hoffman's face appears in close-up as the airline captain announces landing and Simon and Garfunkel start singing "The Sound of Silence," I loved that movie. I thought, as crazy as it sounds, that it was a movie about me.

Around the same time I read a novel about a young man who wants to escape, who wants freedom from the moral and societal expectations placed on him, who wants to run. I had never even heard of John Updike when I took the green, yellow, and blue striped book off the library shelf. But just like that opening sequence of *The Graduate*, the opening pages of *Rabbit, Run* drew me in and held on to me until its final words: *"His hands lift of their own and he feels the wind on his ears even before, his heels hitting heavily on the pavement at first but with an effortless gathering out of a kind of sweet panic growing lighter and quicker and quieter, he runs. Ah: runs. Runs."* From my perch at the top of the stairs, that's what I imagined. Running.

RABBIT, RUN WAS published in 1960, over a decade before I read it. John Updike said that when he looked around in 1959, he saw a number of scared, dodgy men who could not make commitments, men who had peaked in high school and existed in a downward spiral. Their idea of happiness, Updike noted, was to be young. Harry Angstrom, *Rabbit, Run*'s eponymously nicknamed protagonist, is only twenty-six, yet on page two of the novel he refers to himself as old. Updike himself was only twenty-eight when he wrote the book. At the age of fourteen, I was more than willing to accept that Rabbit was indeed old. Twenty-six? Definitely old. In fact, rereading the novel recently I was stunned by how young he actually is in it because he *feels* so old, so disheartened and beaten.

A former high-school basketball star, Rabbit is married with one young son and a baby on the way, working at a job selling a kitchen gadget called a MagiPeel when the story opens. Julian Barnes described Angstrom in an article about all four Rabbit books in *The Guardian*: "Harry is site-specific, slobbish, lust-driven, passive, patriotic, hard-hearted, prejudiced, puzzled, anxious. Yet likeable—for his humour, his doggedness, his candor, his curiosity and his wrong-headed judgments—for example preferring Perry Como to Frank Sinatra." The description is fitting; yet as a young reader I developed a literary crush on Rabbit, as I did on Dr. Zhivago and Jay Gatsby. The allure of Zhivago and Gatsby is obvious. Angstrom—hard-hearted and anxious man that he is—less so. But in his introduction to *Rabbit Angstrom: A Tetralogy*, Updike himself comes close to capturing what I found so appealing in Rabbit: "The character of Harry 'Rabbit' Angstrom was for me a way in—a ticket to the America all around me . . . an Everyman who, like all men, was unique and mortal."

In my blue-collar mill town, I recognized Rabbit's own hometown of Brewster, and the people who populated it. "My subject," Updike said, "is the American-Protestant small-town middle class. I like middles. It is in middles that extremes crash, where ambiguity restlessly rules." Rabbit and I wanted to escape the very small town, the very middles, that Updike described. That ambiguity fed our restlessness, and therein lies the effect Rabbit had on my teenage self. He is, after all, a middle-class guy who is "*overwhelmed by the shifting world around him.*" So overwhelmed that Rabbit does exactly what I dreamed of at the top of the stairs—he runs away. "*He had thought, he had read, that from shore to shore all America was the same.*" He wonders, "*Is it just these people I'm outside, or is it all America?*" As the *New York*

Times put it in their November 6, 1960, book review of *Rabbit, Run* it's "a tender and discerning study of the desperate and the hungering in our midst." If ever a word was perfect to describe how Rabbit and I felt, that word is *hungering.*

Isn't this the magic of books? That a fourteen-year old girl can exactly identify with the fictional character of a twenty-six-year-old, married, former basketball star from Pennsylvania just as readily as that same girl—Italian American, blue-collar, Catholic in a small town—exactly identifies with Marjorie Morningstar, an upper-middle-class Jewish girl in New York City? When I read *Rabbit, Run*, I understood that Rabbit, and John Updike, knew me. The me I didn't think anyone else saw.

JOHN UPDIKE LEFT New York City in 1957 for Ipswich, Massachusetts, because, as he said, "I was full of a Pennsylvania thing I wanted to say," and he could not write that in the city. The novel, written entirely in present tense and with multiple points of view, has an urgency made even more apparent by all the ways in which Harry runs. After he joins young boys in a basketball game at the start of the book (a scene that Updike imagined cinematically, with the title and credits playing above it), Rabbit runs home: "*Running,*" the paragraph begins, and then we get a description of the street where he lives as he is "*running uphill,*" with its "*block of big homes, small fortresses of cement and brick,*" and then halfway up the block "*a development built all at once in the thirties,*" until finally, "*There are a dozen three-story homes, and each has two doors. The seventh is his.*" It is there on the worn wooden steps that Rabbit finally pauses.

"*Don't run off on me,*" his wife, Janice, admonishes him. Janice, who "*just yesterday, it seems to him, she stopped being pretty.*" Janice, who, in one of the most harrowing scenes I have ever read to this day, gets drunk and accidentally drowns their infant daughter Rebecca in the bathtub while Rabbit has, once again, run off on her. And he runs from her again at Rebecca's funeral: "*He hates his wife's face. She doesn't see . . . A suffocating sense of injustice blinds him. Again he turns and runs.*" Not just runs, but "*uphill exultantly. He dodges among gravestones.*" Perhaps escaping the death of his soul that he so acutely feels but can't articulate. "*I'll tell you*," Rabbit says, "*when I ran from Janice I made an interesting discovery . . . if you have the guts to be yourself, other people'll pay your price.*"

AFTER I READ *Rabbit, Run*, I read the other three John Updike books on the library shelf: *The Centaur, Couples*, and *Bech: A Book*. Although I remember being equal parts shocked and seduced by *Couples*, none of these other books had the effect on me that *Rabbit, Run* did. I took that book out of the library over and over, growing more certain with each reading that Updike had stared unflinchingly straight into my heart.

In 1974, I graduated from West Warwick High School in a ceremony held in the Warwick Musical Theatre, a giant tent on Route 2 that hosted the likes of Engelbert Humperdinck, John Davidson, and Liberace on summer nights. That fall, my parents drove me and my brand-new stereo thirty-one miles south to the University of Rhode Island and my new home in the Barlow dormitory, Room 401. For one day, I was a journalism major. When the teacher told us that in journalism we had to tell the truth—"No making things up!"—I immediately switched my major to English. In 1974, at URI, there were no creative writing classes, only remedial writing classes. My first English class was a general American literature survey. The teacher handed out the syllabus, and to me the reading list was like a gift. Someone had chosen all of these books for me to read. I didn't have to scour library shelves and haphazardly select books anymore. Here was *My Ántonia* by Willa Cather, *The Falconer* by John Cheever, *Humboldt's Gift* by Saul Bellow, and—I blinked to be sure I was reading it correctly—*Rabbit Redux* by John Updike.

As if she'd read my mind, the teacher asked, "How many of you have read John Updike's *Rabbit, Run*?"

I alone raised my hand.

She smiled at me, and gave me a little nod.

"The rest of you read *Rabbit, Run* first, before *Rabbit Redux*," she said.

My heart was beating hard against my ribs. For my whole teenage life, I'd read to understand who I was and where I was going and what it was I was yearning for so desperately. And sitting in that warm, stuffy classroom in Independence Hall on that September day in 1974, I realized I'd somehow, through serendipity and curiosity and doggedness and intelligence and just plain luck, done it right. I'd taught myself how to live the life I'd dreamed by reading books.

Soon I had other English classes, and professors who told me to read Shakespeare, Anne Sexton, Flannery O'Connor, and so many more authors that I cannot even begin to name them all. I discovered *The New Yorker*, and the *New York Times Book Review*, and I made friends who loved to read, and then friends who wanted to write, and then I was doing it, living this life I'd dreamed about. I stepped into this big, beautiful world with an open, eager heart. I opened my arms to it, all of it

This is why we all read, isn't it? To know the world and ourselves better. To find our place in that world. Even if you did have access to readers and guidance on what to read, even if you grew up in a family that loved to read and owned shelves of books, still, still, one day a book falls into your hands—perhaps it's

Beloved or *A Wrinkle in Time* or *A Tree Grows in Brooklyn*; perhaps it's *Great Expectations* or *Pride and Prejudice*— whatever book it is, it falls into your hands at just the right moment when you need to read it. It transforms you. Perhaps it lifts you up when you are at your lowest; perhaps it shows you what love is, or what it feels like to lose love; perhaps it brings you places far away or shows you how to stay put when you need to.

In a 1966 *Paris Review* interview, John Updike said, "When I write, I aim in my mind not toward New York but toward a vague spot a little to the east of Kansas. I think of the books on library shelves, without their jackets, years old, and a countryish teenaged boy finding them, and having them speak to him."

I was more than a little east of Kansas, and a daughter of Italian immigrants, but those books on library shelves called out to me too. Thick, beautiful old books. They called out, and I heard them. Gratefully, I heard them.

Acknowledgments

I would like nothing more than to thank every writer who helped me become the person I used to dream of becoming, but the list would be too long and never ending.

Many, many thanks to my brilliant agent, Gail Hochman, who recognized how books had shaped me and urged me to write about that; and to my brilliant editor, Jill Bialosky, who agreed.

As always thanks to all the people at Brandt and Hochman and W. W. Norton who work tirelessly for me. And to Sam and Annabelle, my kids who are passionate readers too and put up with a mom who reads and writes all the time.

And to Michael, ybv.

Available in Paperback

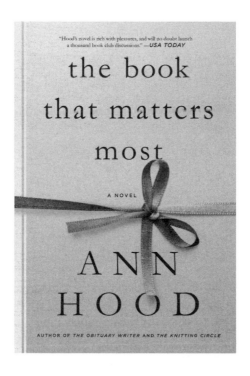

"Rich with pleasures, and will no doubt launch a thousand book club discussions."   —*USA Today*

Finding Buck McHenry

by Alfred Slote

HarperTrophy
A Division of HarperCollinsPublishers

Finding Buck McHenry
Copyright © 1991 by Alfred Slote
Printed in the United States of America.
For information address HarperCollins Children's Books,
a division of HarperCollins Publishers,
10 East 53rd Street, New York, NY 10022.
Typography by Joyce Hopkins

Library of Congress Cataloging-in-Publication Data
Slote, Alfred.
  Finding Buck McHenry / by Alfred Slote.
      p.   cm.
  Summary: Eleven-year-old Jason, believing the school custodian
Mack Henry to be Buck McHenry, a famous pitcher from the old
Negro League, tries to enlist him as a coach for his Little League
team by revealing his identity to the world.
  ISBN 0-06-021652-2. — ISBN 0-06-021653-0 (lib. bdg.)
  ISBN 0-06-440469-2 (pbk.)
  [1. Baseball—Fiction.   2. Afro-Americans—Fiction.]   I. Title.
PZ7.S635Fi   1991   90-39190
[Fic]—dc20   CIP
                                                               AC

First Harper Trophy edition, 1993.

For Jim Shaw
scholar, source, second baseman

Finding
Buck
McHenry

1

Dad says it's wrong to make up scenarios for real life. (As though I did it on purpose.) He says real life has a way of telling you off.

He's talking about Mr. Henry, of course.

Mr. Henry is the custodian where I used to go to school. My name is Jason Ross. I'm eleven years old and I live in Arborville, Michigan.

There's no reason you should have heard of me. But there was, I thought, every reason you should have heard of Mr. Henry. Not under that name, of course. But under his real name—Buck McHenry.

I'm jumping the gun now. Dad says that if I insist on telling this story, "which doesn't do you a lot of credit, Jason," he adds, I ought at least to start at the beginning.

The beginning was when I got kicked off the Baer Machine baseball team. And that happened during our last intrasquad practice game of the

3

spring. I was the batter and I'd just hit a hard ground ball down the third-base line.

"Run, Jason, run!" the guys on my side yelled. (We'd divided the team in half for this practice game.)

I ran hard. If I beat out the ball for a hit, Greg Conklin would score from third and we'd tie them and go into extra innings. I knew I could beat it out too, because as I took off for first, I watched Art Silver, our third baseman, back up on my ball. Ahead of me I saw Tim Corrigan, our first baseman, stretching to receive Art's throw. It would be close but I could make it, I thought. I lunged for the bag and hit it with my right toe just before, I thought, the ball arrived.

"Out," Mr. Borker called. He's our coach and was umping from behind the pitcher.

"Out?" I couldn't believe it.

"Yes, out, Jason. When you should've been safe. For Pete's sake, when you run that slowly to first, are you thinking about something?"

"Jason's thinking about baseball cards, Coach," Pete Diaz, our center fielder, said running by us to the bench.

"Jason's always thinking about baseball cards," Greg Conklin laughed.

Kevin Kovich chimed in, "Jason was thinkin'

that soon as practice was over he was goin' down to The Grandstand and buy more cards."

"Okay, guys," I said, getting down on the bench with them. "Take it easy, huh?"

I try not to let their taunting get to me. Some athletes collect cards; others don't. I'm one who does. Baseball cards are an important part of my life.

Mr. Borker shook his head. "Ballplayers don't think about baseball cards while they're playing, Jason."

I wanted to tell him that I wasn't thinking about baseball cards. I wasn't thinking about anything except beating Art's throw to first. But I had the sense to keep my mouth shut. You never get anywhere arguing with a coach. In any sport. Coaches are always right. Even when they're wrong.

"Daydream while you're playing ball, Jason," Mr. Borker went on, "and you'll never win a game for your team."

That stopped me. Not the daydream part but the way he said, win a game for *your* team, as if my team wasn't Baer Machine. As if Baer Machine wasn't *our* team. I guess I should have sensed then what was coming. But I didn't.

"All right, everyone down on the bench and let's have some quiet," Mr. Borker said, even though he was the only one talking.

He looked at his clipboard. "Next Wednesday we've got our first real practice game. Against the Bank team. Who *cannot* make it?"

No one raised their hand. He looked at me. "I'll be there," I said, wondering why he was singling me out. Did he *not* want me to be there? I was the backup catcher. If Tug Murphy ever got hurt, I'd be taking his place. Of course, I'd get into the game anyway. By league regulations, everyone has to play at least one inning. If we're way ahead, Mr. Borker lets me catch the last inning. If it's tight, he sticks me in right field.

"We'll all be there, Coach," Tug said. "This year we're gonna get those Bank guys."

"We shoulda got 'em last year," Tim Corrigan said.

"That's right," Mr. Borker said. "We should've taken them last year. But this year we will. We've got the pitching, the hitting, and the depth." His eyes roamed from one player to another. "Maybe too much depth," he added, and once again those eyes settled on me.

And still I didn't think anything of it. I was wondering how a team could have too much depth. In the major leagues depth helps a team overcome injuries. You don't have too many injuries in Little League. But what you do have are kids going on vacations. Vacations are Little League injuries. So even in Little League you need extra bodies.

"We've got fourteen players," Mr. Borker said. "A team in the eleven-year-old league shouldn't carry more than thirteen. Most of the other teams have extra players too. Last night we had a coaches' meeting and Chuck Axelrod, our new league president, said—"

"Chuck Axelrod, the sportscaster?" Art Silver interrupted.

I was glad Art had the nerve to ask. I think we were all wondering that. Chuck Axelrod was Channel 4's top sportscaster. His Saturday night *Sportsline* show was the most popular sports show on TV. None of us could believe someone as famous as Chuck Axelrod would live here in Arborville.

"That's right, Art," Mr. Borker said. He seemed annoyed at the idea of Chuck Axelrod living here in Arborville and being involved with our league. "We're supposed to be honored to have Chuck Axelrod become our league director."

"I didn't know he lived in Arborville, Coach," Kovich said.

"He moved here about a month ago and some

genius in the Recreation Department got the idea we could get a lot of publicity for the Arborville kids' baseball program if we asked him to be director of one of the leagues. Since he's got an eleven-year-old kid he wants to get on a team, they asked him to direct our league. Right away Axelrod decided there were enough extra players and brand-new players like his own kid to form a new team. To make a long story short, Baer Machine has agreed to contribute one player to the new team."

He said "Baer Machine" as though it was one of his toolmaking machines that had made the decision. Mr. Borker was part owner of the Baer Machine Company and *he'd* made the decision. I wondered who he was going to cut. I looked around. None of the other guys were looking around. They were all studying their mitts or their shoes as though they'd never seen them before.

And then it hit me. No, I thought, he wouldn't do that. He wouldn't cut me. I'm not the worst player on the team. I'm not the best but I'm not the worst. And suppose Tug gets hurt? Who would catch then?

I looked at Mr. Borker, hoping by now he was eyeing someone else. But he was still looking

8

at me. My heart began to pound. My face felt hot. I knew it had turned red.

"Jason, this is as hard for me as it is for you."

His words hung in the air in front of me. I wished I was a million miles away and couldn't hear them.

"But catcher is your position, Jason, and you'll be a starter for the new team."

I didn't want to be a starting catcher for a new team. I liked being Tug's backup. He was the best catcher in the league. It was no disgrace being his backup. Besides, this was the only team I'd ever played with.

"It could be a great opportunity for you, Jason."

I felt my eyes getting moist. I gritted my teeth. Whatever you do, I told myself, don't cry!

"What's the name of Jason's new team?" Greg Conklin asked quietly. I think he felt bad for me.

"The team hasn't been formed yet, Greg. It will be getting a new sponsor and a new coach."

"It'll be like an expansion team, won't it, Coach?" Tug asked. He was trying to make me feel better too. Tears sprang into my eyes. I cry when people are nice to me more than when they're mean.

9

"That's right, Tug, that's just what it'll be like. A major-league expansion team. Lots of good ballplayers got their start on expansion teams, Jason."

He didn't have to tell me that. I had an Ace Bubble Gum Expansion Player set. It included people like Bill Stoneman (Ace 550), who pitched two no-hitters after he'd been let go, and Dean Chance (Golden Ace 215), who became a Cy Young winner with his new team.

I could feel everyone looking at me now. I took a deep breath. "What do I do now, Mr. Borker?" I asked.

He looked relieved. "You just sit tight, Jason. I'll turn your name in to Chuck Axelrod soon as I get home. He'll be in touch with you and with all the other expansion players. And the new players."

That meant all over town kids were being cut this morning. I wasn't alone. That made me feel a little better.

Mr. Borker went back to his clipboard. "All right, let's move on. Wednesday we play the Bank right here at Eberwoods at five o'clock. I'll pitch Cal for the first two innings and then bring in Tim and—"

He looked up and his eyes fell on me again.

10

I could see him wishing I was gone already. (Even though he'd just told me to sit tight.)

"Jason, how'd you like to do me a big favor?"

He's figured out a way to get rid of me, I thought.

"Those bases out there, I borrowed them from the school. Mr. Henry, the custodian, is up there. There's an adult-league basketball game going on and he has to keep the school open. How'd you like to return the bases to him?"

I didn't want to return the bases for him. I didn't want to do him any favors. But what choice did I have? I was off the team. I might as well be gone.

"Okay," I said, and stood up.

"Thanks, Jason. And listen"—his face took on a phony sincere look—"I know everyone joins me in wishing you good luck with your new team."

"Yeah, good luck, Jayce," someone said.

And the others mumbled, "Yeah, good luck, Jayce. Take it easy, Jason. We'll see ya around. Yeah, see ya, Jason. See ya, see ya, see ya . . ."

And that's how it goes when you get cut from the only team you've ever played with. That's how you say good-bye to guys you've known since kindergarten.

11

It's "See ya, Jason, see ya, man, see ya, see ya, see ya."

I looked at them. "Yeah," I said. "See ya."

I ran out on the field to get the bases. I ran hard. I didn't look back.

2

Two years ago when I was in third grade, my family moved across town. I don't go to Eberwoods School anymore, but I remembered Mr. Henry, the custodian there, real well. He was a tall, gray-haired old man who always had a friendly word for everyone as he pushed his broom down the hall. He knew every kid's name, too.

I doubted he'd remember me now, though.

Mr. Henry was sitting by the back door of the school. The school's up a slight hill past center field. It was like center-field bleachers in Tiger Stadium. If Mr. Henry had been out there awhile, he probably had seen our intrasquad game.

"Hi, Mr. Henry," I said. "I got some bases for you."

"I see that, boy." He got up. "And I thank you for bringing 'em up here."

13

"That's okay."

He peered down at me. "Say, aren't you the one made that last out?"

I felt my face turn red all over again. This just wasn't my day. "Yes, sir."

He laughed. "Well, you sure run a lot harder picking up those bases than you run to first."

"Did *you* think I was out, Mr. Henry?"

"You were out by four feet. Four big feet. You stayed in that batter's box so long I thought the train was going to leave without you."

I laughed. It was funny how he put it. It didn't hurt. "I guess maybe I *was* out."

"You were out all right. But you got the right attitude, bouncing back like you did, running hard to pick up bases. I always said you can't keep a good man down. All right, you can give me those bases now and head on back to your team."

I looked back at the diamond. They were still there. I'd have to go back for my bike and glove. Better to hang out here till they were gone. I didn't want any more "see ya's."

"I can take the bases into the gym for you, Mr. Henry."

"That's nice of you, son. But your coach is going to be mad at you if you don't get back right away. I'll take them from you."

14

I held on tight to the bases. "He's not my coach anymore." I tried to sound cheerful about it. "He just cut me from the team. I don't want to go back there till they're gone."

Mr. Henry's lips pursed in a surprised silent whistle. "He cut you?"

"Yes, sir."

"For not beating out that ground ball?"

"I guess so."

His tongue made "tsk, tsk" sounds against his front teeth. "Well, that's how it goes sometimes. Sometimes they cut the best along with the worst."

"Thanks, but I'm not the best."

"You aren't the worst either." He held the back door open for me. "I've seen lots better ballplayers than you cut from ball clubs." I marched into the school with my arms full of bases. I could hear the sounds of the adult basketball game coming from the gym.

"You ever hear of Willie Mays, boy?"

"Ace 675," I said.

"What's that?"

"That's the number of my 1955 Mays baseball card. It's a pretty valuable card. It's not worth near as much as a 1952 Mickey Mantle, but it's worth a lot."

"How come?"

15

"How come what?"

"How come Willie Mays isn't worth as much as Mickey Mantle?"

"I don't know." Nobody'd ever asked me that before. It wasn't the kind of thing you ever thought about. It was enough to know the prices of baseball cards. They were always changing.

"Willie Mays was a greater player, wasn't he? They played the same position in the same years, didn't they? Willie Mays had better numbers, didn't he?" Mr. Henry was challenging me. I wondered what he was so upset about.

"I think Mays did have better stats than Mantle."

"Well, if Willie Mays had better numbers than Mickey Mantle and he was a better ballplayer, how come his card's worth less?"

"I don't know."

"You ought to find out. You've got to think about those things, young man. You've got to ask yourself how come things are the way they are."

Jim Davis, who owned The Grandstand, would know, I thought. I'd stop there on the way home and ask him.

"Willie Mays was the greatest center fielder who ever lived," Mr. Henry said emphatically.

16

"If he was so great, Mr. Henry, how come he got cut?"

Mr. Henry blinked. Then he laughed. "You come back with a good pitch, boy."

"Well, you said he got cut."

"He did get cut. And they were right to cut him."

"Who cut him?"

"The New York Giants when he first came into the major leagues. Willie was strikin' out all the time. He was too anxious to show the New York folks that he'd be as good up there as he'd been with the Birmingham Black Barons."

"The Birmingham who?"

"The Birmingham Black Barons. Willie played center field for them when he was sixteen." Mr. Henry's voice turned soft as he began to remember. "Willie Mays was a boy among men way back then, but you could see the greatness in him already. He could run like a deer, hit like a mule, and throw you out from deep center field. He could do it all. It was there from the beginning. I saw it with my own eyes."

I stared at Mr. Henry. He'd seen Willie Mays play when he was sixteen?

"Willie Mays was put on earth to play baseball.

17

Not football. Not basketball. Just baseball. It was in his chromosomes. You know what chromosomes are, boy?"

"They're what makes us look like our parents."

"That's right. Well, Willie Mays had chromosomes for baseball."

"Wow."

"The Black Barons were good. But when he played for them, Willie made them great."

"I never heard of them."

"That right?" He didn't seem surprised. "You probably never heard of the Kansas City Monarchs neither."

"No, sir."

"Or the Homestead Grays?"

I shook my head.

"Or the best of them all. The Pittsburgh Crawfords?"

Was he making these teams up? I went on shaking my head.

"Josh Gibson caught for the Crawfords. Now I suspect you may have heard of Josh Gibson."

I was really embarrassed. "No, sir." This was kind of awful. I had over two thousand baseball cards and there wasn't a Josh Gibson on any of them. Nor a Crawford nor a Homestead Gray.

"Josh Gibson was only the greatest hitter who ever lived. That's all he was."

"Was he a better hitter than Willie Mays, Mr. Henry?"

"Yes, he was. He was better than Hank Aaron. Better than Mickey Mantle, Ted Williams. Better than Pete Rose, George Brett, Wade Boggs, your Cansecos and Strawberries. Better than any of your players today. You name 'em and Josh was better than. Better than Ty Cobb and Babe Ruth. Why, I saw Josh hit a home run out of Yankee Stadium. Up and over and out of it. Now Babe Ruth, great as he was, and I'm not denying his greatness, Babe Ruth never did that."

Mr. Henry looked at me under my load of bases. They were getting heavy. I was hoping he'd offer to take them again. But he didn't.

"I expect you *have* heard of Satchel Paige?"

Finally I'd heard of someone beside Willie Mays. "Sure. He pitched for the Cleveland Indians." I had a 1949 Satchel Paige (Ace 129).

"Well, before Satchel pitched in the so-called big leagues, he pitched for the Pittsburgh Crawfords. And Josh Gibson was his catcher. What a pair they were. Old Josh in his rocking-chair squat and Paige firing those bullets. I tell you another great one was on the Crawfords those years. Cool Papa Bell. You hear of him?"

Here we go again, I thought. "No, sir," I said.

"Fastest man ever to play the game. Cool Papa was so fast, he'd often get hit by his own line drives."

I laughed. Mr. Henry stopped walking. He stopped so suddenly, I bumped into him with the bases. We were smack in the middle of the school where the two main corridors intersected.

"What's your name, boy?"

"Jason Ross."

"You don't look familiar. You go to school here?"

"I used to. We moved when I was in third grade. I go to Sampson Park School now."

"That's okay. It doesn't matter where you go so long as you go. Now, Jason Ross, you set those bases down."

"Here?"

"That's right. Right there on the floor."

I didn't hesitate. I set down the bases on the floor. And rubbed my arms and wrists to get the circulation back.

Mr. Henry didn't notice. He had taken a key from his big key ring attached to his belt and was unlocking a closet door that said on the front: MACK HENRY, CUSTODIAN.

"You know why you run so slow to first, Jason Ross?"

"No, sir."

"You stood there at the plate looking at where you hit the ball."

The second he said that, I knew that was just what I'd done. I'd stood there watching Art back up on my ground ball.

"Nobody in this world can run and look at the same time."

He rummaged around in the closet and came out with a long push broom.

Had I brought dirt in with my spikes? I didn't see any. Though I probably shouldn't be wearing baseball shoes inside the school. They could ruin the wax on the floors. Luckily, Mr. Henry hadn't spotted my shoes.

"You can see without looking. You've *got* to see without looking."

He unscrewed the stick from the broom and tossed it at me.

I caught it. It would have bopped me on the nose if I hadn't.

"I'm going to prove that to you, Jason Ross. That's your bat."

He picked up two of the bases, leaving one near me. He marched down the hall with the other two and dropped one of them at his feet.

"All right, Jason Ross," he called down the

21

hall to me, "step up to the plate."

I didn't move. I wanted to know what he was going to do first.

"C'mon, boy. I haven't got all day. That's home plate there. You just step up to it."

He was standing about sixty feet from me.

"Jason, you are trying my patience. Get in there."

Still I didn't move. I don't like to do things unless I know why I'm doing them.

"Jason," he said softly, "this lesson isn't going to hurt you any. It might even do you some good. Now get up there and get your bat back."

What kind of lesson was he talking about? Well, there was only one way to find out. I stepped up to the plate. At least no one was watching.

"Good. Now get your front elbow up a bit. That's it. Now, boy, as soon as this imaginary ball arrives, you are going to hit an imaginary ground ball down that other corridor. That's where third base is. But you are not going to look once at where you hit the ball. You can see out of the corner of your eye where your ball went. You can see without turning your head to look. You are just going to run like the wind to this base, which is first base. You are going to run, Jason Ross, like there were hot coals under your feet. You understand me?"

"Yes, sir."

"Get set now. I'm throwing smoke."

And then right there in the middle of Eber-woods School, old, gray-haired Mr. Henry, the school custodian, went into a full windup.

And as he did, something strange happened. He didn't look so old. He looked tall and young and powerful as he kicked high and came down over his head with a smooth motion and fired the imaginary ball.

I swung.

"Run!" he yelled.

I ran. I didn't look down the other corridor where the imaginary ball went. I lifted my feet and ran hard and hit first base with my left shoe. The base slid far down the smooth, waxed floor.

Mr. Henry laughed and slapped me on the back. "Now, if you'd moved like that when you hit that ground ball, you'd still be on your team. You run like that and you'll be getting your share of hits and then some."

He walked back to home plate. "You know who you remind me of, son?"

I shook my head.

"Roy Campanella. You ever hear of him?"

"Sure. He played with the Brooklyn Dodgers.

I've got two Ace Campanella cards."

"Well, before that, my friend, he played with the Baltimore Elite Giants and some other clubs. Just like Jackie Robinson—you've surely heard of him—played with the Monarchs before he was signed by Mr. Branch Rickey and sent to Montreal. Campy now, he was chubby like you. And he was a catcher too. And he could beat out ground balls!"

"How'd you know I was a catcher, Mr. Henry?"

"I've seen you catching."

"Well, I don't catch very much. I don't play very much."

"You will if you hit. If you hit, they've got to play you. Now you go back and tell that coach of yours to give you another chance."

Mr. Henry screwed the stick back into the broom and leaned it against the shelves of cleaning powder, wax, shelves of paper towels, toilet paper, soaps. Then he shut and locked the door that said MACK HENRY, CUSTODIAN on it. He picked up home plate.

"He won't give me another chance, Mr. Henry. I'm gonna be on a new team."

"Well then you're just going to have to come back with your new team and beat that man's socks off. Speaking of which, boy, before you take another step, you take those spikes off. You're wrecking my floor."

And with that he went off toward the gym carrying the bases as though they weighed nothing.

I had to laugh. He'd just proved that you could see without looking. I walked out of the school in my socks. The team meeting was over. The diamond was empty. I sat down on the grass and put my shoes back on. Then I raced over to my bike and glove. I wanted to get down to The Grandstand as fast as possible and check on those players and teams he'd mentioned. If they were real—those Crawfords and Monarchs and Black Barons and Cool Papa Bells and Josh Gibsons—then there'd be baseball cards for them.

Jim Davis down at The Grandstand was always saying, "Truth's in the cards." I believed that. I hurried down there.

3

Southeastern Michigan, where I live, is a hotbed of baseball card collecting. There are lots of baseball card stores around. But The Grandstand is the best of them. And that's mostly because of Jim Davis, who has a great way with kids and also because he has a lot of great stuff in the store.

As you enter The Grandstand, the first thing you see are packs of new Ace bubble gum cards. They sell for fifty cents each. You get one stick of gum and fifteen cards. The gum is terrible but no one buys Ace bubble gum baseball cards for the gum.

Just past the new cards is a table of old cards. There are three long boxes there. One box is marked 5 CENTS EACH, anothor 10 CENTS EACH, another 25 CENTS EACH. There are about two hundred cards in each box. Unless

Jim changes them often, I know what's in those boxes by heart.

After buying a pack or two of new cards, most kids will make a beeline here hoping to find their favorite player for a nickel. This is Detroit Tiger country, so kids are always hoping to come up with a rookie all-star Matt Nokes or an oldie like a 1968 Al Kaline as though Jim would be careless enough to put either a 1968 Kaline or a rookie Nokes or a Cecil Fielder in the nickel, dime, and quarter boxes.

Around this table a lot of trading also takes place. Jim Davis doesn't mind kids trading but he won't let adults trade. He says there are adults who come to the store not to buy but to use it as a trading post.

"No way," says Jim. "I'm paying the rent here."

After you get past the new cards and the old cards there's lots of wonderful things in The Grandstand. There are T-shirts—Detroit Tigers, Lions, Pistons, Red Wings. There are Tigers window insignia, key rings, bumper stickers, wristbands, decals, buttons, baseball caps, backboards for wastepaper baskets, big posters of all different superstars like Wayne Gretzky, Mark McGwire, Ozzie Smith, Magic Johnson, Isiah Thomas, Joe Dumars, Dennis Rodman.

27

There are warm-up jackets, American League baseballs, old football and baseball programs.

There are books and magazines about every sport imaginable.

Near the cash register are the glass cases with some valuable baseball card sets: traded sets, complete sets, team sets, rookie sets, theme sets like sluggers versus pitchers, record breakers, superstars. Decade Greats—Sportsflicks puts them out.

On the wall behind the glass cases are autographed bats. Jim has a Cecil Fielder bat for fifty bucks. He has a regular Alan Trammel bat for $79.95 and an autographed one for one hundred bucks.

He also has an empty Wheaties box autographed by Pete Rose. Rose's picture is on the box.

"How'd you get the autograph?" I asked Jim once.

"Baseball card show in Dearborn. It cost me eight dollars to get in. So I'm making fifteen dollars on the deal."

"If you sell it."

Jim laughed. "Oh, I'll sell it, Jason."

I wasn't so sure about that. I didn't have twenty-five dollars, but if I did I wouldn't spend it for Pete Rose's name and picture on a Wheaties box. Jim's probably gonna have to go down to Cincinnati to sell it.

Around the other side of the wall is a room with a coffeepot, a small round table, and some chairs. Jim does his private dealing back there.

That Saturday when I went into The Grandstand, it was packed with little kids and their fathers. Jim was behind the counter kidding with people, watching, but never pressuring anyone to buy. He's a collector himself and knows how to talk to kids.

He spotted me right away. "Jason, how's the Baer Machine team doing?"

I still had my Baer Machine baseball shirt on.

"Okay. But I'm not on it anymore. Jim, I want to ask you something."

"What do you mean, you're not on it anymore?"

"I got cut."

"You're kidding?"

"No."

"You've been on that team for years. What'd they cut you for?"

I shrugged. "Not beating out a ground ball."

"That's it?"

"Also, Mr. Borker never liked me. He thinks I think about baseball cards too much." I grinned as I said that. I kind of like teasing Jim a little.

"Does he? Well, I don't think I like *him*. As far as I'm concerned, you can never think about baseball cards too much." We both laughed. "What are you gonna do now, Jason? Try to hook up with another team?"

"I don't know. Mr. Borker says there's going to be an expansion team in the eleven-year-old league. I may play on it. What I came here about, Jim, is to ask you if you've ever heard of the Birming—"

"Wait a second, Jason. You say there's going to be an expansion team in your league? A new team?"

Jim leaned over the counter. He suddenly had a very interested look on his face.

"Yeah, there's going to be a new team."

"Do they have a sponsor for it yet?"

"I don't know. Why?"

Two little kids had come up behind me to buy some stuff. They could have been on another planet as far as Jim was concerned.

"I've been thinking for some time that The Grandstand ought to sponsor a kids' baseball team."

I almost jumped at the idea but I restrained myself. "We'd be a lousy team, Jim. We'd all be rejects from other teams. We'd give The Grandstand a bad name."

"C'mon, Jason, get a good coach, a couple of key players, and we'll be great." Jim grinned at me. "And every time we win, Jason, instead of going for Dairy Queens, I'll treat you kids to a pack of Ace bubble gum cards. How does that hit you?"

I laughed. "That's a pretty good deal if we win any. Would you coach us, Jim? You could be an owner-manager like Connie Mack (Ace Old Timers 212). He was the last owner-manager, wasn't he?"

"I wouldn't mind being another Connie Mack, Jason. But Connie Mack didn't have a baseball-card store to look after. No, we'll have to find a coach. Someone's father."

"Excuse me," a little voice said from behind me. "Could we buy these cards?"

Two little six-year-olds stood there clutching new packs of Ace gum.

"You sure can. Sorry I didn't see you there. Stick around, Jason. What've you got there, gentlemen?"

"Bubble gum cards."

"I hope you got some good ones."

"We do too, don't we, Mikey?"

"Yeah," Mikey said.

The kids paid for their cards with pennies, nickels, and dimes the way I used to when I

31

was their age. I started to step back up to the counter when a teenage girl slipped in ahead of me. She was holding a poster of Isiah Thomas, the Pistons' great guard.

"How much?" she asked shyly.

"Seven fifty," Jim said.

"That much?"

"You think he's good?"

"I love his smile."

Jim laughed. "All right, for Isiah's smile I'll shave twenty-five cents off the price. Seven twenty-five. That's as low as I can go."

"I'll buy it," the girl said.

"Hey, Jim," I said, "I like the way Mickey Mantle smiles on his 1952 Ace card. Would you let me have it for seven twenty-five?"

That Ace 1952 Mickey Mantle (which I'd been telling Mr. Henry about) fetched two thousand five hundred dollars. Jim didn't own it, of course. But it reminded me of the other thing I had to ask Jim about, even though I still hadn't even asked him about the Birmingham Black Barons and Josh Gibson and Cool Papa Bell. I waited till the girl and her Isiah Thomas poster left.

"Jim, I got a couple of things to ask you about. First, do you think Willie Mays was a better ballplayer than Mickey Mantle?"

"Jason, let's talk about our new team first."

"Just tell me," I begged. "Mantle or Mays. Who was better?"

"Okay. Most people think Mays was the greater ballplayer. Mantle was a superstar too. But most of the time he could only really beat you with his bat. He was a great offensive player. Mays could beat you every which way. Arm, legs, bat, glove. Mantle was injury prone too. Mays had a longer career. Now can we go back to this expansion team?"

"If Mays is considered better, how come Mantle's cards are always worth more?" I was asking Mr. Henry's question.

"It's the market."

"What's that mean?"

"It just means there's a greater demand for Mantle's cards than for Mays's. And it's demand that sends up the price."

"How come there's more demand for Mantle if Mays had the better stats?" Mr. Henry would have asked that.

Jim shrugged. "Who knows? Maybe it's because kids who collect cards are mostly white. I don't know. I just sell cards. I don't analyze them. Now who do I call about sponsoring the expansion team?"

I thought about what Jim just said. It was true you didn't see many black kids collecting, but there had to be some. But even if that was the reason, it was the wrong kind of reason for one card to be worth more than another. It was dumb.

"Jason, I just asked you a question. Who do I call about sponsoring the new team?"

"Huh? Oh. Chuck Axelrod."

"The sportscaster?"

"Yeah."

"Are you kidding me, Jason?"

"No. Mr. Borker says Chuck Axelrod just moved to Arborville and they asked him to direct the eleven-year-old league to get publicity. Mr. Borker says he took it cause he's got a son who's eleven years old and wants to get on a team."

Jim whistled. I could see the wheels turning inside his head. "I like it, Jason. The possibilities are tremendous. Chuck Axelrod living in Arborville, directing the eleven-year-old league, The Grandstand sponsoring a team in his league, his son is on the team, and he gets interested in doing a feature story on The Grandstand for his Saturday *Sportsline* show. How does it grab you, Jason?"

I laughed. "Sounds good."

He opened up the Arborville phone book and started looking through it.

"Now what're you doing?" I said.

34

"Lookin' up Chuck Axelrod's phone number."

"Can I ask you something else while you do that?"

"You can ask me anything, Jason. But will I have the answer? That's the question. Axelrod, Axelrod. Axel—"

"Did you ever hear of a team called the Birmingham Black Barons?"

"That was a team in the old Negro leagues. Here we are. . . . Axelrod."

"The old Negro leagues?"

"Yeah, those leagues were in operation from about 1900 to 1946, when Jackie Robinson broke the color barrier. There were some great teams too. . . . Axelrod, Alan and Susan; Axelrod, Barry; Axelrod, Bernard . . ."

"Like the Pittsburgh Crawfords?"

"Yeah. And the Homestead Grays and the Kansas City Monarchs and the Detroit Wolves and the Chicago American Giants and the Newark Eagles and . . . and there's no Axelrod, Chuck or Charles. It goes from Bernard to Lawrence."

"Are there baseball cards for those old teams?"

"It's probably a new number. What did you say?"

"Are there baseball cards for those teams?"

"What teams?"

35

"Jim, for Pete's sake, the teams in the old Negro leagues."

"Andy Armstrong has just put out a collection he put together himself. Here . . . I haven't had a chance to look at them yet."

With one hand Jim dug under the counter and brought up a small white box. With the other he started punching phone buttons.

On the mailing label of the box it said in blue letters: ARMSTRONG. And there was a return address in Wassau, Wisconsin.

Anyone who is a serious baseball card collector knows that Mr. Andy Armstrong of Wassau, Wisconsin, is one of the biggest baseball card dealers in the country. If not the biggest.

I opened the box.

"Arborville," Jim said into the phone. "I'd like the phone number for a party named Chuck Axelrod. I don't have his address. It's probably a new number."

I took out a bunch of cards and looked at them. They were like nothing I'd ever seen before. They were old black-and-white baseball photos. Fuzzy. Out of focus some of them. Maybe copied from old newspapers. Old pictures of old black ballplayers. I started spreading them out on the counter. I was looking into another world.

"Are these for sale, Jim?"

"Sure."

"How much?"

"Oh," Jim said into the phone. "Well, thanks anyway." He hung up. "Wouldn't you know it? He has an unlisted number. It's real smart having a celebrity for a league director. Now what? I've got it. Your old coach'll have his number. What's his name again?"

"Mr. Borker."

"His first name, Jason?"

"Bob. Robert, I mean. Jim, how much does—"

Just then a bunch of kindergarten-age kids came up to the counter with cards. Naturally, they all started talking at once.

"Jason, take those cards into the back room. You can spread out there."

"Thanks, Jim."

Between me, the kindergartners, and trying to get hold of Chuck Axelrod, Jim had his hands full.

"What've you got, gentlemen?" I heard him ask the kindergartners as I headed for the back room.

4

Truth in baseball cards? You bet. There they all were. The ballplayers Mr. Henry had told me about. One second I'd never heard of Cool Papa Bell. The next second I had him in my hands.

And there also was Josh Gibson. The greatest hitter who ever lived, according to Mr. Henry. Standing there looking at the camera, broad shoulders, roundish serious face, the word GRAYS across his uniform shirt. That had to be the Homestead Grays. It was all real. Everything that Mr. Henry was talking about.

And there were others too. Lots of others. Players I'd never heard of. And with great names. Bingo DeMoss, Bullet Rogan, Crush Holloway, Rats Henderson, Judy Johnson (a guy!), Jelly Jackson, Smoky Joe Williams, Double Duty Radcliffe. What was that nickname about?

There looked to be over a hundred cards in

this set. The teams each guy played for were on the backs of the cards. And it looked like each guy played for a whole bunch of teams. Mr. Henry had just mentioned a few. But there were also the Indianapolis Clowns and the Cuban X Giants and the New York Black Yankees and the Cleveland Buckeyes and the Newark Eagles and the Chicago American Giants. Jim had known about some of those too. There were the St. Louis Stars and the Baltimore Black Sox and the Baltimore Elite Giants. (Mr. Henry had mentioned the Elite Giants. Roy Campanella, he said, had played for them.) There were the Nashville Black Vols, the Brooklyn Royal Giants, the Bacharach Giants. So many teams named Giants. So many teams period, and till today I'd never heard of a single one of them.

How could I know so much about baseball and all of a sudden know so little?

There were no stats on the backs of the cards like you have on Ace or Topps or Donruss or Fleer. Just the team names and maybe little bits of information and stories. Like how fast was Cool Papa Bell? Mr. Henry said he was the fastest. And I guess he was. Because on the back of one of Cool Papa Bell's cards, Satchel Paige, who roomed with him on the Crawfords, said Bell was so fast he could turn off the light switch and be in bed before the light went out.

I laughed out loud at that one.

More names: John Henry Lloyd was the first superstar of the Negro leagues; Martin Dihigo played every position on the field; Rube Foster, a pitcher, won fifty-one games in 1902; Cannonball Dick Redding once struck out twenty-four men in a nine-inning game; Buck McHenry once struck out fifteen straight batters. I read the whole of the Buck McHenry card. Something had caught my eye.

McHenry was a powerful right-handed fireballer who pitched in the late 1930's. He pitched only three seasons for the Crawfords but won over ninety games. After several scrapes with the law, McHenry retired early from baseball and worked as a school janitor in Michigan. He later said he made more money sweeping than pitching.

I stared at the words "school janitor in Michigan." It couldn't be. I turned the card over. It was a fuzzy old black-and-white photograph of . . . of . . . My heart almost stopped. It was him. It had to be. It was Mr. Henry!

I just stared and stared. I don't know how long I looked at Mr. Henry, and then I grabbed the card and took for the main part of the store.

"Jim," I yelled, "I've got a coach for our team!"

I almost ran over three little kids looking at Detroit Pistons sweatshirts. I dodged between two mothers buying magazines. At the counter were two adult customers. I wriggled between them and shoved Mr. Henry's card at Jim.

"I know him, Jim. He lives here in Arborville. He could be the coach of The Grandstand team."

"I'll be with you in a second, Jason. What you really want, sir, is a Donruss favorite player pack. That would give you . . ."

Jim, I thought, stop with business as usual. This is important.

But Jim wouldn't be interrupted. Which told me he wouldn't have made a good coach for our new team in the first place. Baseball always comes first for a real coach. Like this morning when he was supposed to be minding the gym, Mr. Henry was outside watching our practice. And then inside the school he showed me how to take off out of the batter's box, how to run to first, even though my spikes had to be messing up his floor. Baseball came first with Mr. Henry.

While Jim did business, I looked again at Mr. Henry's picture. It was probably taken from an old newspaper. There were no statistics on the back. Just that little bit of information.

None of the cards had stats on the back. I wondered why not.

41

Oh, there was much I had to learn. When did the Negro baseball leagues start? Why did they start? What was life in them like? Why did they stop?

Mr. Henry could tell me. I wondered if he'd let us call him Buck McHenry. Well, not Buck McHenry, but Mr. McHenry.

It was clear as pie what he'd done. He'd changed his name by dividing it into two parts. McHenry became Mack Henry—the name on the custodian's closet at Eberwoods School.

No wonder his pitching motion had looked so good. And him saying he'd been there when Josh Gibson hit his home runs. He'd probably been on the field with him. Maybe he'd pitched the day Gibson had hit a ball out of Yankee Stadium.

Why had Mr. Henry quit baseball? The clue was right there on the card. *Scrapes with the law*. I wondered what that was about. Maybe he'd tell us. It was going to be fantastic having a baseball legend as a coach.

"Okay, Jason, what's the problem?"

"No problem, Jim. No problem at all. Truth in the cards, Jim? Isn't that what you're always saying? Well, do you see this card?"

"What are you going on about, Jayce?"

"This card is Buck McHenry. Did you ever hear of him, Jim?"

"Sure. He was a great right-handed pitcher in the old Negro leagues."

"Well, I've got news for you, Jim. Buck McHenry lives right here in Arborville. He's the custodian at Eberwoods School."

Jim started to laugh. So did another adult customer who'd come up behind me. "Department of wishful thinking," the man said.

Adults never believe something wonderful can happen.

"Just to start with, Jason," Jim said gently, "if Buck McHenry lived here in Arborville, we'd all know it. Secondly, he played in the 1930's. That was about sixty years ago. The odds are he's no longer alive. Now be a sport, Jason, and step to one side so I can earn a living."

I stepped to one side and waited while the man paid for his shirts. When he left, I said, "Jim, you don't understand. I saw Buck McHenry pitch in the corridor at—"

"Jason, I don't have time for nuttiness. Saturday's my busy day. And I've already put time in on our team."

"Our team? Does that mean . . . ?"

Jim grinned. "It sure does, pal. I talked to

43

Chuck Axelrod himself. Your old coach had his number. Axelrod seems like a nice guy for a celebrity. He allowed as how a baseball card store sponsoring a kids' baseball team might be the greatest idea since sliced bread. We're in, Jason. But we've got to move fast now. Practice games are already being booked between teams and we don't even have a team yet. Axelrod has a list of expansion players plus new kids in town who are eligible for our team. Two we know about already."

"Who's that?"

"You and his daughter."

"His daughter?"

"That's right. His daughter."

"But Mr. Borker said he had a son."

"Mr. Borker got it wrong. He has a daughter. Her name is Kim and he says she's a heckuva ballplayer."

"I doubt it."

Jim smiled. "Secondly, it's got to be a big plus having the league director with a special interest in our team. He wants us to have a team meeting at four o'clock today over at Sampson Park. Which means we don't have much time. All the kids on his list have to be called before four o'clock. I volunteered you to go over to his house and help his daughter make those calls. Here's the address. Put it in your pocket. 1800 Devonshire. Get on over there, Jason. And try to get as many fathers as possible to the meeting. One of them is going to have to coach our team."

"But that's what I'm trying to talk to you about, Jim. I've got a coach already. Buck Mc—"

"Jason, stop with this Buck McHenry nonsense and get over to Chuck Axelrod's house right now."

"Jim, would you *please* read this card? It says how Buck McHenry became a school custodian here in Arborville."

I pushed the card so close to Jim's face he had to read it. "It doesn't say anything about Arborville, Jason. It says he became a school custodian in Michigan."

"Isn't that close enough? And why did he change his name? He got into scrapes with the law. And how did he change his name? He divided it into two. McHenry became Mack Henry."

That shook Jim up a little. But he was stubborn. "Jason, it's impossible. I'll believe it when *he* tells me he's Buck McHenry, not you. And another thing." He tapped the card. "This picture is so old and out of focus it could be a picture of anyone."

"Jim, if I prove to you that Mr. Henry really is Buck McHenry, will you agree that he can coach our team?"

"Sure. And while you're at it you can prove to me that Sparky Anderson is my uncle. Meanwhile, get over to Chuck Axelrod's house."

"Jim, it's more important for us to get a coach first. And if we get Buck McHenry, we won't have to recruit kids. Every kid in Arborville will want to play for The Grandstand."

"Jason, I can't deal with you when you get like this."

"Jim, if Mr. Henry really is Buck McHenry, can I keep this card?"

"Jason," Jim said slowly, "if a school custodian in Arborville, Michigan, turns out to be one of the greatest right-handed pitchers who ever lived, you can have the whole set. And I'll throw in a poster of Isiah Thomas too."

"You mean that?"

"I do."

"Will you shake on it?"

"Gladly."

He stuck out his hand. And we shook on it. A whole bunch of customers came up then, which suited me fine. I had to get out of there right now.

The clock behind Jim said five minutes to

twelve. I was certain the adult basketball league ended at noon. I'd never make it to the school in time. I could probably catch him at home.

"Jim, can I look at the phone book?"

Jim didn't answer. He was busy. I slipped around the counter and grabbed the phone book.

It was kind of nice being behind the counter with him. Like we were running the store together.

There were a whole bunch of Henrys living in Arborville but only one Mack Henry—332 North Fourth Avenue. That was downtown, not far from the river. The other way from my house. I probably ought to call my folks and tell them I had to skip lunch for the sake of our new team.

No, better not. They'd get upset and tell me to come right home. Better to just head down to North Fourth Avenue and face the music later.

Which is what I did.

5

North Fourth Avenue is one of the oldest streets in Arborville. Two years ago our third-grade class visited a stone house there that had once been part of the Underground Railroad.

Before the Civil War, people in Michigan used to hide runaway slaves who were escaping to Canada. In that stone house there were trapdoors and tunnels and secret passageways. It was interesting and scary. It also made you realize what it was like for black people then.

332 North Fourth Avenue, where Mr. Henry lived, was in the same block as the Underground Railroad house. Only it wasn't half so big. It was a little white house with blue shutters and an aluminum awning over the front door. There was a flower garden in front and a white picket fence.

It was neat and tidy. The way you'd expect a custodian's house to look.

A sign hanging from the gate said: WEL-

COME. THE MACK HENRYS. I looked at it and hesitated. Suppose Mr. Henry said he wasn't Buck McHenry? Did I still ask him to coach?

Worse, suppose he didn't even remember me from this morning. Then what?

Stop, Jason, I told myself. You've come all this way. Go in and get it over with. Be tough.

I unlatched the gate and wheeled my bike in. I could hear a television set playing loudly inside the house.

I laid my bike down near the front steps and unlooped my mitt from the handlebar. That TV set was really blasting. Maybe his wife was hard of hearing. Maybe they wouldn't be able to hear the doorbell. If that was true, I could turn around and go home. Besides, my folks were probably worrying what had happened to me. The practice was long since over. I hadn't even had lunch yet. I might as well go home.

I took a deep breath and rang the bell.

Nothing happened. I rang it again. If no one came on this second ring, I was definitely going to leave. There was probably no one home. They'd probably left the TV on by mistake.

The door opened. A woman not much bigger than me looked at me with sharp eyes. "What can I do for you, young man?" Her voice was sharp too.

"Is Mr. Henry home?"

"He might be."

What kind of answer was that? Either he was home or he wasn't.

I must have looked flabbergasted because she went on, "It depends on what one wants to see Mr. Henry about. I'm his wife. You can tell me why you want to see him."

His wife and his bodyguard, it looked like. Maybe it had to do with those scrapes with the law. If so, I couldn't very well tell her I wanted to find out if he was Buck McHenry.

"Would you . . . uh, tell him that Jason Ross from Eberwoods School this morning is here?"

"Young man, if you left something inside the school, you are just going to have to wait till Monday. Mr. Henry is on his weekend and he's planning on going fishing this afternoon."

"I didn't leave anything, Mrs. Henry. I don't even go to Eberwoods anymore. I used to go there."

"Who's there, Jessie?" Mr. Henry's voice sounded over the TV noise.

Before she could answer, I shouted, "It's me, Mr. Henry. Jason Ross. From Eberwoods School this morning. You gave me a baseball lesson on how to run to first. Remember? I was delivering bases to you . . ."

Before I finished, Mr. Henry appeared behind his wife. He towered over her.

"Don't tell me you've got more bases to return, boy?"

I laughed. "No, sir. I just wanted to talk to you."

"What about?"

I looked at Mrs. Henry, who was looking very curious. Mr. Henry understood right away. "Jessie," he said, "would you go into his bedroom and get him to turn that TV set down so I can hear what's on Jason Ross's mind?"

"Mr. Henry, are you going to take up your Saturday with school business?"

"This boy doesn't go to my school"—which I'd already told her—"so it can't be school business. Go and tell him I hung the mattress out back and want him to try it out."

Try out a mattress out back? What was that about?

"It will take more than a mattress to get him moving, Mr. Henry."

She didn't understand he was only trying to get rid of her for a few minutes.

While they talked, I looked around the living room. Like the front yard, it was small and neat. There was a sofa and two soft chairs. They were each covered with clear plastic. There were little

51

tables with color photographs on them. There was a bookcase with books in it. And small statues of shepherds and people like that on top. On the walls were more color photographs. Mostly of a young man in an Army uniform.

I didn't see any sports photos or trophies. No pictures of Mr. Henry in a baseball uniform. Of course, if he'd had trouble with the law, the last thing he'd want around the house were pictures of himself in a baseball uniform.

After more talk, Mrs. Henry finally left the room and Mr. Henry turned to me. "How'd you find out where I live, boy?"

"The phone book."

In the other room the TV got turned down a little.

"You know, when I first started working for the schools, Mrs. Henry wanted me to have an unlisted number. I said no. She said kids'll be calling you. I said no they won't. Well, they called. But you're the first to actually come. All right, boy, what you want to talk about?"

He clearly wasn't sore about my coming over here. But still I hesitated about coming right out and asking him if he was the great Buck McHenry. For one thing, face to face, he didn't look as much like him as he had back in The Grandstand. I stuck my hand in my pocket and felt the hard edge of the card. It was reassuring.

"Spit it out, boy. It can't be that bad."

"No, sir. It's good really." I took a deep breath. "On my way home from Eberwoods, I stopped at The Grandstand. That's the baseball card store on the corner of State and Packard."

"I know where it is."

"Well, you remember some of the players and teams you were telling me about? The Pittsburgh Crawfords and the Birmingham Black Barons and Cool Papa Bell and—"

"I remember," he interrupted. He was wondering where this was all leading.

"Anyway, I asked Jim Davis who runs The Grandstand about those teams and he showed me some baseball cards from the Negro leagues and I found this card."

I whipped out Buck McHenry and gave it to him. My heart began to pound as he examined it. At first his expression didn't change. But then he smiled.

"Old Buck McHenry on a baseball card. Wonder of wonders."

It's him, I thought. It's him!

Mr. Henry turned his card over and read the stats side, which told how he had become a school custodian in Michigan. In the other room a car-rental commercial was now playing on the TV.

They always play the commercials louder than the program.

"That's an interesting card, boy, very interesting." He handed it back to me.

I cleared my throat. "Mr. Henry, are you Buck McHenry?"

He looked at me as though I was crazy. "Am I Buck McHenry? Boy, what on earth makes you ask a question like that? Buck McHenry was a great baseball pitcher." He laughed. "I wish I *was* Buck McHenry."

"Are you sure?" I persisted.

"Am I sure who I am?" The laughter got louder. It rose from inside his body and filled the room. "Jason, there've been times I wasn't so sure who I was. And times I wished I *was* someone else. But I'm pretty sure I've been Mack Henry for some sixty-eight years now."

He laughed so hard tears came into his eyes. It had to be an act. He was laughing too hard. It wasn't that funny.

"Your names are pretty close, Mr. Henry. McHenry and Mack Henry. And you never mentioned Buck McHenry this morning when you were talking about those old ballplayers."

He slapped his hand on his knee. "Boy, there's lots of ballplayers I didn't mention. Did I mention Sid Morton?"

"No, sir."

"Well, I'm not him either. Did I mention Bill Byrd or Cannonball Dick Redding or Mule Suttles?"

I shook my head. He was teasing me now. Trying to get out of it.

"I'm not any of them either."

I felt my face burning. I tried to keep my voice calm and even. "On the stats side it says that Buck McHenry became a school custodian."

"I saw that. I always wondered what happened to him. He quit while he had his best years ahead of him."

I bet you wondered what happened to him, all right. Well, I would have to take a chance now. It was risky, but I had to let him know I knew why he got out of baseball.

"It says Buck McHenry got into scrapes with the law," I said.

"I saw that." His eyes were twinkling. "All I can say is if you ever meet up with Buck McHenry, you might ask him what that was about."

"You think he's alive, Mr. Henry?"

We were playing cat and mouse with each other.

"Well, let's see. Old Buck played in the late 1930's and early 1940's. That would put him into his late sixties today. I bet he's alive and kicking. . . ."

Alive and kicking in Arborville, Michigan, I thought.

". . . Which is," he added softly, "more than I can say for most of those boys. Most of 'em died young and poor. And now some smart businessman has come along and figured a way to make them immortal and make himself a pot of money. Somehow that doesn't seem fair, does it, Jason?"

"I think it's right that there's baseball cards for them, Mr. Henry. I want to know about them."

"Well, maybe you've got a point there. Who else did you see on those cards?"

"Cool Papa Bell and Josh Gibson and Bullet Rogan and Crush Holloway and—"

"I saw Rogan play many times."

And played against him too, I thought. Well, I thought, I wouldn't push it. I knew. And he knew that I knew. And I knew that he knew that I knew. Stop. You're making yourself dizzy.

"Mr. Henry, can I ask you another question?"

"Not if you're going to ask me if I'm Josh Gibson too."

"No, sir. This is something else."

"Go ahead then."

56

"You remember this morning when I told you I was cut from my team?" He nodded. "And I told you there was going to be a new team?" He nodded again. "Well, Jim Davis who manages The Grandstand is going to sponsor the new team. Only we need a coach. I was wondering if you'd be our coach."

This time Mr. Henry was really surprised. He wasn't playacting now the way he had when I asked him if he was Buck McHenry. Now he didn't laugh. He stared at me.

"You'd be a great coach, Mr. Henry. You gave me a great baseball lesson this morning."

"Jason," he said solemnly, "you are nice to ask an old man to coach your ball team. I am flattered. But I'm too old to be coaching baseball."

"You're not too old, Mr. Henry! Connie Mack coached when he was over eighty. And Casey Stengel was still coaching when he was over sixty."

Mrs. Henry came back into the room. "I can't get him moving, Mr. Henry. You will have to do it."

I don't think Mr. Henry even heard her. He went on talking to me. "I don't know about Connie Mack and Casey Stengel, boy, but Mack Henry is too old. Still, it was nice of you to ask

57

me. And I won't soon forget that."

"Ask you what, Mr. Henry?" Mrs. Henry was one of those people who always have to know what's going on. It would be hard if not impossible for Mr. Henry to have kept any secrets from her. I was sure she knew who he was.

"Jessie, young Jason Ross here has just offered me a job." He smiled, making a joke out of a serious offer.

"What kind of job?" Mrs. Henry didn't smile.

"He wants me to coach his Little League baseball team. That's what." Mr. Henry laughed.

Mrs. Henry didn't laugh. She turned to me and asked abruptly, "How old's your team, boy?"

What a question. Why would she want to know that? What did that have to do with anything? "It's brand-new, ma'am."

"No, boy. How old do you have to be to *play* on your team?"

"Oh. You have to be eleven. We're in the eleven-year-old league."

"Well," she said, turning back to Mr. Henry, "what are you going to do, Mr. Henry, or don't you see it yet?"

"You mean, am I going to coach a baseball team at my age?"

"That's *exactly* what I mean."

58

"The answer, Missus, is I am *not* goin' to coach a baseball team."

"If I were you, Mr. Henry, I'd think that over. If I were you, I would seriously consider the young man's offer."

They were funny the way they talked to each other. Like they were onstage in front of me. Which, in a way, they were.

"What are you trying to say, Jessie?"

"I'm saying, Mr. Henry, that we have an eleven-year-old grandson living with us who does nothing all day but watch TV. Or follow us around like a stray dog. How about that child following you to a baseball team and making friends with other children?"

So that was who was playing the TV set. An eleven-year-old grandson. Maybe he was a ballplayer.

Mr. Henry was silent.

"I'm going to fetch the boy right now," she said, and walked out of the room.

Mr. Henry's lips pursed and he blew one of his silent whistles. "Jason," he said softly, "I am beginning to regret I ever met you."

"But you'd be a great coach, Mr. —" I hesitated and then said boldly, "McHenry."

"Hey, you stop that McHenry foolishness right

59

now. My name is Mack Henry. Not McHenry. And don't you ever forget that."

"I promise I won't tell anyone."

"Jason," he said exasperatedly and then stopped. The door had opened. Mrs. Henry came back in followed by the kid my age. Except he was bigger than me. He was bigger than anyone on Baer Machine. Bigger than Cal Borker or Tug Murphy. He had wide shoulders. He was awesome for an eleven-year-old.

"Aaron," Mrs. Henry said, "this is Jason Ross, who used to go to the school where your grampa works. Jason, this is our grandson Aaron Henry, who has moved up from Memphis to live with us."

"Hi," I said to Aaron Henry, who sure looked like a ballplayer.

Aaron Henry stared at my Baer Machine shirt and my mitt and then he looked down at the floor. He was shy. And with muscles like that.

"Aaron," Mrs. Henry said, "Jason Ross has just said hello to you. I want you to say hello back to him, boy."

It was an order. "Hello," Aaron Henry mumbled. He still wouldn't look me in the eye.

I wondered what was wrong.

6

Mrs. Henry broke the silence that followed.

"Back in Tennessee," she said, "Aaron Henry was supposed to have been a very good baseball player."

"Is he on a team now?"

We were talking as though Aaron Henry wasn't there.

"Why don't you ask him yourself?"

It felt odd but I repeated the question to Aaron Henry. "Are you on a team in Arborville?"

Still not looking at me, Aaron Henry shook his head.

"You've got a tongue, Aaron Henry—use it," his grandmother snapped at him.

"I ain't on a team," Aaron Henry mumbled.

"I'm *not* on a team," she corrected.

"I'm not on a team," he repeated.

"That's better." She turned to me. "Aaron was a pitcher on his baseball team in Memphis. Now what I want to know is, Jason, could your team use a good pitcher?"

"Aw, Grandma," Aaron said.

"*Now* you can be quiet, boy. I'm talking to Jason. Jason, can your team use a very good pitcher?"

"Could we ever! We'll be going nowhere unless we get a good pitcher. We're an expansion team." I felt embarrassed. "We're mostly rejects from other teams. We'll need a good pitcher bad." Aaron was looking at me. "Would you come on our team and pitch for us?"

"No," he said.

Bango. Just like that. No. I was stunned by how quick he said it and how final it sounded.

There was a heavy silence. Finally Mrs. Henry broke it. "Well," she said, giving her husband a sharp look, "are *you* going to speak up?"

All this time Mr. Henry hadn't said a word. Like he didn't want to get involved.

"What do you want me to say, Missus?"

"You *know* what I want you to say, Mr. Henry."

You could tell he did and also that he didn't want to say it. But she kept looking daggers at him, and finally he turned to Aaron, who had gone back to staring at the floor.

"Look at me, boy," Mr. Henry ordered.

Aaron looked at him. Grampa and grandson

looked at each other. They looked alike, I thought. And in a few years Aaron would look exactly like Buck McHenry on the baseball card.

"Listen to me, boy. Jason Ross here has biked across town to ask me to coach his new baseball team. If you're willing to play on it, I'm willing to coach it. What do you say?"

My heart leaped up. From nowhere to everywhere. From nothing to everything. It was a genuine twofer. We get a coach and a pitcher in one fell swoop. But—and it was a big but—if we didn't get one we wouldn't get the other. Come on, Aaron Henry, I prayed, say yes.

But Aaron Henry shook his head. "I told you, Grampa. I don't want to play baseball anymore." His voice was husky. His eyes were pleading with his grandfather. I didn't get it.

"You did tell us that, boy. But I thought maybe you'd change your mind. I guess I know why you won't, though. You don't think Jason here can catch your fastball. Well, I got news for you, boy. I saw Jason catch this morning, and he sets up behind the plate just like Roy Campanella used to. Why don't you get a baseball out of the box in the closet and throw a few to him? He's got his catcher's mitt with him. See if he can't catch you."

"Grampa, you're just trickin' me."

"Enough!" Mrs. Henry snapped. She reached over and grabbed Aaron's ear between her thumb and forefinger. "Up you go. You're not going to watch TV all day long in my house. You are coming with me right now."

She twisted his ear hard, making him stand up.

"Grandma, that hurts."

"That's nothing compared to what I'm going to do to you if you don't start behaving yourself." She looked triumphantly at Mr. Henry. "Aaron Henry and I are going to find a baseball, and then he is going outside and playing with Jason. Isn't that right, Aaron Henry?"

"Ouch," Aaron Henry said as she yanked him out of the room by his ear. Seconds later Mr. Henry and I heard boxes being moved about somewhere and her saying, "Keep on looking, boy. It's there somewhere."

"I guess you're wondering what's going on here, Jason," Mr. Henry said to me.

I nodded. I was.

"The boy is grieving. He's mourning."

As he said those words, Mr. Henry's face changed. His eyes, his mouth, began to twitch. Like the features on his face were about to come apart. Like he was going to cry. I winced. I couldn't picture Buck McHenry crying. I didn't

64

want to be around if that ever happened.

He didn't cry though. He pulled himself together. He blew his nose into a handkerchief. And looked at me.

"Last month in Tennessee, Aaron lost his mama and his papa and his brother in a . . . car crash. He . . ."

He stopped, unable to continue. I didn't understand what he'd said. Lost? In a car crash? What did that mean? And then it hit me. Lost meant dead. Aaron's mother and father and brother had been killed in a car crash.

That was just awful. Your mother and father and brother. And Aaron Henry's father must have been Mr. Henry's son. This was terrible. I shouldn't be here. It was crazy of me to come here today.

He must have understood what I was feeling. "It's all right, boy," he said gently. "I'm glad you came now. Maybe you can help us make Aaron his old self again. You see, the reason he doesn't want to play baseball anymore is because that was what he was doing when his family was killed. He was playing in a Little League game in Memphis. That was why he wasn't in the car with them. That's why he's alive today."

He blew his nose again and wiped it. "A baseball game saved the boy's life. But for what? To grieve and grieve and grieve. The doctor down there says he feels guilty because he's alive. I tell him we've all got to come back from what happened. I tell him but he doesn't listen. He doesn't even hear."

In the other room Mrs. Henry said, "That's the box right there. The ball's in it and your glove too. You fetch that box out."

"The doctor down there thought a change of scenery would do him good, so his grandma and I brought him back up here to live with us. He says he doesn't want to live up here. You've got to live somewhere, I tell him, and what you're doing isn't living anywheres. He says he wants to go back to Tennessee. I tell him all you're going to do down there is what you're doing up here, and that's nothing. Watching TV is nothing. I tried to get him to throw a ball with me, but he won't do that. I thought maybe he'd throw a ball to a mattress. So when I came home from the school today, I hung a mattress against the shed in back." He shook his head. "But he won't do that neither."

Mr. Henry looked at me. "Maybe you can help me with the boy, Jason?"

I nodded. I'd help you with anything, Buck McHenry, I thought.

66

"Go out back and see if he'll pitch to you."

"I'd be glad to, Mr. Henry."

Mrs. Henry came back in the room. "I got him as far as the porch steps. He won't go any farther."

"Jason's going to try and throw a ball with him, Jessie."

"Are you? Well, boy, bless your heart. But you got to go slowly with him. You see—"

"I told him, Jessie. He knows."

Her eyes filled with tears. He gave her his handkerchief. She started to cry. "It's . . . through the . . . kitchen."

I got out of there fast. I went down the hall, through a kitchen, and out onto a screened-in porch. It was a big porch with large wicker chairs, a card table, and lamps. There was a door to the outside. And steep steps leading down to the backyard. The backyard was long and narrow. At the far end was a shed, and hanging down on the side was the mattress. Mr. Henry had painted a bull's-eye on it.

Aaron Henry was seated on the bottom step. Next to him on the step was a glove and a ball.

The screen door clicked shut with a sharp noise, but Aaron didn't turn around. I sat down next to him.

"How're you doing?" I asked, and knew right

away it was a dumb thing to ask. How *could* he be doing? His father and mother and brother were dead.

"Wanna see my mitt?"

I held up my catcher's mitt. He glanced at it. And looked away.

"I was backup catcher on Baer Machine but I'll be the starting catcher on The Grandstand team. That's the team your grampa's going to coach, Aaron."

His lips curled scornfully. "My grampa doesn't know anything about baseball. How's he going to coach a team?"

"The heck your grampa doesn't know anything about baseball. He was only one of the greatest baseball pitchers who ever lived. He won ninety games in three years."

"You crazy or something? What're you talking about?"

Although I'd promised Mr. Henry I wouldn't tell anyone who he really was, I had to make an exception here. His grandson had a right to know!

"I'm talking about this," I said. I started to take the Buck McHenry card out of my pocket and then I thought, No, use it in trade.

"I got your grampa's baseball card right here." I patted the pocket.

"Who you foolin'?"

"I'm not trying to fool you. I got a baseball card with your grampa's name and picture on it."

"Let's see it."

"I'll trade you."

"I don't have any baseball cards."

"I'll trade for something else."

"What?"

"I'll let you look at your grampa's baseball card if you pitch to me and let me see how good a pitcher you really are."

"Now I know you're fooling. Grampa sent you out here. I bet you don't even have a card in your pocket."

"I do too."

"Let's see."

"All right, I'll show you a little bit of it."

I took the card carefully out of my back pocket and showed him just enough so he could see it was a genuine baseball card.

"And you're saying my grampa's on that card?"

"I'm not saying. I know he is. I even showed it to him."

That stopped him. He thought about it.

"What's your name again?"

"Jason. Jason Ross."

"Okay, Jason. You go down by Grampa's dumb

mattress. I'll pitch to you. Then you're going to show me his card. Right?"

"Right!" I ran down to the other end of the yard and stood in front of the mattress with the bull's-eye on it and looked back at the house and the back porch that was supported by iron poles. To the right of the porch was a window, and in it Mr. and Mrs. Henry were watching us. Aaron couldn't see them. He had his back to them.

"You want to warm up?" I called out.

He nodded. "I haven't pitched in a while."

He threw some easy tosses at me, and while I couldn't tell yet if he was a pitcher, I could tell he was a ballplayer. He had a nice easy motion.

"How long's it been since you threw?" I asked. I was just trying to make conversation, but it was a pretty dumb thing to say. Pitching was what he had been doing when his family was killed. I shouldn't be reminding him of that. That was a subject to stay away from.

He didn't answer right away, and I said, "I'm ready. You ready?"

"Yeah," he said. "I'm ready."

"Okay," I said and squatted down, "fire away."

The moral of what happened next is that "fire away" is a dumb thing to say when you don't

70

know who you're asking to fire away.

Aaron went into a slow windup that reminded me of his grampa. He was Buck McHenry on a smaller scale. The same motion, the same high kick, and then he fired the ball at me.

Only this wasn't an imaginary ball in a corridor at Eberwoods School. This was a real baseball coming at me like a bullet. I ducked at the last split second and the ball whistled past me and smacked up against the mattress. It made a smashing sound. And, for all I knew, a hole in the mattress.

I stared at Aaron Henry. Never in my life had I seen a kid my age throw that hard. Not Cal Borker, not Tim Corrigan, not Manny Fernandez who pitched for the Bank team. If Aaron Henry pitched for The Grandstand, we'd beat Baer Machine any day of the week and the Bank team twice on Sundays.

He was talking to me.

"What'd you say?" I said.

"How come you didn't catch it?"

"Are you crazy? It would've broken my hand. I'll need a sponge in my glove to catch you. No, correct that. Two sponges."

He saw I was serious. And he laughed. He stood there and laughed. I didn't mean to make him laugh but he laughed. Mr. and Mrs. Henry heard that laugh. I saw them smile at each other.

I fetched the ball and went up to him. "You're a pitcher all right, Aaron. We'll be a winning team with you. You want to see your grampa's baseball card?"

His eyes were alive. Alive and interested. "Yeah. Let's see that card."

I took the Buck McHenry card out of my back pocket and handed it to him. As I did so, I remembered my promise to Mr. Henry not to tell anyone. I looked up at the back window. They weren't there now. I guess they didn't want Aaron to think they were spying on him. Maybe it would still be all right. Maybe they wouldn't mind my telling Aaron. It was in a good cause.

"That ain't my grampa. That's someone named Buck McHenry."

"Your grampa's name *was* Buck McHenry. What he did was chop his last name in half when he quit baseball. McHenry became Mack Henry."

Just as that detail had shaken Jim Davis, it also shook up Aaron. But then he looked doubtful. "It don't look like my grampa."

"It don't look like him *now*. But it looked like him then."

"My daddy would've told me if Grampa was a professional baseball player."

"He probably didn't know. It was a secret. Read the other side." It irritated me that he would doubt his own grandfather's greatness.

"There," I said, pointing to the words on the stats side. "It says he became a school custodian in Michigan. And right below it says why. He quit baseball because he had scrapes with the law."

Aaron was silent. He turned the card over and looked again at the picture.

"It still don't look like him," he said, but he was beginning to weaken.

"The picture's out of focus. Jim Davis at The Grandstand says most of the pictures of the Negro league baseball stars are out of focus. Ask him if you don't believe me."

By "him" I meant Jim Davis.

"I will," he said, and took off for the house like an Olympic sprinter.

"Where're you going?" I yelled.

"To ask Grampa like you said," he yelled, waving the card over his head without looking back.

"I didn't mean your grampa," I shouted. "Stop!" But it was too late. He was in the house already.

Mr. Henry was going to be very angry with me, I thought.

7

"Whoa. Slow down, boy. You're talking too fast for an old man."

Mr. Henry and Mrs. Henry were seated on the plastic-covered sofa looking up at Aaron, who was pointing at the Buck McHenry card.

"Jason says you used to be a famous baseball player, Grampa. And your name was"—he looked at the card—"Buck McHenry. Were you him, Grampa?"

I couldn't bear to look at Mr. Henry.

To my surprise, though, he laughed. "No, boy, I'm not Buck McHenry, but I sure did like seeing you throw to Jason. You threw that ball hard."

"Real hard," I said.

Aaron turned to me. "He's not Buck McHenry and he can't coach your team."

"Wait a second, boy," Mr. Henry said. "Where does it say a man has to be named Buck McHenry in order to coach a baseball team?"

"Aw, Grampa."

"Don't 'Aw Grampa' me. This country is full of folks coaching baseball teams whose names aren't Buck McHenry."

Aaron gave me back the card. "You were just tricking me to play baseball."

"What's wrong with playing baseball, boy?" Mrs. Henry said.

"Aw, Grandma."

"Don't you 'Aw Grandma' me either. I'll twist your ear off if you go on behaving like a hermit. You should be out making friends up here." She looked at Mr. Henry. "As for you, sir, I think it's high time you owned up to who you were."

"What are you saying, woman?"

"I'm saying it's time to own up to who you are, Buck McHenry."

I gulped. So did Aaron. Mr. Henry stared at his wife. Talk about being betrayed.

"Jessie, stop talking nonsense," he said.

"I'm not talking nonsense, Buck McHenry. I want your grandson to start living again, and if it means admitting who you are, then you should do that. What is it going to cost you, Buck McHenry?"

Mr. Henry was silent. He didn't look at Aaron or me. I guess when you've had a new name for years, you don't take the old one back easily.

Those scrapes with the law must have been more than just scrapes. Maybe Buck McHenry had killed someone. But I couldn't believe that. Not Mr. Henry.

"Tell him, Buck," Mrs. Henry insisted.

Mr. Henry remained silent.

"Mr. McHenry," she said, "if you want to go on eating meals in this house, you will admit to the boy who you are."

She meant it, too. Mr. Henry looked helpless. He didn't want to do this. But he had to.

"Boy," he said, "look at me."

Aaron looked at him.

"You want me to be Buck McHenry? I'll be Buck McHenry."

But the way he said it was all wrong and Aaron shook his head. "It's okay, Grampa. I didn't think you were him anyway."

"For God's sake, tell the boy clean out," Mrs. Henry snapped.

There was a silence. Then Mr. Henry said, "All right, boy. I *was* Buck McHenry. But it was a long time ago. Before you were born. Before even your daddy was born. And it's all over now."

But it wasn't over at all, I thought. It was just beginning and it was wonderful! I couldn't restrain myself. I clapped my hands.

No one even looked at me. Aaron turned to

76

his grandmother. "Is it true, Grandma?"

"Yes, boy, it's true. Your grampa doesn't like to live in the past, but sometimes you have to. Now, I've had enough of this foolishness. I'm going out front to do some gardening. You behave yourself, Buck," she said as she went out the door.

"You're not makin' this up, are you, Grampa?" Aaron asked. He was still suspicious.

"No, he's not," I said.

"How come you never told anyone?" Aaron slid onto the floor at his grampa's feet.

"How come I never told anyone?" Mr. Henry frowned. "I guess I didn't think it was worth telling. That's how come."

"But you're on a baseball card. That's worth telling."

"Not to me, boy."

"Didn't you ever tell Daddy?"

"No."

"Why not?"

"Because like I just told you, it all took place before he was born. It took place before I even met your grandma."

"But you told her."

Mr. Henry smiled. "Had to. A man can't keep secrets from his wife. Especially your grandma." He chuckled.

Aaron's face was serious. "Can I see the card again, Jason?"

I gave him the Buck McHenry card and then slid down next to him on the floor.

Aaron read the stats side again. "It says you were a great pitcher, Grampa. It says you won ninety games in three years."

Mr. Henry laughed. "Don't believe everything you see in print, boy."

"Did you or didn't you, Grampa?"

"I probably did."

"Mr. uh—" I began and stopped. I didn't know what to call him. Henry or McHenry?

He knew what I was worrying about. He smiled. "You keep calling me Mr. Henry, Jason. That's my name now."

"Okay, thanks. Mr. Henry, can I ask you some questions?"

"What kind of questions?" He sounded suspicious. I didn't blame him. He hadn't wanted to admit who he was and now I wanted to know even more.

"How come there are no stats on the backs of these cards?" I asked.

He looked relieved. He probably thought I was going to ask him about those scrapes with the law. But I wouldn't do that. That would be really mean. You'd have to be a TV reporter, the kind that ask a family whose house has just burned down how they feel.

"How come there's no stats on the cards?" he repeated. "Well, that's easy to answer, Jason. Who was going to keep statistics in those leagues? There wasn't any money to pay someone to keep records. There wasn't even money to pay players. Most of those boys played for the love of the game and carfare home. And they were lucky if they got carfare."

He kept saying "they," not "we." He was still being cautious, but at least he was talking about the old days. This was the most exciting thing that had ever happened to me. Talking with a living baseball card.

"How come there were Negro leagues in the first place, Mr. Henry?"

"That's history, Jason. You've got to know your history."

"I don't know it."

"Me neither," Aaron said.

"Well, you both heard of Jackie Robinson, didn't you?"

"Sure," we said.

"Well, till Robinson broke the color bar they wouldn't let colored ballplayers into regular organized ball. I'm talking about major *and* minor leagues. Oh, a couple of fellows'd sneak in from time to time as Indians and Cubans. Like Chief Bender. But Charley Grant, who was a fine second baseman, couldn't make it as an Indian even though John McGraw, manager of the New York Giants, gave him an Indian name—Chief Tokahkoma. That was a long time ago."

"Before you played, Grampa?"

"Yep, boy, even before I played. Fact is, from the very beginning white folks wouldn't let black folks play baseball with them."

"How come?" I asked.

"How come? How come folks don't like other folks just because the color of their skins is different? How come? I don't know how come. You've got to ask a white man that. Ask your father how come."

"I will."

"Then you tell me what he says, because I don't know. All I know is that when baseball leagues first started way back after the Civil War, they didn't want black men playin' with white men. That's when it started. Lincoln freed the slaves but he didn't free them to play ball."

"Were they any good?" Aaron asked.

"Were who any good?"

"The slaves."

"Slaves didn't play baseball," Mr. Henry said crossly.

80

"So who are we talking about, Grampa?"

"I'm talkin' about what came afterward. When there were colored ballplayers better than the best white ballplayers. Men like Gibson and Satchel Paige and before them John Henry Lloyd, Rube Foster. Better than any white players."

"Better than Babe Ruth?" Aaron asked.

"That's right, better than Babe Ruth."

"Josh Gibson hit a ball out of Yankee Stadium once," I said to Aaron. "Babe Ruth never did that."

"How do you know, Jason?"

"Your grampa told me. Mr. Henry, did you know Satchel Paige personally?"

Mr. Henry leaned back on the couch. "I knew them all, boy."

"Was he as great as they say—Satchel Paige?"

"Better. There were those who said Smoky Joe Williams was better, but I never saw him pitch. Matter of fact," he said, chuckling, "I never saw much of Satchel's pitch either. Especially his fastball. He called it 'trouble' or 'jump ball.' 'Trouble' because that's what it gave to batters. And 'jump' cause it took a little jump at the end and disappeared."

"Where'd it go?" asked Aaron.

Mr. Henry laughed merrily. "Into the catcher's

glove, boy. That's where it went." We laughed too.

"Who was the best all-around player in the Negro leagues, Mr. Henry?" I asked.

He didn't take long to give an answer. "John Henry Lloyd was the best baseball player ever lived, Jason. Colored or white."

"His card was in that set," I said.

"Was he better than Josh Gibson?" Aaron asked.

"Not as great a hitter. No. Not that. But a greater ballplayer. Greater than Ty Cobb. Greater even than Honus Wagner. I bet you heard of Honus Wagner, Jason."

"Sure. He was in the original Hall of Fame. A mint-condition Ace 1911 Honus Wagner is the most valuable card around. One sold last year for over a hundred thousand dollars."

Aaron's mouth fell open. "A hundred thousand dollars? For a baseball card?"

"That's right."

Mr. Henry smiled. I couldn't tell whether he believed me or not. But it was the truth.

"Would you two like to hear a little story about the great Honus Wagner *and* John Henry Lloyd?" Mr. Henry said.

I inched up closer. I loved getting the inside scoop like this. Mr. Henry hadn't just read about these guys. He had played with them. He was one of them!

"One day a reporter in his newspaper column called John Henry Lloyd 'a black Honus Wagner.' Someone asked Honus Wagner to comment on that. And you know what Mr. Honus Wagner said?"

"What did he say?" we asked.

"He said, 'I am proud to be compared to John Henry Lloyd.' That is exactly what the great Honus Wagner said. 'I am proud to be compared to John Henry Lloyd.' Now what does that tell you about John Henry Lloyd?"

"That he must have been better than anyone who ever played ball," I said, thinking it also told you something about Honus Wagner. He must have been a good man besides being honest.

"John Henry Lloyd was the best," Mr. Henry said.

"I bet he wasn't better than you, Grampa," Aaron said. His eyes were shining.

Mr. Henry smiled. "He was a lot better than me, boy."

"But you could've pitched in the big leagues if they'd let you, Grampa."

"I like to think so, boy."

"Can I ask you another question, Mr. Henry?"

"You do enjoy asking questions, don't you, Jason?"

"I guess," I laughed, a little embarrassed. "My dad says I'm going to be a lawyer like him. Lawyers ask lots of questions. Except they're only supposed to ask questions they know answers to."

"What're they asking for then?" Aaron said.

"To trap people in court."

"That's ugly," Aaron said.

Mr. Henry laughed. "I agree with you, boy. I think it's better to ask questions because you don't know the answers. Not because you do. How else are you going to learn anything? Go ahead, Jason. You were asking . . ."

It was wonderful. Now Mr. Henry really wanted to open up about the old days. I'd done him a favor. I inched up closer. So did Aaron.

8

"How come the Pittsburgh Crawfords were called Crawfords?" That was my question.

"Who were they?" Aaron asked me.

"Best black team ever brought together," Mr. Henry said. "That's who they were. I pitched for them. So did Paige. Gibson was our catcher. Cool Papa Bell played in the outfield and Judy Johnson played third base."

"Judy?" Aaron said.

"Short for Judah, though his first name was Bill."

That didn't make much sense, but I didn't want to interrupt.

"On that same team was Oscar Charleston. And who else? Oh, Jimmie Crutchfield, Rap Dixon, and Double Duty Radcliffe."

"I saw his card. How'd he get a nickname like Double Duty, Mr. Henry?"

"The way it happened, Ted Radcliffe pitched

the first game of a doubleheader and won it. And caught the second game. Some reporter gave him that name right then and there. Because he did double duty. Let's see, who else was there? Oh, lots. We jumped around a lot. Mostly we didn't belong to a league. Just went around the country, playing who'd ever play us. We played hard, though we might ease up on a poor team. A batter'd hit a ball down to third with no one on base and Judy Johnson'd whip it to Sam Bankhead at second and he'd whip it to Oscar at first and they'd still get the runner out at first by a step. That's how good that Crawford infield was."

"What'd they do that for?" Aaron asked.

I was about to ask that too. It seemed like a really unprofessional thing to do.

"To have fun," Mr. Henry said gleefully. "To make a close game out of a poor one."

"I bet they wouldn't've done it if Cool Papa Bell was running out that hit," I said.

"No, we wouldn't've done that, Jason. Just to start with, Cool Papa was on our team. He was our center fielder. But if he was on an opposing team, well, no one, not even our boys, would fool around like that. The only way you could get Cool Papa out on a ground ball was, let's say with no one on he hits a ground ball to third. Well, if the third baseman had his wits about him, he'd fake throwin' to first, fake throwin' to second, and then tag Bell out as he came slidin' into third."

I laughed. Aaron, grinning, said, "He was fast all right."

"Fast isn't the word to describe Cool Papa. He was a strong breeze goin' by. You felt him, you didn't see him.

"Oh, they were all good, you know. Born to run, born to hit, throw, catch. You didn't have to teach them. There was no one to teach them. There was no coaching. There was no spring training. You put on a uniform and you started playing. You learned by playing. No one brought you along. They figured if they paid you, you were good enough. And they were good enough. We'll never see them again. The Crawfords, the Homestead Grays—"

"How did the Homestead Grays get their name?" I asked.

He hadn't told me yet how the Crawfords got their name, but maybe he didn't know. Ballplayers don't always know stuff like that. They're too busy playing.

"Homestead Grays got their name from the old Homestead Steel Works outside Pittsburgh. We all lived around there."

"It was like Little League then," I said. "Having teams named after businesses."

"Well now, I never thought of that. You could be right, boy. Of course we didn't do much philosophizing about our profession. We lived to play ball. Teams came and teams went. Sometimes a fellow would play for three or four teams in the course of one season."

"How could he do that, Mr. Henry?"

"He'd jump teams. Everyone did it. Paige did it all the time before he finally settled down with the Kansas City Monarchs. He'd go where the money was. And the money was there for him. He made a lot. Of course it's nothing compared to what they make now, but it was a lot for then. Josh Gibson didn't make half as much as Paige and we didn't make half as much as Gibson. The owners made money, all right. But there was no players' union. No lawyers. No agents. Just the idea that someone would pay you to do what you loved to do, that was enough."

"Did you have all-star games, Mr. Henry?"

"Yes we did, Jason. There was an all-star game between the Negro National League and the Negro American League."

"Were you in one, Grampa?"

"More than one, boy."

"Did you get the wins?"

"I expect I did. You could look it up. They kept records on the all-star games."

"Was it fun or was it hard being in those leagues, Mr. Henry?" I asked.

Mr. Henry smiled. "As I remember, it was a little bit of both. Sometimes it was hard and sometimes it was fun and sometimes it was fun and hard at the same time. Going around the country, especially the South, we played in some hostile ball parks and with some hostile fans. The home clubs paid the umps, so when you were a visiting team you often got cheated and that was hard to accept. But . . . we had fun too. Everyone could play just about any position, though of course you were apt to be better at one position than another. The managers all played. We didn't have more than thirteen, fourteen players on some teams." (Like Little League again, I thought.) "You got hurt, you played. You made do with what you had. You made something out of nothing. There were no whirlpools, no clubhouses, no hot tubs, no fancy hotels. You slept in old buses, in old cars, in ratty hotels. Unless you were Satchel Paige, you didn't get rich. But there you were, playing ball, being paid to do what you'd do for nothing, and that's the best job anyone can have."

"I'm going to have that job," Aaron said quietly.

"That so?" Mr. Henry looked amused. "And who's going to give it to you, boy?"

"The big leagues."

Mr. Henry chortled. "Maybe they will, but first you've got to earn it. And I don't know about that. I've got to see how good you are."

"Oh, he's good all right, Mr. Henry. He throws harder than anyone," I said.

"That right? Well, only thing I saw this boy throw till today was stones in a river while I was trying to fish. In those old leagues we had boys not much older than him throwing complete games, and throwing them harder than full-grown men."

"I could pitch in those leagues, Grampa," Aaron said firmly.

"Put that in the past tense, boy. You'd have a hard time finding one of those leagues now. They are *long* gone. When Mr. Jack Roosevelt Robinson went up to the Brooklyn Dodgers in 1947, that was the beginning of the end for the old black leagues. After that lots of black ballplayers came into white ball. And black fans, they went to the big white ball parks to see how their boys did in the major leagues. It was integration that ended the old Negro leagues."

"Did that make you sad, Mr. Henry?"

"No, Jason, that didn't make me sad. That's progress. And progress means money and fame for the new black ballplayers. The Jackie Robinsons, Willie Mays, the Monte Irvins, Hank Aarons, Frank Robinsons, Bob Gibsons. Sure, sometimes I look back and wish I could have been born a little later. Me and Josh and Satchel and Cool Papa and Oscar and Judy and Buck Leonard and oh, there's so many that could have been stars. Martin Dihago, we haven't even talked about him and he was one of the great ones. He was from Cuba. And Smoky Joe Williams before my time and Dandridge who almost did make it to the big leagues. Well, Satchel used to say, never look back. You've always got to look ahead. I like being me now. I like being who I am now, what I am, where I am. Of course," he added with a chuckle, "at my age I don't have a baseball future."

"Sure you do, Grampa," Aaron said. "You're going to coach our team."

Coach our team? I jumped up.

"We've got to get moving," I said. "All we've got so far is a sponsor and a coach. We're supposed to have a team meeting today over at Sampson Park."

"Grampa, we have to go to the meeting," Aaron said.

"I'm planning on fishing this afternoon, boy."

"Grampa. Please."

"Well, I guess if I'm going to coach a team, I better meet up with them. But you two have to promise me something first."

"What's that?"

"You both have to promise you won't tell anyone who I used to be. Especially kids. People in this town, they've known me for thirty years as Mack Henry. I don't want to confuse them. To everyone around here my name is still Henry. Mr. Mack Henry. You've got to forget about my ever being Buck McHenry."

"But Grampa, kids should know who you were." Aaron looked unhappy. I didn't blame him one bit.

"Unless I get your promise, boy, I'm not coaching your team."

"I promise not to tell kids," I said. I'd already promised once about not telling who he was and broken it. But I hadn't told any of the kids. That was a promise I could still keep.

"Aaron?" Mr. Henry asked.

"I promise," Aaron said reluctantly.

"What time's the meeting, Jason?" Mr. Henry asked.

"Four o'clock. At Sampson Park. But I don't know how we can have a team meeting. We don't even have a team yet. I was supposed to call up kids on Chuck Axelrod's list—the expansion players—and tell them about the meeting. The list's at Chuck Axelrod's house."

"Chuck Axelrod? The Channel 4 man?" Mr. Henry's eyes opened really wide.

Here we go again, I thought. The power of TV. If there was another Chuck Axelrod living in Michigan, no one knew it.

I nodded. "He lives in Arborville. They asked him to be director of the eleven-year-old league. His daughter's going to be on the new team. I'm supposed to help her make phone calls." I looked at Aaron. "You want to come help with the phone calls?" I wasn't sure I wanted to be alone with Chuck Axelrod's daughter. She could be a real jerk.

"Can I go with Jason, Grampa?" Aaron asked.

"Of course you can, boy." Mr. Henry looked pleased.

"I'm on my bike, Mr. Henry. Does Aaron have a bike?"

Aaron shook his head.

"Yes, you do too have a bike," Mr. Henry said to him. "There's an old bike of your daddy's in the shed. I kept it oiled. Go get it, boy."

93

For a second I wondered if maybe riding a bike of his father's would sort of scare Aaron, but it didn't. He got up and ran out of the house.

"Isn't that somethin'," Mr. Henry said, his eyes following Aaron as he left.

"It's great."

"I better make sure he doesn't mess up my shed."

Mr. Henry went out the back way and I went out the front door. Mrs. Henry was working in the flower garden on her hands and knees. She looked up as I came down the steps. She was looking into the sun. She shaded her eyes with one hand to see me better.

"Mr. Henry's going to coach and Aaron's going to play, Mrs. Henry. And Aaron's coming with me now to help me make phone calls. We don't have a lot of time and we've got to recruit kids for the team."

"Well, well," Mrs. Henry said, "think of that. One second he doesn't know anyone. The next he's going to meet a lot. Well, we have something to thank you for, Jason Ross."

I felt myself blushing. "I'm the one who should be doing the thanking, Mrs. Henry. You helped us get the great Buck McHenry as our baseball coach."

"That's right. I did. Tell me something, boy.

94

Did Mr. Henry say he didn't want you telling folks about him?"

"Yes, ma'am."

"Well then, you be sure you do as he says. It's got to be a secret."

"Oh, it will. We won't tell a soul. I promised. And Aaron promised too."

Just then Aaron and Mr. Henry came around the side of the house pushing Aaron's dad's bike. Aaron looked happy.

Mrs. Henry gave him a severe look. "You're going into society now, Aaron. You behave yourself, you hear?"

Aaron grinned. "I will, Grandma."

"You keep an eye on him, Jason."

"I will, Mrs. Henry."

Mr. Henry laughed. "They'll be all right, Jessie."

"See you at four at Sampson Park," I shouted at Mr. Henry as we took off.

"I'll be there," he called after us. "And remember you aren't goin' to tell anyone, especially kids. . . ."

Those were the last words we heard as we took off down the block.

Funny how you remember something like that.

9

Aaron and I rode up North Fourth Avenue, up Huron, then Washtenaw. We went past a lot of buildings I could point out to him. Starting with the big old stone house on North Fourth Avenue that had been part of the Underground Railroad.

Then City Hall on the corner of Huron and Fifth. Then the *Arborville News* building. I detoured us past some of the university's athletic buildings and then we headed up Washtenaw, going by the big fraternity and sorority houses.

Aaron took it all in, looking from one side of the street to the other.

"This town at all like Memphis?" I asked him.

"Memphis is bigger."

"I know. If we had a minor-league team, it'd only be Class A. Memphis has got a Double A team. The Chicks."

"How do you know something like that, Jason?"

96

"Baseball cards. Heck, everything I know is from baseball cards."

Aaron hesitated. Then he said, "What're you going to do with my grampa's card?"

"Give it to you."

That just popped out of me. I'd never given away a card before. You're not supposed to *give* away cards. If you want to get rid of one, you trade it. Even duplicates. Especially duplicates. You've got to treat cards like a major-league ball club treats players. Trade them, sell them, and if they get too shabby, dump them. But out of nowhere I'd shot my mouth off and given away a baseball card. One I didn't even own yet, as a matter of fact.

"Thanks, Jason," Aaron said softly.

We pumped up the sidewalk past the First Presbyterian Church. It was uphill here. Aaron wasn't breathing hard and it was a one-speed he was pedaling.

"Heck," I said, trying to make myself feel better about the freebee, "I'm gonna get the whole rest of the set for nothing. Jim Davis said he'd give it to me for free if your grampa turned out to be Buck McHenry."

"We're not supposed to tell anyone, Jason."

He was right. I hadn't thought of that. How was I going to get the set for free then? Wait.

I'd made the bet with Jim before I'd made the promise to Mr. Henry. And, at that, I'd really only promised not to tell kids. I was in the clear.

I told Aaron all that. And added, "Jim didn't believe me. All he said was that he had to hear it himself from your grampa before he'd believe it."

"Well, Grampa won't admit it to him, Jason."

"Then I'll buy the set. How much could it cost anyway?"

"I wish Grampa would admit it. I wish he'd tell everyone who he is. I don't know why he's bein' like that."

I knew why. It had to do with scrapes with the law. Mr. Henry was probably still on the run. But I couldn't very well tell *that* to Aaron.

"Well, maybe he doesn't want to be bothered by folks. If the kids in Arborville found out he was the great Buck McHenry, they'd be pestering him to death for his autograph. And the kids who go to Eberwoods would be the worst. They'd be after him all the time in the halls even. He'd never be able to do his job."

Aaron thought about it. He nodded. "I guess you're right. You know what bothers me most, Jason?"

"What?"

"That my dad and mom and Louis aren't ever

goin' to know. I wish there was some way I could tell them."

A chill ran down my spine as he said those words. The last thing I wanted was to set him to thinking about his family and get him all sad and closed up again. I had to change the subject fast.

"We only got about two blocks to go. You getting tired?"

"No. My daddy had a good bike."

"That's Devonshire up there," I said quickly, "the street coming in on the left."

"We have to cross?"

"Yeah."

There was a lot of traffic on Washtenaw. It's a state highway. Finally lights stopped the traffic down at Hill and Washtenaw and up at Brockman and Washtenaw. No cars were coming. We ran our bikes across the street to Devonshire Road.

Now the neighborhood began to change. At Devonshire Road begins the fancy part of Arborville. Big houses, big lawns, no sidewalks. That's how you can tell a rich part of town. No sidewalks.

Of course, it's how you can tell a poor part of town too, no sidewalks. But the streets in the poor parts of town aren't paved and the houses are small and all you ever see in front of them are pickup trucks and motorcycles. Here Mercedes and BMWs were parked on the circular drives off the streets with no sidewalks.

1804 Devonshire, two houses up from the corner, was a big house with a big lawn in front. There were all kinds of trees and bushes and flower beds.

We got off our bikes and walked them quietly up a long curving brick walk. I think we were both a little intimidated. The house was big. Halfway to it, Aaron turned to me. "Your house this big, Jason?"

"Are you kidding?"

I couldn't tell if he was disappointed or not. I think he wanted my house to be this big so maybe I'd know how to behave here. I didn't know any more than he did.

We finally got to the front door. We laid our bikes down and confronted it. The door was big and thick. There were ivy vines growing around a tiny stained-glass window toward the top.

"This is like a castle," Aaron whispered.

"No, it's not. Castles have moats and drawbridges. This place doesn't even have a doorbell."

Aaron pointed at a lion's head sticking out on the door. "That's the doorbell," he said.

It was a door knocker in the shape of a lion's

head. Lion's whiskers fanned out into a solid bar you were supposed to yank up and let go.

"Go ahead, do it," I said.

"You do it," he said.

"Let's both do it."

"Okay."

We reached out together and pulled the lion's whiskers up. It was solid. It would bang hard when we let go.

"One, two—" Aaron began.

The door suddenly opened. We were holding on to the door knocker so tightly that we almost got pulled into the house. We caught ourselves on the sides of the doorway.

A girl our age stood there looking at us. She had short dark hair and wore a sweatshirt that said BINGHAM FARMS.

"What do you boys want?"

"Does, uh, Chuck Axelrod live here?" I asked.

"Yes."

"I'm supposed to see him."

"Are you Jason Ross?"

"Yeah."

"If you're Jason Ross, you were *supposed* to be here an hour ago," she said.

It was pretty snotty the way she said that. I decided to go on the attack. "I was busy getting my new team a coach. Are you his daughter

101

who's *supposed* to play on the team?"

"I'm *going* to play."

There was no "supposed to" in her reply.

"What's your position?" Aaron asked in a friendly tone.

"Infield. I can pitch too. Are you on the team?"

"Yep." Aaron grinned. "And my grampa's goin' to coach us."

"Your grampa?" She sounded doubtful.

"Hey," I said, "his grampa only happens to be—" I caught myself just before I let out the secret—to a kid!

"Go ahead, tell her," Aaron whispered.

"No!" I said.

"Tell me what?"

"Nothing."

"Kim," a familiar voice called out from inside the house, "who're you talking to?"

It was the voice of Channel 4 sports. I'd know it anywhere.

"It's Jason Ross and another boy, Dad."

"Bring 'em in, honey."

She nodded to us and opened the door wide. We stepped into a large front hall.

"This way," she said. After we went through the hallway, we followed her into a room big enough to have a basketball game in. Three on three. There was hardly any furniture. The walls

102

were bare. No pictures. There were no shelves or bookcases. It didn't look very lived in. There was a big TV set in one corner. That and one chair was about it.

After that we went through another mostly empty room. We could hear Chuck Axelrod talking to someone.

"You ever get lost in this place?" I asked her.

"Once," she said.

Aaron laughed.

We went down two steps into another hall that was lined with cardboard cartons.

"You just move here?" Aaron asked her.

"About a month ago."

"Me too," Aaron said.

They were both new to town. I hadn't thought of that till now.

Chuck Axelrod's voice was getting closer.

Finally we entered a large office-den. This was where the furniture was: chairs, tables, a couch, and pictures. Lots of pictures.

At the far end, seated behind a desk, was the man himself, looking just like he did on TV. Hair falling over his forehead, horn-rimmed glasses, large pop eyes behind them, and a mouth that was always moving.

He was talking into the phone, and as he talked he motioned for us to sit down. Sit down where, I wondered? Every chair had something on it: papers, magazines, video cassettes, audio cassettes. His desk was piled high with papers and cassettes. There were two phones on his desk, one red and one black. There was a computer, a printer, a photocopier, a fax machine, a VCR, and an audio cassette player. The walls were covered with black-and-white glossy photos of famous athletes.

"Jimmy," Chuck Axelrod said into the phone, "did I ever not deliver when I said I would?"

I looked at the pictures on the wall. They were pictures of Tigers, Pistons, Red Wings, Lions. All the Detroit teams. There were pictures of former players, current players, and, as far as I could tell, each picture was autographed to Chuck Axelrod from so and so.

It was just the opposite of Mr. Henry's little house where, if he wanted to, he could have put up pictures of a hundred great players he'd played with. Not just interviewed. And Mr. Henry didn't have a one. He just had family pictures.

"Jimmy, you worry too much," Chuck Axelrod said. "Stop asking me because I don't know yet. Just make sure I have a crew standing by. Tony's if I can have them. If nothing happens I'll make something up. No, no. For the next hour I'll be tied up with Kim's baseball team. I know, I know. But it's something I have to do. Listen, I've got visitors right now. I'll get back to you in two minutes."

He hung up and winked at us. "My producer is getting nervous about tonight's show. I lost a live interview with Sparky and now I've got five minutes to fill. Okay, which of you is the famous Jason Ross?"

"Him," his daughter said, pointing to me.

"Jason, you did good work getting a baseball card store to sponsor the new team. But you're late getting here and time's of the essence. This afternoon we've got to—where did I put the darn thing?"

"What're you looking for, Daddy?"

"That list of names. I had it on my desk. If you'd come when you were supposed to, Jason . . ."

Kim Axelrod slipped out of the room.

"I was getting us a coach, Mr. Axelrod," I said.

"Who? Your father? That couldn't have taken that long." He peered under a stack of video cassettes.

"No, sir. I got Aaron's grandfather."

"Who's Aaron?"

"Him. My friend."

Chuck Axelrod looked up from his search at

Aaron. "Your grandfather know anything about baseball, Aaron?"

His condescending tone got to me.

I spoke up. "His grampa was only one of the greatest right-handed pitchers in the history of the old Negro leagues."

Aaron looked shocked. "You told," he whispered.

"Your grampa said especially not kids," I whispered back. But I'd done wrong. He'd said not to tell anyone. If I could have yanked those words back into my mouth, I would have. But it was too late. Chuck Axelrod had stopped looking for the player list and was gazing at the two of us with intense interest.

10

"Are you making a joke, Jason?"

A lot of grief would have been saved right then and there if I'd answered "yes" to that question. But that would have been lying. I may shoot my mouth off, but I'm not a liar.

"No, sir. I'm telling the truth."

Chuck Axelrod turned to Aaron. "That a fact, son? Your grandfather played in the old Negro leagues?"

"Yes, sir."

"What's your grandfather's name?"

Aaron hesitated. He shot me a should-I-tell-him? look.

No, you shouldn't, I tried to message him with my eyes. What we've got to do is change the subject. Something I was becoming very good at.

"Do you know about the old Negro leagues, Mr. Axelrod?" I asked.

"Of course I know about the Negro leagues," Chuck Axelrod said. "I did a show on them once. I did an interview with Cool Papa Bell at Cooperstown when he was inducted into the Hall of Fame. Let's get back to—"

"I didn't know Cool Papa Bell was in the Hall of Fame."

"Well, he is. And so are Josh Gibson and Paige and John Henry Lloyd."

I was impressed with Chuck Axelrod. He wasn't just TV show biz. He knew his stuff. "Is Double Duty Radcliffe in the Hall of Fame too?"

"Never heard of him." (And that, in a way, made him even more legit. He was honest.)

He was looking at Aaron. "What's your grandfather's name, son?"

When Aaron didn't answer, Chuck Axelrod shook his head disgustedly. "You kids are making jokes while your team is running out of time."

"No, Mister," Aaron said, "Jason and me aren't jokin'. My grampa was a great pitcher. Only we're not supposed to tell anyone."

"Is that so? And why aren't you supposed to tell anyone?"

"Because he changed his name a long time ago. That's why," Aaron said.

Chuck Axelrod laughed. "The story gets better and better. But kids, I don't have time for jokes." He got down on his hands and knees and started going through papers that had fallen off his desk.

Aaron looked at me. I could tell he wanted to tell Chuck Axelrod his grandfather's name in the worst way. Well, we'd gone this far. Besides, not telling made us look bad. Chuck Axelrod thought we were fooling around.

"His name was Buck McHenry," I said.

Chuck Axelrod looked up. "Buck McHenry?"

"Yes, sir. Did you ever hear of him?"

"Buck McHenry pitched for the Pittsburgh Crawfords. If I recall correctly . . ." Chuck Axelrod sat back up on his chair, "Buck McHenry pitched on the same team with Satchel Paige. He was supposed to have thrown as hard as Paige, but he quit early in his career."

"And went to work as a school custodian in Michigan. You got the card, Aaron?"

"You still got it, Jason."

And so I did. In my pocket, where it was beginning to get creased. I whipped it out and handed it to Chuck Axelrod.

"That's Buck McHenry. And he's Aaron's grampa."

Just then Kim Axelrod came back into the room with a sheet of paper in her hand. "I've got it," she said.

Her father didn't even look at her.

"On the back is where it says about him working as a school custodian," I pointed out.

"I see it."

"Well that school's here in Arborville. It's Eberwoods School, where I used to go."

Chuck Axelrod looked over the top of the card at us. "Did *he* tell you he was Buck McHenry?"

"Yes," we said.

"How do you know he wasn't putting you on?"

"Because," I said, "he didn't want to admit it in the worst way. Aaron's grandma made him confess." For a brief moment I thought about mentioning the scrapes with the law, but I didn't. He surely had spotted it on the card. He could put two and two together just as well as me.

"Dad," Kim Axelrod said.

"One second, honey. What's your grampa's name now, son?" he asked Aaron.

"Mack Henry," Aaron said softly.

Chuck Axelrod saw it right away. McHenry to Mack Henry. His eyes gleamed, just the way Jim Davis's had when I told him there was going to be a new team in the league. They were each like dogs after a bone. I could understand Jim

110

Davis's interest. But I was pretty slow figuring out Chuck Axelrod's. Maybe you've figured it out already. I hadn't.

"Buck McHenry is your grampa," Chuck Axelrod repeated slowly. He was trying to be cautious and it wasn't in his nature.

"Who's Buck McHenry?" Kim Axelrod asked.

"His grampa," I said.

"My daddy's daddy," Aaron said.

Warning signal again. We've got to stay away from that.

Before I could change the subject, Chuck Axelrod asked Aaron, "What's your grampa's phone number?"

"Mr. Henry's going to be at the team meeting at four at Sampson Park," I said.

"That's fine, but I've got to know ahead of time that he is who you and he say he is."

Why did he have to know it ahead of time?

"You know your grampa's phone number, Aaron?"

"Mr. Henry's not home now," I said. "He was going fishing till the team meeting."

Chuck Axelrod looked exasperated. "All right, is your grandma home?"

"Yeah, my grandma's home," Aaron said.

"So what's the phone number?"

"I don't know."

111

Chuck Axelrod was getting irritated.

"Aaron just moved here," I explained, and wondered if I should explain further that Aaron lived with his grandparents. But then he'd ask why and that would bring up the car crash in Tennessee. And that had to be a secret. A real secret. Compared to that the secret of Buck McHenry was nothing. Absolutely nothing.

But Chuck Axelrod was already punching buttons on the red phone.

"Will someone tell me what's going on?" Kim Axelrod asked.

"Aaron's grampa was Buck McHenry, a famous ballplayer in the old Negro leagues," I explained.

"That's fine, but we've got to start calling kids. I've got the list."

"Let's see it," I said.

"A party named Mack Henry living in Arborville," Chuck Axelrod said into the phone.

The first few names on the list were familiar, all right. They were terrible ballplayers.

"Do you know any of them?" Kim asked.

"All of them. And they're all lousy."

"There's no answer at your grandparents' house, Aaron," Chuck Axelrod said.

"Grandma's probably outside still working in the garden, isn't she, Jason?"

"I'm sure."

Chuck Axelrod's fingers tapped impatiently on a video cassette while the phone in his ear kept ringing busily. He was coming to a decision. He hung up, picked up the phone again, and punched more buttons. I hadn't the slightest idea who he was calling now.

"Dad," his daughter said.

"What is it, honey?"

"I've got the list. You gave it to me."

"Then for Pete's sake, start calling. Carol, let me talk to Jimmy. It's urgent."

"I knew we were wasting time," Kim Axelrod said. "Come on, let's go."

"Jimmy . . ."

Aaron and I started to follow her, but Chuck Axelrod's next words stopped us in our tracks.

"Jimmy, I've got the missing story for tonight's show. . . ."

If someone had had a camera and taken a picture of Aaron's and my faces just then, it would have shown two stunned kids.

"Are you guys coming?" Kim Axelrod called from another room.

We were not going anywhere. We were frozen.

"Gold, Jimmy, gold just fell into my lap. A fantastic local story . . ."

"Jason," Aaron whispered, "he's goin' to—"

113

"I know."

There was no way we could stop him, either. Even if we wanted to, which deep down neither of us did. Something had gone into motion that no human being could prevent. Chuck Axelrod was waving the Buck McHenry card around as he talked. At one point he saw us still there. "Don't worry about this card, kids. I won't lose it. I've got to hold on to it for a little longer. I'll get it back to you. No, Jim, I'm talking to a couple of Kim's teammates. This is what we're gonna do. I'll do a voice-over for the game shots and coaching shots. I'll do an interview with some kids, with our star—he's an old man, a guy who played in the old Negro leagues, which you are too young to know anything about but you will when I'm done. We can lay his interview over some stills too. In fact, I've got the prize still right here in my hand. Would you believe a baseball card, Jimmy? A baseball card!"

Aaron turned to me. "He's goin' to tell the whole world about my grampa."

"I guess so. I'm glad."

"Me too," Aaron said.

"There's nothing we can do about it now. We better go help with those phone calls."

"Yeah. Let's go help her."

What was going to happen was going to happen. It was like the sun coming up in the morning or the rain falling or the wind blowing. It was life! It was natural! It was good!

We ran to catch up with Kim Axelrod.

11

We ended up in a family room that was as big
as the living room. No furniture but, sure
enough, more telephones. One red and one black.

"You got phones in every room?" Aaron asked
her.

"Just about."

"Bathrooms too?" I said, kidding.

"In one of them." She was serious.

Aaron whistled. "How many bathrooms you
got anyway?"

"Four."

"Wow."

"That's a lot of toilet paper," I said. I didn't
think Aaron should be impressed by lots of bathrooms.

"We don't *use* every bathroom," she retorted.

"Jason just means you got a big house," Aaron
said gently.

She shrugged. "Where we used to live was

bigger." She wasn't bragging. Just stating a fact.

"Where'd you used to live?" I asked.

"Birmingham."

"That's near Detroit," I explained to Aaron. "Aaron just moved here from Tennessee."

"Where in Tennessee?" she asked him.

"Memphis."

"We used to live in Nashville. My dad worked in a TV station there before we moved to Michigan."

"I've never been to Nashville."

"What's the sweatshirt stand for?" I asked her.

She looked down at the BINGHAM FARMS across her chest. "That was the name of my school in Birmingham."

Birmingham was less than fifty miles from Arborville. "Why'd you move to Arborville?"

"My parents got divorced."

"So?"

"So in the settlement my mom got the house and furniture and my dad got me."

Ouch, I thought. That had to hurt.

There was a silence. It's hard to know what to say after someone says something like that. But Aaron found the right words. "Your dad got the better deal," he said softly. He really was nice.

Kim Axelrod blushed. "Thanks."

"Hey, your folks divorcing is no big deal around here," I said. "Half the kids I know in Arborville, their folks are divorced." That was true, too. Tug's folks were divorced. So were Kevin's and Silver's and Diaz's. And then there was Aaron with no folks at all. But I wasn't going to get into *that*.

"Okay," Kim Axelrod said, getting business-like again, "what about these kids?" She handed me the player list.

"Well, like I said, they're all pretty bad. This first guy, Gerald Kofer. He played for Bob's Tex-aco. His teammates called him 'Glue' because his bat never left his shoulders."

Aaron laughed. Kim didn't. "What about the others?"

"Well, there's Andy van Gasse. He played for Garnet Realtors. He's a fat kid whose father makes him play. Victor Perles collects baseball cards and can't hit the side of a barn. Norman Fahler throws like a girl."

Oops. Dumb thing to say. She yanked the pa-per out of my hand. "I can throw as good as you, if not better," she snapped.

"Bring your glove to the park and we'll see."

"I will."

"Good."

The day a girl could outthrow me in baseball was the day I'd hang up my shoes. But I had the sense not to say that out loud. That would be like pouring gasoline on a fire.

"Anyway," I said, "all the guys on that list are rejects."

"Aren't you a reject too? In fact, I think your name's on that list. Here it is. Jason Ross, Baer Machine, catcher."

I felt my face get red. "Okay, so I'm on the list, but I'm a lot better than those guys. I was backup catcher to Tug Murphy, who's the best catcher in the league. Tug'll probably be a major leaguer when he grows up. And I can hit okay. These guys can't hit, field, run, throw. They're hopeless. H-O-P-E-L-E-S-S." I spelled it out for her.

"So what should we do? Not call them?" she said.

"Call them. It's better to play and lose than not play at all."

"That's a great attitude."

"I'm just being realistic."

"You don't know how good I am. Or him." She pointed to Aaron.

"Oh, I got an idea how good he is all right.

119

He was an all-star in Memphis."

"I made the all-star team in Birmingham last year."

"Girls' league."

"Boys' league."

"Girls *here* play softball."

"They do in Birmingham too, but I like hard-ball. Have you asked enough questions? Are we going to call these kids or not? We're supposed to have a team meeting in about an hour."

The timing was impossible, I thought. But I guess we had to give it a try.

"Okay, give it to me. I'll call Glue first." As I took the list from her, one of the telephones rang.

The three of us stared at it. "That's our home phone," Kim said. She picked it up. "Hello." Pause. "Yes, he's here." She handed the phone to me. "It's for you."

"Me? You're kidding. Is it a kid?"

"A man."

It had to be Jim Davis, I thought. He was the only one besides Mr. Henry who knew I was supposed to come here.

"Hello."

"Jason . . ."

It was my dad. My heart sank. I knew I should have called my parents from The Grandstand.

Or from Mr. Henry's house. They had expected me home after practice. They must be worried about me. How had he even found out where I was?

"Dad, I'm sorry."

"Jason, we've been trying to track you down for hours. I called Mr. Borker, Tim Corrigan, Tug Murphy. They're worried about you too. In fact, they're probably running around now looking for you. I finally had the sense to try The Grandstand. Jim thought you might be at this number. Jason, what's going on?"

"Dad, the most exciting thing has happened. The most fantastic thing in the world. Did Mr. Borker tell you I got cut?"

"Yes, he did. That's why they're worried about you."

That stopped me. I hadn't put those two things together. I guess the Baer Machine guys thought that because I got cut from the team, I might want to throw myself in the Huron River. That was kind of funny.

"I'm okay, Dad. Better than okay. I'm great. I'm on a new team. The Grandstand. Jim's going to sponsor it."

"I know all this, Jason."

"What you don't know, Dad, is I got the team a new coach. A great coach. Dad, it's unbelievable, but Mr. Henry, the custodian at Eberwoods School, do you remember him, he's going to be our coach. Only he's not really Mr. Henry. Who he is really is Buck McHenry, one of the greatest pitchers who ever lived. He pitched with Satchel Paige in the old Negro baseball leagues. In three years in those leagues he won ninety—"

"Jason, stop," Dad said quietly but firmly. "We want you to come home for lunch. It's almost three o'clock. Your mother and I are having a hard time remembering what you look like."

"Dad, what I'm trying to say is I can't come home just yet. Aaron and me and Kim Axelrod have got to recruit players for a team meeting at four at the park. Aaron's my new friend. He's Mr. Henry's grandson. And Kim Axelrod is Chuck Axelrod's daughter. She's going to be on the team. We've got to make a whole bunch of phone calls right away."

"Make your phone calls from here, Jason. Bring your friends here. Jason"—Dad's voice got very gentle—"don't make me come get you."

When my father's voice gets gentle is when he is most serious.

"I'll be right home," I said, and hung up.

"I've got to go. I haven't had lunch yet. I'll make the phone calls from my house while I'm eating. Unless you guys want to come with me and call too."

"But we've got two phone lines here," Kim said. "We could call different kids at the same time."

"Your dad's always on one phone. And besides, I *got* to go. You and Aaron can make the calls from here, if you want."

"It'd be better if you were there. They know you. In case they want to know something we don't know about. I'll ask my dad if I can go to your house."

"Aaron and I are on bikes. Do you have a bike?"

She nodded.

"We'll see you out front then. Don't forget to bring your glove. We can go over to the park from my house. We live real close."

She took off.

It wasn't so easy getting out of the Axelrod castle. At one point Aaron and I wandered into the kitchen, which was as big and bare as the rest of the house. They must eat out a lot, I thought. Finally we made it to the front hallway and out the door to our bikes. We didn't have long to wait for Kim. She came pedaling around the house, biking over the lawn. She had a ten-speed boy's bike. A fielder's glove was looped around the handlebars.

"Let's go," she said, and shot past us down the walk and over the curb and into the street, where she made a tight little circle and yelled, "Which way?"

"Left," I yelled back.

Aaron shook his head, smiling. "She's somethin', isn't she?"

"So far she's all talk," I replied.

He laughed. We shoved off. We pedaled hard, trying to catch up with her. But we couldn't. She was all talk and a ten-speed bike, I thought, as she zoomed ahead of us.

12

My mom, Jean Ross, is an artist. Her idea of excitement is to go off with her sketchpad and draw pictures of wildflowers. When she comes to my games, she usually draws pictures of us. At the end of the game she always asks, "Who won?"

She's pretty laid back, and if you hang around her long enough you get pretty calm too.

"Hello, stranger," she said to me as I came into the house with Aaron and Kim.

"I'm sorry, Mom. I lost track of the time. This is my friend and teammate Aaron Henry."

"Hello, Aaron," Mom said. "I'm glad to meet you."

"And this is Kim Axelrod. She's on the team too."

"But isn't a friend," Mom said, and laughed. "Hello anyway, Kim." She turned to me. "Dad told me you have phone calls to make, Jason.

I'm afraid you're going to have to eat lunch first."

"If it's okay with you, Mrs. Ross, Aaron and I can call while Jason eats," Kim said.

"It's not okay with me," I said. "I'm making the first call."

"Why should you make the first call?"

"To show you guys how to do it."

"What makes you think we don't know how?"

"I know these kids. I know how to talk to them."

"That's all well and good, Jason," Mom said. "But first you're going to eat a sandwich. So please sit down." She turned to them. "Have you two eaten?"

"Yes, ma'am."

"It's just peanut butter and jelly and we have a lot of it."

"No, thanks," they said.

"Please feel free to change your minds." She got a carton of milk out of the refrigerator.

"Please, Mom, no milk," I said.

"What do you mean, no milk?"

"Milk cuts down your wind."

"Oh?" Mom said, pouring out a big glassful. "And where did you hear that?"

"On the back of a Diamond Stars card."

Kim Axelrod laughed. "You believe the stuff on the backs of those cards?"

I was surprised. Diamond Stars are old cards. Put out by the National Chickle Company in the 1930's. Not too many kids today know about them.

"You heard of Diamond Stars?"

"I've got some. They have hints about how to pitch, catch, steal, bunt. They came with Chicklets."

"So you collect cards?"

"Yep."

"Eat, Jason," Mom warned.

I took a big bite of peanut butter and jelly. "Howmanycardsyougot?" I asked, my mouth full.

"About thirty thousand."

Aaron whistled. "She's got thirty thousand cards, Jason," he said.

"I heard, I'm not deaf." I washed the peanut butter and jelly down with milk. I burped.

Mom said, "Jason, you're going to get sick if you eat that fast. Please chew your food."

"It's quality not quantity that counts in cards," I pointed out to Aaron. "I've met kids at card shows who have two hundred thousand cards." I burped again and pounded my chest. "What's your most valuable card?"

"An Ace 1952 Mickey Mantle."

That was too much. "You've got *that* card?"

"Signed too."

That was the card I'd been telling Mr. Henry about at Eberwoods this morning. When he asked me why Mantle was worth more than Mays. That Mantle card was worth over $2500. I couldn't begin to guess what it was worth with Mantle's signature on it.

"Do you know Mickey Mantle?" Aaron asked her. He was awed. So was I, for the moment.

"No. My dad did an interview with him and asked him to sign the card."

"If your father wasn't a sportscaster, you probably wouldn't have anything," I said.

"And if your father wasn't a lawyer, you wouldn't be talking that way." A new voice had entered the conversation.

I spun around. Dad was standing there looking amused. He had on gardening gloves. He'd been working in the backyard. I wondered how long he'd been listening to us.

"Who are your friends, Jason?"

I introduced him to Kim and Aaron. He looked at Aaron with interest. "You must be the one whose grandfather is Buck McHenry?"

"Yes, sir," Aaron said proudly.

"Have you heard of Buck McHenry, Dad?"

Dad got himself some coffee and joined Mom at the dining-room table. "A few years ago someone published a history of the old Negro leagues.

128

Buck McHenry was in there along with Cool Papa Bell and Josh Gibson and Satchel Paige."

"I didn't know you knew about those guys."

"I don't know an awful lot. But Grampa told me that when he was a kid he saw the Homestead Grays play in the old Polo Grounds."

"My grampa Ross lives in New York City," I explained to Aaron. And to Kim, I explained, "The Homestead Grays were a team in the old Negro leagues."

"I know that. I've got a set of Negro League Baseball Stars."

"No, you don't," I said. "There are no Negro league sets. No Ace, Topps, Fleer, Donruss—"

"I'm not talking about a set you buy with gum. Andy Armstrong in Wisconsin printed his own set last year. He sent one of the first batches to my dad."

I stared at her. Wherever I went, I met this girl coming back.

"Look," she said, "we've only got a half hour before the team meeting. Can we start calling kids now? Can we use this phone, Mrs. Ross?"

"Of course, Kim."

"I'm making the first call, remember?"

"You'll do nothing, Jason, until you finish your milk," Mom said.

"But you gave me so much."

"Drink it slowly."

"Aaron, you want to start?" Kim asked.

Aaron shook his head.

"Okay, I'll do it. Do we tell kids about your grampa being famous?"

"Sure," Aaron said.

"We can't do that," I said.

"Why not?" Kim demanded.

"Because we promised his grampa we wouldn't tell kids."

"But you told my father. He'll tell the whole world."

"That's different."

"I don't get the difference," Aaron said.

Dad laughed. "You don't get it, Aaron, because there isn't any difference. All it means is that your friend Jason is on his way to being a politician. Leaking information rather than giving it."

"A promise is a promise," I said, my face turning red.

"All right, we won't tell," Kim said. "The first kid on the list is Gerald Kofer."

"The first and the worst," I said.

"Maybe we can make him better," she snapped. She dialed Kofer's number.

"Can I speak to Gerald Kofer, please?" she said. "Oh. Do you know when he'll be in? I see.

Well, if he does come back, would you tell him there's going to be a meeting of his new team at Sampson Park today at—oh." She listened. "Well, if he changes his mind. Okay. Thanks anyway." She made a face as she hung up.

"His mother said he was so upset about being cut that he's never going to play baseball again."

"Good news for everyone," I said. "You're 0 for 1. You bat next, Aaron."

Aaron looked grave as he took the paper from Kim and read: "Andy van . . . ?"

"Gasse," I said. "And that's what he's full of too."

"That's not very nice, Jason," Mom said.

"Jason doesn't like anyone," Kim said. She was miffed, being 0 for 1.

"Excuse me," Aaron said softly into the phone. "Is Andy in? Oh. I'm, uh, Aaron Henry. I'm calling about our new baseball team. We're having a team meeting at Sampson Park today at— Oh—sure, that's okay. If you change your mind we uh— Sure. So long."

Aaron hung up. He looked embarrassed, as though it was his fault. "He says he was only playing baseball because his father was making him. He says his father has quit making him."

I finally finished my milk. "You're batting zero too, Aaron," I said cheerfully. "Now I'll show you guys how it's done. And why I wanted to go first. You can't just *ask* them to be on a new team. You've got to *sell* the team to them. Listen and learn."

"Pride goeth before a fall, Jason," Dad warned. He and Mom were sitting at the dining-room table watching us. I guess we were better than a floor show to them.

Next on the expansion-player list was Victor Perles. He was a tall, skinny kid who collected baseball cards. He wasn't a bad kid but a dreadful ballplayer. I dialed his number. I knew how to approach Victor.

The phone rang. And rang. And rang and rang and rang. No one was home.

Kim, grinning, nudged Aaron. "Jason can't even get it to answer. That's like not getting into the game at all. You never left the bench, Jason. My turn." She held out her hand for the phone.

What a snot. Well, I'd show her. "Hello," I said to the ringing in Victor Perles's house.

Kim stopped grinning.

I kept a straight face. "Victor, this is Jason Ross," I said to absolutely no one. "I'm calling for your new team—The Grandstand. That's right. The baseball-card store. Isn't that great? And we're going to get free baseball cards from

132

Jim. Win or lose. Pretty good deal, huh?"

"Is that right?" Kim whispered to Aaron.

"I don't know," Aaron said.

"This afternoon, Vic," I went on, "we've got a meeting at Sampson Park. Bring your glove, because our coach'll want to look us over. We've got a great coach, by the way. He's Buck McHenry, one of the greatest right-handed pitchers of all time. He pitched with Satchel Paige in the old Negro leagues. He's even on a baseball card."

"Wait a second," Kim said, "you said we couldn't tell kids. You're changing the rules. That's not fair."

That almost broke me up. If she thought that wasn't fair, she should only know what I was doing now.

I went on merrily. "We've also got some great players, Vic. Buck McHenry's grandson is going to pitch for us. He was an all-star pitcher in Tennessee." I hesitated and then I couldn't resist it.

"We've also got a girl on the team who, if she's as good as she says she is, is going to sign a pro contract before the season ends. She—"

That was as far as I got. Kim grabbed the phone from me. *Ring, ring, ring* it went in her ear.

"Just as I thought," she yelled. "There's no one there."

"You didn't think that at all," I said, breaking up. "I fooled you." I howled with laughter. Aaron realized what I'd done and started laughing too. Mom and Dad were laughing. Pretty soon everyone but Kim was laughing.

"I . . . fooled . . . you." I was laughing so hard my stomach hurt. I could hardly talk. I could hardly breathe. I began to feel nauseous. I could feel the milk I'd drunk so fast rising in my esophagus to smite me. I put my hand on my chest and tried to force it back down.

"You fooled me all right," Kim said. "We've got about fifteen minutes to call eleven kids. And you fooled me for two of those minutes. You think that's so smart?"

I stopped laughing. She was right. I'd been fiddling while Rome was burning.

"Okay," I said. "No more gags. I'll make three calls. You three. Aaron three. We'll go fast. Agreed?"

They nodded.

After that we went fast. Too fast. Only one of my kids was at home and he was sick and not interested. Aaron called three kids. One wasn't home and the other two didn't want to play ball this summer. Kim called three and none of them were home. That left two more kids to call. Kim called them both. Neither were there.

Well, we made all the calls in less than fifteen minutes. We also didn't recruit a single player for The Grandstand team. We had a great pitcher, a great sponsor, a coach who was a living legend. But no team.

I felt nauseous all over again. And this time it had nothing to do with milk.

13

"I better call my dad," Kim said gloomily. "He's got a camera crew coming in from Detroit."

I explained to Mom and Dad about Chuck Axelrod wanting to tell the story of Buck McHenry on tonight's *Sportsline* show. Even though Mr. Henry didn't want anyone to know.

"Well," Dad said, "at least you don't have to worry about that now."

"My grampa's probably at the park, Jason," Aaron said.

It was already after four.

"You better go there, Aaron, and tell him what happened," Dad said. "Kim, you ought to call your father right now and tell him to contact his camera crew. I'm sure they have a phone in their truck. Jason, why don't you show Aaron where the park is? I'll walk Kim over after she's talked to her dad."

Aaron rose to go. I didn't feel like going anywhere.

"Jason," Dad said, "the world's not coming to an end because you didn't recruit a baseball team."

"It's not just that, Dad," I said. "It's other stuff too. It's the story of Buck McHenry. People ought to know about him and now it won't get out. And the stories of those other great players too. People don't know about them either. They don't know how good those guys were and how they never had a chance to play in the big leagues because of the color of their skin. It was so unfair. Those guys were great ballplayers. Josh Gibson hit a home run out of Yankee Stadium. Babe Ruth never did that. John Henry Lloyd. Honus Wagner said he was the best player who ever lived. People don't know about Josh Gibson and John Henry Lloyd and Buck McHenry and Cool Papa Bell. They don't know about the kind of life those guys led. Mr. Henry said that half the time they never got paid. They never had coaching. They never had spring training. They just got out their gloves and played ball. They made do with what they had, Mr. Henry said. They were always making something out of nothing. They were great and no one knows

137

about them and now no one will." I felt like crying.

"That's good," Kim Axelrod said.

"What's good?" What a dumb thing to say that was.

"What you just said. Making something out of nothing."

"I didn't say that. Mr. Henry said that."

"My dad could do that too."

"Do what?"

"Make something out of nothing."

"What are you talking about?"

"It could be part of the story."

"Part of what story? There is no story. There's no team, there's no story, there's nothing."

"Jason, the storyline could be we don't have enough players for Buck McHenry to coach. So we advertise for players on Dad's show."

"That's crazy."

"Why's it crazy? There's got to be kids around who didn't play on any team last year who no one knows about. Kids that maybe don't even know there's an eleven-year-old league. New kids."

"There are no new kids."

"Aaron and I are new."

"You're probably the only new eleven-year-old kids in town."

"Probably is probably. You don't *know* that."

"This isn't Detroit. This is a small town."

"What's the population of Arborville?"

"A hundred thousand. Maybe a little more."

"Let's get the little more," Aaron said.

"You're as nuts as she is."

"Listen, kids," Dad said quietly, "you ought to stop arguing and go over to the park and let Mr. Henry know what's going on. And maybe, just maybe, there'll be some eleven-year-old kids playing there who might want to be on a team."

"Dad, by this time every eleven-year-old kid in Arborville who wants to be on a team is on one. I guarantee it."

Kim stood up. "You coming, Aaron?"

"Yeah."

"Aren't you going to call your dad?" I said.

"Nope. Let the camera crew come. Where's the park?"

"I like your spirit, Kim," Mom said. "Come. I'll show you where the park is."

"*I'll* show her, Mom. And please don't you and Dad come. This is going to be really embarrassing. A camera crew coming in from Detroit to shoot a three-man team."

"A three-*person* team," Kim said.

And now that too, I thought. Girls! Who needed them?

"Aaron needs a glove," she said.

"What for? We're not going to have a practice."

"You don't know what's going to happen, Jason. Do you have an extra glove?"

"Yes."

We went to the front hall and I opened the athletic box next to the closet and dug through old tennis balls, Frisbees, hockey pucks, and broken badminton rackets and found my old fielder's glove.

"It's pretty old."

"It's okay," Aaron said. "You got a ball?"

I looked at him. The memory of the fastball he threw at me in his backyard came back to me. "Here's a ball. You guys start walking. Go left. I'll catch up with you."

"Where're you going?" Kim asked.

"To get some sponges."

I ran back in the kitchen.

"Now what?" Dad said.

"Sponges for my catcher's mitt. Aaron throws hard." I looked under the sink.

"I like your new friends, Jason," Dad said.

"I like Aaron but she's not my friend."

"That's too bad because I think she's great," Mom said. "She's a super kid."

"She's spoiled. That signed Mickey Mantle

card. Her Dad being big TV sports show business."

"You're just jealous," Mom said.

"Of her? Not in a million years. She's probably a lousy ballplayer, and if we had a team we'd have to carry her just because her dad is the great Chuck Axelrod and also director of the eleven-year-old league." I stuffed two old sponges into my pocket. "See ya."

"Behave yourself," Dad said. Practically what Mrs. Henry said to Aaron before he and I took off from their house on our bikes.

I caught up with Aaron and Kim at the corner of Ferdon and Granger.

"We were just talking about your folks," she said. "They're really nice."

"They're all right."

She shook her head. "No, they're nice, Jason. I can tell. Most kids I know have all kinds of problems with their parents." She turned to Aaron. "How about you, Aaron?"

Bango. Out of nowhere. Here we are walking in sunlight to the park and she drops a bomb.

Aaron didn't answer right away. I shot her a warning look. She misread it.

"Are your folks divorced too?" she asked.

From bad to worse. Usually I'm terrific at

141

changing subjects. But this time I couldn't think of a thing to say.

"My folks got killed in a car crash," Aaron said quietly. "With my brother Louis."

Now are you happy, I thought. Now look what you've done.

She was shocked.

"I'm sorry," she said.

Aaron pounded the pocket of my old glove.

And then instead of cutting her losses and shutting up, she went on. She asked, "Were you in the crash?"

Was she out of her mind? Had she no sense at all?

Aaron shook his head. "I was home playing ball."

I couldn't stand it any longer. "The park's right there, past that senior citizens' shelter."

But it was like I didn't exist at all.

"Did your father coach your team?"

I could have throttled her.

"He coached my brother Louis's team when Louis was in Little League." Aaron suddenly grinned, remembering. "They were champs. Except Louis was going to be a football player. Always calling himself Mr. Q.B. He could throw a football a long way. He used to make me run and run and run and he could still throw it over my head. . . ."

I was stunned. Aaron was talking about his family and talking easily. He wasn't clamming up and looking the way he'd looked when I first met him. He was talking. About the tragedy.

Kim said, "Was your dad a professional ball-player too?"

"He was a teacher. So was my mom."

"In the same school?"

"Yeah."

"Your school?"

"Yeah," Aaron laughed. "That's where they met. Before I was born though."

"That's like my folks," she said. "They met where they were working too. Only it was a TV studio. My mom did the weather. Dad did the sports. Where'd your folks meet, Jason?"

"I, uh . . ." I was tongue-tied. Confused by what had just happened. Her getting him to talk about stuff that used to shut him up. She'd somehow done what all the doctors in Tennessee hadn't been able to do, get Aaron to open up about his family. As for her question about where my folks met, I didn't know the answer to that either. I'd never asked my folks where they'd met.

"I guess they met here in Arborville," I said lamely.

"Were you born in Arborville?"

"Yeah. Where were you born?" Let's get off me, I thought.

"In Nashville. Do you have brothers and sisters?"

"No. Do you?"

She shook her head. Aaron didn't say anything. He didn't have any either now, I thought. We must have all thought that, because a silence suddenly descended on the three of us.

But it wasn't a bad silence. It was the kind of silence that happens when everyone's thinking the same thing and you don't *have* to talk.

We walked inside that silence together, the three of us, the rest of the way to the park.

14

Some parks are better than others. Sampson Park is a park for everyone, from little kids on jungle gyms to senior citizens playing cards. In between are parents and kids flying kites, dogs chasing sticks, tennis matches, baseball games, soccer games, kids riding bikes, college kids playing basketball or throwing Frisbees. It's a great big park for everyone.

It was fun seeing it through Kim's and Aaron's eyes as they saw it for the first time.

"Neat," Kim said, her eyes shining.

"It's nice," Aaron said softly.

I felt good. There are kids who come to Sampson Park and wonder what's so special about it. It's just another city park, they say. But it isn't. And Kim and Aaron felt that immediately.

"You see your grampa?" I asked.

"That's his truck. The yellow pickup. There he is."

"Where?"

"Leaning against the backstop."

Sure enough there was Mr. Henry, fingers in the metal mesh of the backstop, watching some college kids playing slow-pitch softball on diamond one, next to the parking lot.

"That's Buck McHenry?" Kim asked.

I guess she expected to see a baseball card picture, a ballplayer in a uniform. And all she was seeing was an old man in a fishing hat leaning against a backstop.

"You bet that's Buck McHenry," I said. "But remember, we don't call him that."

"Not even after my dad's *Sportsline* show when everybody knows?"

"*If* that comes off. Maybe then."

"Don't worry. It'll come off. If the crew gets here, Dad will use them. It costs too much not to."

It sounded like she knew a lot about the TV business.

"I wonder if we should tell him a crew is coming," I said.

"He could get mad," Aaron said.

"Better not tell him then."

"Hey, Grampa," Aaron yelled.

Mr. Henry turned around. It took him a second to see who was calling him, but when he did

146

he smiled and waved to us to come down to the diamond.

Aaron started running slowly. I turned to Kim. "Let's see how good of a runner you are."

She didn't need to be asked twice. She took off like a shot. She passed Aaron like he was standing still. When I got there, she was looking up at Mr. Henry and he was looking down at her, amused.

"You got fine runnin' legs, girl," he was saying. He turned to Aaron. "You been behavin' yourself, boy?"

"Yeah, Grampa."

"That's good." He looked at me. "Where's the rest of our team, Jason?"

Here we go, I thought. "There is no rest of the team, Mr. Henry."

Mr. Henry pursed his lips in a silent surprised whistle.

"We couldn't get any of the kids on the list to come," I explained.

"What do you know about that?" He didn't sound too disappointed.

On the other side of the backstop the softball game was ending. The players were shaking hands.

"Well, we can't have us a team with only three players," Mr. Henry said cheerfully.

"My dad'll recruit players, Coach," Kim said. And the word "coach" crackled in the air.

Mr. Henry smiled at Kim. "How's your daddy goin' to recruit players, young lady?"

"He has a TV show."

"I know about that. But they don't make ballplayers on Channel 4, do they?"

"He could advertise on the show for eleven-year-old ballplayers."

"Advertise?" Mr. Henry laughed.

"He could. My dad can do just about anything. Here he comes now. We can ask him."

We looked where she was looking. A white Lincoln Continental had pulled into the parking lot. Inside it, Chuck Axelrod was still on the phone.

He pulled the Lincoln up to the edge of the parking lot, only a few yards from where we were standing. He popped the trunk.

"Grab the bag, kids," he called out the window and then went on talking on the phone. We could hear him clearly.

"Tony, you're only about a mile from the State Road exit. Take that exit. Make a right turn and all you've got to do is follow State Road into town. You'll go past a golf course, under a bridge. You'll see a street called Granger on your

148

right. Take it and follow it to . . ."

He was talking to the film unit who were on I-94. They were almost in town. I got a shaky sensation in my stomach. I looked at Mr. Henry. He was watching Chuck Axelrod, fascinated. He had no idea what was coming down the Interstate toward him.

Aaron and Kim hauled an equipment bag that had ARBORVILLE REC LEAGUES stenciled on it out of the Lincoln's trunk.

"Imagine that," Mr. Henry murmured. "Chuck Axelrod himself, delivering me bats and balls."

Chuck Axelrod hung up his phone, jumped out of the Lincoln, and came running up to Mr. Henry, his right hand pumping in front of him.

"Chuck Axelrod," he said.

Mr. Henry shook his hand and smiled. "Now you don't have to tell me that. I see you on TV all the time."

Chuck Axelrod laughed. "Well, I've heard a lot about you too, Mr. Buck McHenry."

And there it was again. The secret that wouldn't stay a secret. Mr. Henry's face didn't change expression. Maybe he hadn't heard it and maybe Chuck Axelrod wouldn't repeat it.

Kim and Aaron were taking stuff out of the bag. They took out a pair of shin guards, a chest

149

protector, four bats, a catcher's mask, and five new baseballs. What did they think was going to happen anyway?

Chuck Axelrod said, "When the kids told me that the great Buck McHenry was living right here in Arborville, I couldn't believe it."

Mr. Henry heard that, all right. He gave me a sorrowful look.

"The boys have lent me your baseball card, Mr. McHenry," Chuck Axelrod went on. He had it out and was looking at the stats side. "It says you're working in town here as a school custodian."

It didn't say that at all. I'd said that. All the card said was that he was a school janitor in Michigan.

"I don't know why you quit at the height of your career. But I figure that's something we can bring out on the show."

Mr. Henry cleared his throat. "I'm afraid there's been a mistake here, Mr. Axelrod." He sounded worried. Scrapes with the law were coming back to haunt him. And it was all my fault.

"Oh, there's been no mistake, Buck. I know you've taken another name. But that's all part of the story. You know what I like best about it, Buck? What I like best is that it's not just

150

going to be about the past but about the present and the future. I mean, sir, here you are. Come out of a self-imposed obscurity, anonymity, if you will, to coach a kids' baseball team. And not just any kids' team but a team made up of rejects. Rejects the way fifty years ago you and your teammates were rejected from baseball. Do you see it, Buck? That's how we'll start. Interview you, show you coaching your team . . ."

As Chuck Axelrod went on outlining the TV show, he began steering Mr. Henry toward the diamond. A powerful little tugboat pushing a big old ocean liner out to sea. The big old ocean liner was helpless.

I went over to Kim. "Listen," I whispered, "please tell your dad there's no story. Tell him no more kids are coming. Tell him there's no team."

"It won't make any difference, Jason. My dad'll get us a team." She was pounding the pocket of her glove with one of the new baseballs.

"You worried about my grampa being mad 'cause of the secret?" Aaron asked.

I couldn't very well tell Aaron I was worried about what those scrapes with the law had been. For all I knew, Mr. Henry was still a fugitive from the law.

"Grampa's goin' to be okay, Jason. He's going

to get used to being Buck McHenry again."

Chuck Axelrod must have run out of breath for a second because now Mr. Henry was talking. "I watch your *Sportsline* show every Saturday night, Mr. Axelrod. I like it. But I can't be on it."

"Yes, you can, Grampa," Aaron cried out.

Mr. Henry wouldn't look at him. "First of all, there isn't even going to be a team for me to coach. The kids haven't told you that, have they?"

"What do you mean there isn't going to be a team for you to coach?" Chuck Axelrod looked over at us.

"We couldn't get any of the kids on the list to come out for the team," Kim said. "But I thought you could advertise on the show for players. Couldn't that be part of the storyline?"

For the first time in his life, I think, Chuck Axelrod was at loss for words.

"Couldn't you advertise for players for us, Dad?"

"I don't believe this, Kim. Are you saying you couldn't recruit *any* kids?"

She nodded.

"When you called them, didn't you tell them Buck McHenry was going to coach them?"

"No."

"Why not?"

"Jason said it was supposed to be a secret."

"That's right," Mr. Henry said firmly. "And it's got to stay a secret."

"A secret?" Chuck Axelrod laughed half hysterically. "I've got a camera crew coming in from Detroit and you're telling me it's all supposed to be a secret. Why in heaven's name would you want it to be a secret anyway? Here you are, the legendary Buck McHenry, coming out of a self-imposed anonymity to coach a bunch of kids—why in heaven's name should that be a secret? Why, we ought to holler the news from the rooftops. It should be broadcast to every corner of the land. It would be an inspiration to every American."

It was like he was on TV right now. I felt like clapping.

Then I looked at Mr. Henry and his face was tight and anxious.

"Mr. Henry," I said, "can I say something?"

He didn't even look at me. He didn't trust me anymore. I didn't blame him.

"Those scrapes with the law, Mr. Henry. I just know they couldn't mean anything after all these years."

Chuck Axelrod held up the baseball card. "I saw that too. Is that why you don't want the world to know about you, sir? Because you didn't pay a parking ticket thirty years ago?"

Mr. Henry looked trapped.

"Buck, whatever it was, it's ancient history now. Secondly, who hasn't made mistakes in their youth? But all that's long ago. As the boy said, it's dead material. What remains is alive and immortal."

Chuck Axelrod was really flying now. But Mr. Henry wasn't listening. "Get your bike, Aaron. We're going home."

"Listen, Buck, if you're worried about not having a team to coach, you can stop worrying now. Kim's right. I can get you kids. And that *will* be the storyline. Thanks, honey. What do you say, Buck? Do we let the world know?"

"Mr. Axelrod, my name is not Buck McHenry. It's Mack Henry. It has been Mack Henry for a long, long time. Folks are confused enough these days. I don't want to confuse them any more. Where's your bike, boy?"

"At Jason's house," Aaron said reluctantly.

"We'll go get it and put it in the truck."

He started to walk off. Chuck Axelrod jumped in front of him. Mr. Henry looked old and tall and dignified and puzzled.

Chuck Axelrod grinned. "If you're worried about confusing people, Buck, let me tell you something. I've been in the media business a long time. And when TV wants to, it can unconfuse people faster than it can confuse them. Especially when they're presented with the truth. And that's what we are after. The truth. Listen to this storyline. That's all I ask you, sir. Listen to the storyline. . . ."

Chuck Axelrod went into a crouch as he talked. A storyteller's crouch.

"Buck McHenry comes out of the past to coach a team fighting to be born. But what happens? Only three kids show up. Will the team die before it was born? Only some eleven-year-old viewers in Arborville, Michigan, can write a happy end for this story. So if anyone out there is eleven years old, living in Arborville, and is not already on a baseball team, Buck McHenry needs you. Call him at, and we give them your phone number. What do you say? Is it a winner or isn't it? Do you like it?"

"Yes," I said.

"Yes," Kim said.

"Yes," Aaron said.

Mr. Henry shook his head. He was smiling faintly. "I admire your talent, sir. I surely do. But no youngsters showing up here today, I think that's God's way of sending us a message. And that message is we better not have a team this year. So my grandson and me are goin' home. Get in the truck, boy. We're going over to Jason's house to get your bicycle."

"Please, Grampa," Aaron begged. "Let him do the show."

"Boy," Mr. Henry said, anger coming into his voice, "I am going home. You coming with me or not?"

"But you said you'd coach us, Grampa."

"There's no one to coach, boy. There aren't even enough bodies for a practice."

"Wait a second," Chuck Axelrod said. "What do you mean there's not enough bodies? I'm a body. You're a body. That makes five of us already. And—" He looked around the park. And then he started to laugh. "Talk about messages from God. We're receiving one now. Do you all see what I see? A bunch of kids with baseball gloves coming toward us? Tell me those kids are not looking for a little action, Buck. I defy you to tell me that."

Coming across the park on bicycles were kids our age. "I bet my bottom dollar those kids are looking for a team to join," Chuck Axelrod said.

Considering Chuck Axelrod's income as a big TV sportscaster, Mr. Henry and I could have made a lot of money right then and there. We were the only ones there who knew those kids weren't looking for a team to join. They were already on one. My old team. Baer Machine.

There was Cal Borker and Art Silver and Diaz and Tug Murphy and Kevin Kovich and Tim Corrigan and Greg Conklin and a couple of others. They must have heard about our team meeting and had come down to laugh at us. And that, I thought, was just about the last thing we needed.

I ran out to ask them to go away.

15

"What're you guys doing here?"

"That's a nice greeting, Jayce," Pete said. "Here we been looking all over town for you and you ask what we're doing here. What're *you* doing here? What's Mr. Henry doing here?"

And then they all started peppering me at once.

"Is that your new team?"

"You're short a few players."

"Who's the girl?"

"Who's the black kid?"

"What's the deal on Mr. Henry?"

"Is the girl on your team?"

"She's pretty but can she hit for power?"

"Hey, that looks like Chuck Axelrod."

"No, it don't."

"Sure, it's him."

"He looks fatter on TV."

"He *is* fatter on TV."

"What's he doing here, Jason?"

"Come on, Jason, what's going on?"

"All right, if I tell you guys what's going on, will you all leave then?"

"Jason sounds like he's ashamed of us."

"I don't blame him. I'm ashamed of us too."

"It's a free country."

"I'm serious. If I tell you, will you leave?"

"Maybe," Tim said.

I'd have to settle for "maybe." "Okay. The Grandstand's going to sponsor my new team. Chuck Axelrod is helping us organize it. The girl is his daughter. The boy is Mr. Henry's grandson. And Mr. Henry is going to coach our team."

"Mr. Henry?" Diaz broke up. "What's he know about baseball?"

"A lot more than you ever will, Pete," I shot back. The idea of Pete Diaz sneering at a baseball legend like Buck McHenry was too much for me. "It just so happens Mr. Henry played in the old Negro leagues. His name was Buck McHenry then and he was a big star. I've even got a baseball card of him."

They looked at me as though I was nuts. Then Tim Corrigan started laughing. "Mr. Henry on a baseball card? Jayce, you just collected one card too many."

That broke them up.

"Okay, I told you guys what was going on. Why don't you go now?"

"We want to meet Chuck Axelrod."

"He doesn't want to meet you guys."

"If he doesn't want to meet us, how come he's yelling for us to come over?" Greg Conklin said quietly.

I looked back toward the diamond. Chuck Axelrod had made a megaphone of his hands and was shouting, "Jason, bring those kids over here."

"That's it. We are being summoned," Kovich said.

"Maybe he wants to put us on television," Pete said. "How's my hair look?"

"Ugly."

"Let's go," Cal said.

"Last one there's in love with Chuck Axelrod's daughter," Art said.

They raced their bikes to the diamond. I ran after them. By the time I got there the air was filled with greetings to Mr. Henry. "Hi, Mr. Henry. How ya doin', Mr. Henry? How's it going, Mr. Henry?" All the while they were looking out of the corners of their eyes at Chuck Axelrod.

Chuck Axelrod knew what was going on, all right. He had to be used to people looking at him on the sly. Meanwhile Mr. Henry answered their greetings.

"Hello, Pete. Calvin. Kevin. Greg. Tug, Art, Jim."

Often the only people in a school who know all the kids' names are the principal and the custodian. And the custodian always knows them first. Starting with the kids who mess up the lunchroom.

"I guess you know these boys, Buck," Chuck Axelrod said, his eyes gleaming.

I wondered if the guys had heard that "Buck." I couldn't tell.

"I guess I know some of them since they were in kindergarten."

"I get it. You're the custodian in *their* school?"

"You've got it right, sir."

"Love it, love it." Chuck Axelrod took out his pad and started making notes. He paused. "How old are you kids?"

"We're eleven," Diaz said.

"Eleven and a half," Greg Conklin said.

"You're eleven like the rest of us, Conklin."

"I'm gonna be twelve in July," Kovich said.

"Kovich got left back."

"Hold it," Chuck Axelrod said. "All I'm trying to find out is if you're eligible to play in the eleven-year-old league."

"Yes," they all said.

"Good. Then I've got a proposition for you. How'd you like to join a brand-new team coached by one of the greatest right-handed pitchers of all time — Mr. Buck McHenry."

With a sweeping gesture, like a circus ringmaster, Chuck Axelrod pointed to Mr. Henry.

The guys were stunned. They hadn't believed me when I told them that, but now it was the voice of Channel 4 sports talking. That made it true.

Mr. Henry looked as though he'd just been shot.

"Mr. Henry," Pete said humbly, "is it true what Jason told us, that you're on a baseball card?"

This was worth everything.

"He sure is, son," Chuck Axelrod said and whipped out the Buck McHenry card. "I've got it right here. Mr. McHenry is too modest. He won't blow his own horn but by God I'll blow it for him." He held the card up. They crowded around.

"Don't push, Borker."

"I can't see it."

"Is that really you, Mr. Henry?"

"It don't look like him."

"It's an old picture, man."

"When was it taken, Mr. Henry?"

162

"Who'd you play for?"

"How come you never told anyone?"

"I bet my dad heard about you."

"It says on the back who he played for."

"It says he became a school custodian."

"Where?"

"In Michigan, jerk."

"I mean, where on the card?"

"There."

"Don't bend it, Kovich. You're goin' to tear it."

"Does it say Eberwoods?"

"Quit shovin', Corrigan."

"Take it easy, guys," Chuck Axelrod said, laughing. I looked at the others. Aaron was so proud. Kim was smiling. But Mr. Henry stood silent as a statue.

We're getting him into trouble, I thought. I felt so guilty.

"Easy now, this card has to stay in good shape," Chuck Axelrod was saying. "I've got to take pictures of it. Let's have it back. Here we go. Thank you, gentlemen, thank you."

He put the card in his shirt pocket. "Kids, my name's Chuck Axelrod, and I do sports for Channel 4."

They all laughed.

"We know *that*."

"We watch your *Sportsline* show all the time, Mr. Axelrod."

"It's my favorite show on the air."

"Mine too."

"Good. Then how would you all like to be on tonight's show?"

That really stopped them. And no one more so than Pete Diaz, for all his jokes about being on TV. "What'd I tell you guys?" he said, and began nervously patting his hair.

"What do we got to do?" Tug asked.

"Join this new team—The Grandstand."

Silence. They looked at each other. I spoke up for them.

"They're already on a team, Mr. Axelrod. My old team—Baer Machine."

Chuck Axelrod looked at me reproachfully. "Thanks a lot, Jason. You could have warned me."

"How could he have, Dad?" Kim said. "He couldn't have got a word in edgewise."

She was defending me!

Chuck Axelrod laughed. "Honey, you're absolutely right. I'm a victim of my own scenario. I just wanted something to happen real bad. But . . ." He turned to the rest of us. "You know what I always say?"

164

No one had the slightest idea what he always said.

"I always say, if you can't join 'em, beat 'em."

It was the opposite of what you're supposed to say, but no one laughed because we couldn't tell if he had mixed up the language or meant it.

It turned out he meant it.

"Here's what I propose. I've got a camera crew coming in from Detroit. They should be here any minute to shoot a feature story on Buck McHenry for tonight's show. I'm going to need game action to run copy over. I want to have Mr. McHenry coaching in a game situation. So here's the plan. A three-inning practice game between Baer Machine and The Grandstand. What do you say?"

"They've only got three players, Mr. Axelrod," Art said.

"We can beat you with three players," Kim snapped.

I hoped she played as tough as she talked.

"And just how are you going to beat us with three players?" Kevin asked her.

"Aaron can pitch, Jason can catch—"

"That's a matter of opinion," Pete cracked.

She ignored him. "—and I can play the field."

165

Chuck Axelrod grinned at Mr. Henry. "How do you like your team's spirit, Coach?"

Mr. Henry, who hadn't said a word since being introduced as Buck McHenry, was silent. I could tell that he still wanted out.

"What do you say, Coach?" Chuck Axelrod repeated.

Mr. Henry sighed. "I admire your daughter's spirit, sir. But I've got to agree with my boys from Eberwoods School. Nine against three can't be a ball game. So I guess we better all shake hands and go home. Let's go, Aaron."

Chuck Axelrod laughed. "Buck, it's a darn good thing you don't have to produce a TV show every week. You give up too easy. Kim, you remember a segment we did last year with Fast Eddie Phipps?"

"Sure. My dad did a show with a fast-pitch softball team that had only three players on it."

"Fast Eddie Phipps, king of the fast-pitch softball pitchers," Chuck Axelrod said. "And all he had on his team was a pitcher, catcher, and first baseman."

"I saw that!" Pete said, excited. "He didn't even need the first baseman. He was unhittable."

"Well, Aaron's unhittable too," I said, nodding in Aaron's direction. They all looked at him.

"You a pitcher?" Cal asked.

"I pitch some."

Just the way he said that, so modestly, you could see they were impressed.

"You eleven?" Kevin asked. I knew they probably thought he was older. He was so big and strong-looking.

"I'm eleven," Aaron said shyly.

The real leader of the Baer Machine team was Tug Murphy. He was quiet. He led by example. Right now I watched Tug making up his mind. I could tell that he wanted to bat against Aaron. Tug was a jock; Aaron was a jock. You could see jock juices flowing back and forth between them.

"I'm willing to play them a three-inning practice game," Tug said quietly.

That settled it. "Me too," Pete said. "Anything to be on TV."

"Sure. Okay. Let's do it," they chorused.

"Good. The game will start in fifteen minutes," Chuck Axelrod said.

"What about the camera crew?" Pete, of course, asked.

"They're here now," Chuck Axelrod said. "I'll be right back."

None of us had seen it arrive—a large white van with a tall antenna on top and the words

167

WVID-TV, DETROIT on the side. It was parked not far from Chuck Axelrod's Lincoln.

"You believe this?" Kovich said, awed as we watched two men come out of the van. One carried a camera and wore a fat belt around his waist. The other carried what looked like a recorder and a pole with a microphone.

Chuck Axelrod was talking to them and pointing toward us.

"Unreal," Diaz said.

"Wait till I tell my folks," Kevin said. I think all our hearts were beating faster. We were going to be on TV. We were going to be famous.

Only Mr. Henry didn't look happy. Aaron saw it too and went up to him. "It's okay, isn't it, Grampa?" He was pleading with him.

Mr. Henry was silent. He didn't even look at Aaron.

"We're just going to play three innings, Grampa. That's all. Just three innings."

Mr. Henry looked down at his grandson. And then he smiled. A funny sad little smile. "What's got to be has got to be, I guess," he said.

He turned and looked at the Baer Machine guys, who were watching the camera crew haul more gear out of their truck.

"Haven't you boys ever seen a movie camera before? You aiming to be ballplayers or movie stars? Don't you know you can hurt your arm in a three-inning game just as bad as in a regular one? Start loosening up those muscles. Start warming up."

I could have clapped my hands. He was going to take a chance. He was staying. He was coaching!

I grabbed one of the new baseballs. "Aaron, let's warm up. Throw easy. Save your arm and we'll save a few surprises for them."

Mr. Henry chuckled. "Now you're talking, boy. Talking like a real catcher. Like Campy, Gibson, Radcliffe, any of them."

It gave me goose pimples to hear that. It was the greatest compliment any kid could've got. Please, dear God, I prayed, don't let me mess up.

Kim warmed up off to one side with Mr. Henry. I didn't really get a chance to check out how she looked. I was busy warming up Aaron. He threw easy. Saving the surprises for later.

16

Well, the game or the TV show, or whatever you want to call what happened next, started out just fine.

The man with the camera and fat belt—which Kim told me was the battery pack for the camera—was tied by a cable to the man with a recorder and a microphone. The moment they got to the diamond, they set up a little black-and-white TV monitor so we could see ourselves.

Then the cameraman said, "Rolling, Chuck," and after a few seconds the man with the video recorder said, "Speed," and then without warning Chuck Axelrod began interviewing Mr. Henry. This was how it went:

CHUCK AXELROD: Mr. McHenry, you came out of a self-imposed obscurity to coach a kids' baseball team. Could you tell us why?

MR. HENRY (*fiddling with his fisherman's hat*): My grandson moved to Michigan from Tennessee. He was looking for a team to play on up here. And there was a new team looking for a coach. We were starting together. Me and my grandson.

CHUCK AXELROD: Let's have the grandson over here. C'mere, son. What's your name?

AARON (*so quiet you almost didn't hear him*): Aaron.

CHUCK AXELROD: All right, Aaron. Crowd right in. The golden rule of television is when you feel uncomfortable is when you look good. Now, Aaron, speak up and tell the folks at home what it feels like to have your grampa, one of the great ballplayers of all time, coaching your team.

AARON (*grinning, speaking a little louder*): Feels good.

CHUCK AXELROD (*laughing*): I bet it does. Was it your idea?

AARON: No, sir. It was Jason who started it. He found out who my grampa was. I didn't even know who my grampa was, did I, Grampa?

MR. HENRY (*smiling that funny little smile*): No, boy, I guess you didn't.

CHUCK AXELROD: Let's get Jason in here too then. The more the merrier.

He said that as though it was spontaneous, but I could tell he had planned it. I walked into the group and faced the camera with them.

171

CHUCK AXELROD: Folks, this is Jason Ross. Jason, how about telling our viewers just how you found Buck McHenry?

ME: Well, it started with me being cut. . . .

And then I told the whole story. About being cut from Baer Machine, finding out there was going to be an expansion team, returning the bases to Eberwoods School, Mr. Henry coaching me in the corridor, him pitching the invisible ball. Out of the corner of my eye I saw the Baer Machine guys listening fascinated. They didn't know any of what had happened after I left them. And then I told how I discovered the Buck McHenry baseball card at The Grandstand. Jim would love the plug. And then how I went to Mr. Henry's house, met Aaron, how Mr. Henry finally admitted he was Buck McHenry, and then how Aaron and I met up with Kim Axelrod, but we weren't able to recruit any other players— not even rejects from other teams—so here we were at Sampson Park with a great coach but no team.

All this Chuck Axelrod let me say without interruption. When I was done, he turned to the camera and said, "So if there are any eleven-year-olds in the city of Arborville watching our show tonight who want to play on a baseball team, there's a team called The Grandstand, coached by a baseball immortal, looking for you. How do they get on your team, Buck?

MR. HENRY (*startled*): Uh, I guess they call me. Or Jason. Better call Jason. Because I'm appointing him captain right now.

ME (*promptly*): My phone number's 555-8742. They can call me there. Can we start our game now, Mr. Henry?

CHUCK AXELROD: Say that number again, Jason. You never say important things only once on TV.

ME: 555-8742. Can we—?

CHUCK AXELROD: Hang on a second more, Jason. Folks, you just heard Jason here call Buck McHenry "Mr. Henry." Well, therein lies perhaps the most interesting part of tonight's *Sportsline* feature story.

Oh no, I thought. Here it comes. Be nice, Mr. Axelrod. Be kind to Mr. Henry, I prayed.

CHUCK AXELROD (*holding up the Buck McHenry baseball card*): This is the baseball card Jason just mentioned. Can we get a close-up of it? There it is. Now on the back of this Negro League baseball star card, it says . . .

I didn't dare look at Mr. Henry. His scrapes with the law were about to be on TV.

Sure enough, Chuck Axelrod read the part about Buck McHenry quitting baseball and be-

173

coming a school custodian in Michigan. And he told the whole world how Buck McHenry had changed his name by dividing it in half, McHenry becoming Mack Henry.

And then he turned to Mr. Henry—I was watching this on the television monitor.

CHUCK AXELROD: Could you tell our viewers why the great Buck McHenry, at the height of his baseball career, quit the sport to become a school custodian in Michigan?

At that moment I was so scared for Mr. Henry. I looked at his face on the monitor. It was without expression. Was he panicking inside? The silence was deafening. And then Chuck Axelrod, like one of those birds of prey that dive into the ocean after a fish, dove in after Mr. Henry.

CHUCK AXELROD: On the back of the card, Buck, it says you dropped out because of, and I quote, "scrapes with the law." Would you like to comment on that? Or . . . (*he smiled*) perhaps you wouldn't.

Mr. Henry stood there with everyone looking at him. Me, Aaron, Kim, Chuck Axelrod, the Baer Machine kids, the cameraman, the recorder man, and through those guys—the whole world. Mr. Henry stood there alone and helpless.

"It's okay, Grampa," I heard Aaron whisper.

More silence. Then Mr. Henry gave a strange little laugh. "My grandson says it's okay. So I guess it's got to be. You were asking, sir, about those scrapes with the law?"

"Yes, sir," Chuck Axelrod said.

"Well, I didn't kill anyone, if that's what you're after. Or rob anyone either."

He looked past Chuck Axelrod, past the camera crew, past the kids, past, it even seemed to me, Sampson Park. He was looking into years gone by.

"Those scrapes with the law had to do with how us colored ballplayers were treated in the old days. In those days when the season was over, some of us used to go barnstormin' around the country. You know, go from country town to country town playin' the local team. Some of those local boys would be all right ballplayers but most were just strong farm boys. Their fans would pay a dollar to see the local heroes lick a team of traveling professional black baseball players. And if they licked us, we'd get half of each dollar.

"Of course they couldn't have really licked us in a month of Sundays, but if we wanted to get paid, well, we had to let them lick us."

"You mean you threw ball games?" Chuck Axelrod asked. "You lost them on purpose?"

"You could say that, Mr. Axelrod. You could also say we earned our pay, because it was a lot harder to lose to those teams than it was to beat them. And one particular night, as I recall, it was especially hard. One night we didn't lose when we were supposed to. The reason was their fans got down on us pretty good, hollering all sorts of nasty stuff. Racial things, you know. I was supposed to walk a few batters and let the rest hit easy pitches. Anyway, they're hollerin' at me that my daddy had been swinging in a tree in Africa with the rest of the apes and what was I doing playing an American sport. There was so much of that that I got mad, and before I knew it, I started firing my smoker. Well, those white boys had never seen anything like that. They never lifted the bat off their shoulders. Up they came and down they went. My teammates got mad too because of all the nasty name-calling and when they came up to bat, instead of striking out and falling down and looking like clowns like we were bein' paid to do, they began hitting the hide off the ball. Home runs, triples, doubles, and racin' round those bases like we were shot out of cannons. Before you knew it we were fifteen runs up on a team we were supposed to lose to."

Mr. Henry chuckled. "Well, sir, to make a long story short, we won the game but not the war. The boys asked me to ask the promoter if we could at least have expense money to get out of town. We didn't want the hundred dollars they were supposed to pay us. We just wanted enough money to buy gas. The promoter said to me, 'Boy, you're going to be lucky to git out of here in one piece. Git, now, git.' Like he was talkin' to a dog.

"The gate receipts were sittin' on his desk. Maybe a thousand dollars. I grabbed four dollars. Four dollars. That'd buy us enough gas to get us out of town. I grabbed the four dollars and I ran. The promoter came around the desk after me shouting, 'Stop that nigger,' and worse, and pretty soon there were sheriff's deputies and folks with guns coming after me. I jumped into one of my teammate's cars. In those days we traveled in two old cars, and by the time we ran out of gas, we had air conditioning through those cars. We were lucky they thought they'd killed us all and didn't come out to bury our bodies."

He laughed. No one else did.

"That was only one time. But there were other experiences like that. Well, a man can only take so much, you know. I couldn't take it anymore, so I got out. I think the hardest thing in life is to listen to folks call you a lot of names and not be able to hit back. And maybe even worse than that, from a ballplayer's point of view, is to lose to teams you know you can beat with one hand tied behind your back. I told myself there's got to be easier ways of making money. And I found one. I found out that pushing a broom was a lot easier than pitching a ball game, taking abuse, and losing on purpose." He looked Chuck Axelrod straight in the eye. "You ask about my scrapes with the law. And now I told you."

With that he was silent. Everyone was silent. My eyes felt moist. I looked around. Kim's eyes were wet too. Kovich and Diaz had tears in their eyes. The camera kept on shooting us; the recorder kept on recording.

Chuck Axelrod broke the silence. "The past is dead. Today, Buck McHenry is back in baseball. This time as the coach of his grandson's team. Coach McHenry, can you get your team on the field?"

Mr. Henry clapped his hands. "Jason, you're catching. Get your gear on, boy. Aaron, you're pitching. Young lady, you're going to have to play everywhere else. You just play each batter where I tell you to."

Then, while I was putting on my catcher's gear, Mr. Henry did a classy thing. He walked over to the Baer Machine kids. "Calvin, Tim, Tug, seeing as how you don't have yourselves a coach, how'd you like me to coach your team too?"

He did that without consulting with Chuck Axelrod. That's what I mean by a classy move.

Tug said, "Thanks, Mr. Hen—McHenry, we'll keep the same lineup we had this morning."

"You mind if I root for your team too, boy?"

"That'd be great, Mr. McHenry," Pete said.

"Pete, the rest of you, you listen to me, my name's still Mr. Henry. The way it's always been. You forget about that McHenry stuff. Nothing's changed. Tug, get your batting order set. You boys'll be first up seein' as this appears to be The Grandstand's home field."

Mr. Henry walked over to me. "No signals, Jason. Just let Aaron pitch how he wants."

"Yes, sir."

In the infield, Tug was throwing ground balls to Kim so she could warm up. She looked smooth scooping and throwing. She threw like a boy. Fielded like a boy. I wouldn't be a bit surprised if she didn't hit like a boy. I wouldn't also be a bit surprised if her baseball card collection was as good as she said it was.

"Jason, get your mind off baseball cards." I could hear Mr. Borker's voice inside my head. And he was right.

I squatted down. Aaron was doing some landscaping around the mound. Kicking the dirt. Getting the feel of it. Every pitcher's mound is different.

I pounded my glove. My two sponges were in. I'd need them. He'd be throwing his smoker all the time. He'd have to. And throw it high, too, so if they did hit the ball, they'd pop it up to Kim or him. Ground balls and we were dead. We didn't have a first baseman. Strike-outs and pop-ups were what we wanted. And no fly balls. A fly ball was a home run.

While Aaron threw easy, Mr. Henry went out and positioned Kim to play between first and second. I knew he was figuring they'd be swinging late on Aaron's smoker. They were all right-handed hitters too.

The Baer Machine kids eyed Aaron as he warmed up. Even throwing easy, they could see from his motion, his kick, his stride, that he was a thrower. What they didn't know yet was how hard he could throw. Well, in a few seconds they'd find out.

"I'll call balls and strikes from behind the

mound," Chuck Axelrod announced. "You rolling, Tony?"

"You bet, ump," the cameraman said, laughing.

"Speed," called out the man with the recorder.

"Batter up," Chuck Axelrod shouted.

17

Kevin Kovich stepped in.

"No batter," I yelled.

"No stick," Kim yelled.

"Make him get one over, Kevin," Mr. Henry called out, coaching for them too. He was reminding Baer Machine that you should always take one with a new pitcher. See what he's got.

Well, it turned out Kevin didn't see a thing.

Aaron wound up, kicked, and fired, and it came just like the bullet he threw in his backyard. This time I stuck with it. The ball exploded in my mitt. And, despite the two sponges, my hand stung. "Ouch," I said.

"Strike one," Chuck Axelrod said.

"Holy cow," Kevin Kovich said.

"Choke up, Kevin," Mr. Henry called out. "Move back in the batter's box." And then he shouted to Aaron. "Keep firing, boy. Keep throwing trouble."

Aaron and I grinned at each other. "Trouble"

was Satchel Paige's pitch.

"Stan," Chuck Axelrod shouted at the man with the recorder, "are you picking up Mr. McHenry's voice? He's coaching both teams."

"I'm getting it, Chuck," the sound man called back. He was wearing earphones.

"Jayce, I didn't even see that ball," Kevin said to me.

"You won't see the next one either, Kev."

"I hope he breaks your hand," Kevin said. I noticed he choked up on his bat the way Mr. Henry suggested.

"Blow it by him again, Aaron," Kim called out, pounding her glove.

I nodded to Aaron, wiggled one finger just for the heck of it, and braced myself. Aaron pumped, kicked, and fired, and once more the ball exploded in my mitt and once more Chuck Axelrod yelled "strike" and once more Kevin hadn't swung.

I could feel for him. It's hard to swing at what you can't see. And Kevin just couldn't see it. Nor could Cal, who was up after him. Or Tug after Cal. Tug at least swung, but he didn't come close to connecting. I wished he had. I wished someone would hit a few fouls. It would give me a little break. My left hand was beginning to hurt.

Up they came and down they went. Aaron struck out one guy after another. In the next inning it was Tim, Pete, Art standing there with their bats on the shoulders. Not even one foul tip.

Kim yelled. I yelled—once in pain, though I masked it by shouting "wow" instead of "ouch."

Mr. Henry didn't yell. He kept talking quietly to the Baer Machine kids telling them to choke up, stand in the back of the batter's box, don't take a big swing, just make contact. They listened and did what he said, except for making contact. That was easier said than done.

I wondered what Chuck Axelrod was going to make of Mr. Henry coaching both teams. And coaching *them* more than us. After the first two guys went down on strikes, all he ever said to Aaron was, "Keep mailin' trouble, boy."

Kim picked it up. "Mail them trouble, Aaron babe. Be a postman, mail them trouble."

It was hard to believe a girl could pick up on stuff like that, but she did. And in our half of the first inning she put her money where her mouth was with the bat. She jumped on Cal's first pitch and hit it over Greg's head at second for a single. She was for real. Cal is one of the best pitchers in the eleven-year-old league, but

184

she'd pinged him like she owned him. I batted second. When I stood in there, Cal said, "Well, I can get *you* out at least."

"Don't count on it," I said.

But I'm sorry to say he did get me out. I popped up to Tim at first. And that brought up Aaron. I don't think any of us had thought of who would bat next if Kim was still on base and Aaron made out. Could Kim come in and bat again? And me take her place on first? It *was* crazy having only three players.

I'd never seen Aaron hit. I expected Mr. Henry to shout encouragement down to Aaron, but he didn't. Instead he shouted encouragement to Cal. "Send trouble the other way, Calvin."

Tug called out, "Pitchers can't hit, Cal."

Maybe Cal thought differently, because he threw the first one in the dirt and the second one wide and the third one high. He was trying too hard.

"You're overthrowing, boy," Mr. Henry called out. "Just throw to Tug's glove. Don't worry about the batter."

"That's right," Tug called out. "This guy's no stick. He's all show."

"You got to drive Kim in, Aaron," I yelled. "She's up next."

I was trying to tell him to hit the 3 and 0

cripple. It wouldn't do just to hit a single or take a walk. He really had to whack it, and a 3 and 0 pitch is the one to whack.

Aaron nodded. He looked relaxed up there in an open stance, feet apart.

Cal went to a full motion. Kim took off on it and Cal threw a fat one down the middle. Aaron stepped into it and drove it. Oh my, how he drove it! Swinging hips, shoulders, arms, and wrists, he drove it on a line starting low and rising higher and higher like a cannonball.

The prettiest sound in the world is when a bat makes solid on-the-nose contact with a ball. And the prettiest sight in the world is to see that ball keep going off, rising and rising.

In center field, Diaz didn't even move. He stood there and watched the ball shoot over his head like a rocket. It touched down way beyond him, near where some little kids were flying kites. The kids looked around. Where did *that* come from?

By the time Pete got to it, Aaron was back on the bench, not even breathing hard. Kim slapped him five. "Man, you hit that a ton," she said.

"Didn't he ever?" I said, and slapped him and her.

Mr. Henry came up behind Aaron and rubbed

his head. "I guess you did play some in Tennessee, boy."

"I got lucky, Grampa," Aaron said.

"You sure did," Mr. Henry chuckled proudly.

Kim and I laughed. We were a small team, three players and a coach, but we were a team.

Out on the mound, Cal Borker kicked angrily at the dirt around the rubber. Mr. Henry went out and talked to him. "Don't get down on yourself, boy. That was just a fat 3 and 0 pitch. He couldn't have hit your smoker. You'll get him next time around."

The words seemed to calm Cal, and he pitched well after that. He only allowed one more hit and, believe it or not, I got it. And believe it or not, it was a leg hit. I hit a ground ball to short. I don't know if Kevin backed up on it or what he did. I didn't look to see. I just ran to first like there were hot coals under my feet.

"You ran that out like Cool Papa himself, boy," Mr. Henry shouted at me.

I never got off first, though. Cal got Kim to pop up and Aaron lined out to Art and that was the old ball game. We won it 2–0 because Aaron kept striking out people. No one even got a foul tick.

In the middle of the third inning Chuck Axelrod told his crew to stop shooting. They had

187

enough game footage. But he said not to pack up just yet. There was something else he wanted to shoot.

When the three-inning game was over, Chuck Axelrod slapped Aaron on the back. "You've got one heckuvan arm on you, son. You'll be pitching for the Tigers one of these days. You're the grandson of Buck McHenry all right. Now don't anyone leave. We've got one more thing to shoot."

I was hoping he'd interview me again, because I wanted to point out, humbly, if I could, that we could have beat Baer Machine with only two players, a pitcher and a catcher.

But Chuck Axelrod didn't want any more interviews. He wanted shots of kids shaking hands. Like the end of a hockey game.

The Baer Machine guys were okay. "I bet you're glad to be shaking with your meat hand, Jayce," Tug said to me.

I'd forgot all about my left hand hurting. It was red and puffy, but the more they struck out, the less it hurt.

"Isn't he great, Tugger?"

"Best I ever seen," Tug said.

Good old Tug. He was classy. I heard him say to Aaron, "You're good, man."

"Thanks," Aaron said, shyly.

The guys shook hands with Kim without mak-

188

ing too many cracks. After all, she had got a solid hit off Cal. When Cal got to her, he said, "That was a lucky hit you got off me."

"No, it wasn't," Kim said.

The guys laughed. They were impressed with her. Heck, I was too.

After taping the handshaking, the crew packed up their equipment and Chuck Axelrod went over to each kid and thanked him for helping out. To Kim, he said, "Honey, I've got to get to the station and start editing. Do you know how to get home from here?"

"I'm okay," she said, blushing. I don't think she liked being called honey in front of everyone. Certainly not after scoring the winning run. Or maybe it was his suggesting she didn't know how to get home.

"I'll call you from Detroit. There's tuna fish in the fridge." He sort of looked embarrassed. "I've got a housekeeper hired but she can't start till next week," he said to us, but mostly to Mr. Henry. "Listen, all of you, thanks again. And Mr. McHenry, a special thanks to you. You're going to do a lot for kids' baseball in Arborville. In fact," he said with a grin, "between the two of us we just might put the kids' baseball program here on the national map. The Buck McHenry story is the kind of story that could get picked up by the network and the wire services. All right, everyone, remember, *Sportsline*, Channel 4. Nine o'clock tonight!"

As though we would forget.

Chuck Axelrod ran, he didn't walk, he ran over to his Lincoln. He shouted something at the Channel 4 van. Then he burned rubber out of the parking lot. The Channel 4 van followed him out almost as fast.

"Your dad always move that fast?" Tug asked Kim.

"When he's late for a show he does."

"How long is it going to take him to edit the tapes?" I asked.

"A couple of hours."

"He's late all right," Pete said.

"I gotta go home and tell my folks about this. My grandpa too," Kevin said. "He always watches *Sportsline*." Kevin ran for his bike. The others walked to their bikes.

Mr. Henry said to Aaron, "We got to get going too, boy. We got to get your bike at Jason's house."

It was like he'd lost himself in the game, but now that the game was over he was worried again about the TV show. I didn't know what he was worried about. Those scrapes with the law were nothing. Absolutely nothing. Grabbing four dollars when crooks owed you a hundred? *They* were the ones who broke the law.

He couldn't get Aaron moving though. Aaron didn't want it to end. None of us did. Kim pounded her glove. I thought about her going back alone to that huge empty house.

"You want to eat at our house?" I asked her.

She shook her head.

"It'll be okay. My mom's a great cook."

"We've got food."

"Tuna fish," I said.

"I like tuna fish."

"Kim could eat at our house, couldn't she, Grampa? And Jason too. Then we could all watch the show together. My grandma's a great cook."

"I couldn't, Aaron. I got to be home to get the phone calls from kids," I said.

"Let's go get your bike, boy," Mr. Henry said. "We can ride over to Jason's house in my truck."

"What about the equipment bag?" Kim asked.

In the excitement, we'd forgotten to put the bats, balls, and catcher's gear back in the bag.

"The three of you pack it up," Mr. Henry said.

While we were packing up the equipment bag, the Baer Machine kids who were still there came over to us.

"Mr. uh . . . Henry," Cal said. "Can we ask you something?"

"Of course you can, Calvin."

"If The Grandstand doesn't come up with a full team, I know my dad would like to have Aaron play for us."

Kim and I looked at each other. This we hadn't expected. We looked at Aaron. He was stuffing a bat in the bag. "I'm goin' to play for my grampa," he said softly without looking up.

"Sure, man. But I know my dad would really like having Mr. Henry help him coach."

Silence. Then Aaron picked up the shin guards and put them in the bag. "Jason, Kim, and I are friends," Aaron said. "Teammates," he added.

"But suppose you don't get a team?"

"We'll get a team," Kim said, glaring at Cal. She looked like she was ready to punch him.

Cal backed off. Mr. Henry smiled. "Boys, I think we'd best leave things as they be. You've got a team. You've got the chemistry." He cleared his throat. "Only thing is when you come up against a pitcher who throws real hard, all you want to do is get wood on the ball. Let his speed do your work, let his speed be your power. You kids got that bag packed?"

"Yes, sir," we said.

"Put it in the truck."

He might have just given them good coaching,

but when he told us to put the bag in his truck, he was really signing on as our coach. Coaches kept equipment bags. It was like signing a contract. Now all that had to happen to make this day a complete success was for the phone to start ringing after the *Sportsline* show.

18

"See ya, Aaron."

"See ya, Jason. See ya, Kim."

"See ya, Aaron."

"See ya, Mr. Henry."

The yellow pickup with the bike and the equipment bag in back left our driveway. Kim and I watched it make a right turn on Ferdon and disappear. Then Kim got on her bike.

"Do you know how to get home from here?" I asked her.

"Sure."

"How?"

She looked around and then pointed in the wrong direction.

I laughed. "I'll bike you home. Just let me tell my folks where I'm going. They'll be sore if I disappear on them again. Come in for a second."

"Jason, my dad'll be calling to see if I got home okay."

"It's just for a second. They won't believe me when I tell them what happened. You've got to confirm it."

"All right, but I can't stay."

Sounds of typing came from Dad's den. The radio was playing in the kitchen. Mom had her back to us and was fiddling with it when we came in. The dining-room table was set for three.

"Boo," I said.

Mom jumped. She's easy to scare.

"Thanks a lot, Jason." She flipped off the radio.

"You won't believe what happened, Mom. The three of us beat nine Baer Machine kids in a three-inning game. Aaron threw nothing but strike-outs."

"Is that a good thing to throw?"

Kim gasped.

"You see what I have to live with," I said. "Can I get Dad? We want to tell you what happened. The ball game was only part of it."

"He's working on something important, Jason. Tell me."

"Okay. Not only did we win our game but we're all going to be on TV. And Mr. Henry was wonderful, wasn't he, Kim?"

She nodded. "I gotta go, Jason."

"Wait a second. Mr. Henry told Kim's dad what it was like to play in the old Negro leagues. Mom, it was awful. They cheated those guys all the time. You'll see it on *Sportsline* tonight."

"Jason, my father's going to call soon."

"Mom, do we have enough food to invite Kim for supper?"

I blurted it out. It was wrong of me, I know. You're not supposed to invite kids for dinner without asking first if it's okay. What could my mom say in front of Kim? No? It was embarrassing to Mom and embarrassing to Kim. I think the only reason I blurted it out was because I was still bothered at the idea of her eating alone in that big house. Especially after a victory like that.

If Mom was embarrassed or annoyed, she didn't show it. She's real good that way. "It's just lasagna, Kim, and we do have more than enough, as a matter of fact."

"She makes great lasagna, Kim. Change your mind?"

Kim wouldn't look at either of us. "I've got to go," she mumbled and headed for the door.

"Why do you have to go? No one's home in your house."

"Is that right?" Mom said. "No one's home?"

Kim kept going.

"That's right," I said. "No one's home except some tuna fish."

Kim was at the door.

"Her dad's editing the tape in Detroit. Her mom lives in Birmingham."

"Wait a second, Kim," Mom called out.

Kim stopped.

"We really do have more than enough lasagna, Kim. Please stay, unless, of course, you don't like lasagna," Mom said gently.

"I like lasagna," Kim said. Her face got all red. "We have it a lot."

"Frozen, I bet," I said.

"Jason, for goodness' sakes. What kind of manners are those? I'm sure Kim's father is busy and doesn't have time to cook. We'd love to have you, Kim."

Kim bit her lip. I think she wanted to stay but wasn't sure my mom really wanted her to. Maybe if we got away from talking about just feeding her.

"You could look over my baseball cards afterward," I said. "You could tell me what you think my collection's worth."

Like she'd be doing me a favor if she stayed.

"Kim's got over thirty thousand cards, Mom. She's got a 1952 Mickey Mantle. Signed."

"Who's Mickey Mantle?" Mom said.

"C'mon, Mom. You know who Mickey Mantle is."

"Is he a pitcher or a batter?"

Kim laughed. Mom couldn't have said anything better to relax Kim. The sad part was that Mom didn't do it on purpose. She really wanted to know.

"C'mon, stay for supper," I said. "Then I'll bike you home."

Kim looked up questioningly at Mom.

"We'd really love to have you eat with us, Kim," Mom said.

Kim nodded quickly. "Thanks, Mrs. Ross. But I better call my dad and see if it's okay with him."

"How are you going to call him?" I said. "He won't be in Detroit yet."

"I'll call him in his car."

"Neat. Ask him where he is."

It was a regular number she punched up. Kim asked him right off where he was. I heard his laugh. "No," she said, "that's not why. Jason wants to know." Pause. "I'll tell him. Dad, Mrs. Ross has invited me to stay for supper. Can I? Pause. "Thanks. Okay. 'Bye."

"He's just passing Metro airport. And I can stay."

"Great. Now both of you wash up," Mom said.

We washed up. Mom pried Dad out of his den and we sat down to eat some great lasagna. I spent more time talking than eating. I told them everything. Mr. Henry, the TV crew and taping, the game, Baer Machine wanting Aaron to pitch for them, Aaron saying he wanted to play with his friends. And Kim confirmed every detail so they knew I wasn't making it up.

Only once did Dad interrupt, and that was when I mentioned that our phone number was going to be broadcast on the air.

"You're joking," Dad said.

"No."

Dad groaned. Mom quickly changed the subject and asked Kim if she wanted a career in television like her father. Kim shook her head.

"What would you like to be when you grow up?" Mom asked her.

"A teacher."

"I know what I'm going to be," I said.

"What?" Kim asked.

"I'm going to run a baseball card store like The Grandstand. I think it's great to do what you like and be paid for it too. Maybe when Jim retires I'll take over—oh no!"

"What's the matter?" Dad said.

"Jim doesn't know The Grandstand's going

to be mentioned on *Sportsline* tonight. He doesn't know anything about what happened today." I jumped up from the table.

"Where're you going?" Dad asked.

"I'm going to call him."

"You sit right down and finish eating first," Mom said.

"But—"

"Sit down and finish dinner, Jason," Dad said.

I sat down and finished dinner. But what a thing to forget. Luckily The Grandstand stays open late on Saturdays. When I was done, and Mom didn't make me wait for dessert, I called The Grandstand and got Jim. I told him all that happened. While I talked I could hear him doing business. When I got to the Buck McHenry part (which was news to him) and then to the video-taping at the park and Chuck Axelrod mentioning The Grandstand on camera, Jim stopped doing business.

"Jason," he said, "you're making this up."

"I'm not. You know who Kim Axelrod is. His daughter. She's here. Ask her. Kim, c'mere. He doesn't believe me. You tell him."

"Jason, no . . ." She shook her head.

"C'mon, he's our sponsor. Tell him." I stuck the phone in her hands. What a time to be shy.

"Hi," she said timidly. And then I didn't hear

what Jim said but she told him exactly what I had said. When I got back on, Jim was so excited, he was spluttering.

"Jason . . . I apologize. . . . You were right from the beginning. About Buck McHenry . . . about everything. The Grandstand's going to be on TV. Oh, too much, too much. I'm going to close early and go home and watch it. Jason, oh Jason, I'll . . . I'll talk to you later."

"He's closing the store to go home and watch the show," I announced.

"Where are you going to watch it, Kim?" Mom asked.

"Home."

"Alone?" Mom said. She smiled. "That doesn't sound so good. I think the team ought to watch it together. Why don't you stay here and watch it and afterward Jason's father will drive you and your bike home."

What Mom said gave me goose pimples. She was right. The team ought to watch it together. And handle the phone calls together. But there was another person on that team.

"Mom, Dad, can Kim and I bike over to Aaron's house and bring him here? He should be here too. And we could drive them both home afterward, couldn't we?"

"It's all right with me," Dad said, "but why

do you have to bike there? Why can't you phone him and ask him to come here?"

"He won't know how to get here. And I can't ask Mr. Henry. He's spent so much time on us already. It wouldn't be fair. Kim and I could go get him."

"Where do they live?" Mom asked.

"On North Fourth Avenue. We can go right down Washtenaw. You want to come, don't you?" I asked Kim.

"Yes." She looked embarrassed. "But I better call my father and tell him I'm going to watch the show here. He'll be calling home the second it's over."

"Boy, you are really on a short leash."

She blushed. "No, it's just that . . ." She shrugged. "He and I are alone."

Silence. Then Dad said, "Go call him, Kim."

"It's long distance. It's Detroit, Mr. Ross."

Dad smiled. "That's all right. We're the same area code."

"You sure know a lot of phone numbers," I said as she punched up Channel 4, Detroit. The only number I knew by heart was The Grandstand. And sometimes ours.

"Hi. This is Kim Axelrod. Is my dad—?" (Pause.) "Oh. Could you tell him I'm going to watch the show at Jason's house?" (Pause.) "He knows who Jason is." (Pause.) "It's the same phone number that's going to be on the show. Right. Thanks."

"Your dad busy?"

"He hasn't finished editing."

"What a job. Let's go."

"Jason," Dad said, "it'll be getting dark soon. Please ride on the sidewalks."

"We will, Dad. We'll be careful."

19

The way to Aaron's house from my house was pretty much the same as from her house to his. Except she lived on the other side of Washtenaw. Kim and I biked down Washtenaw, past the First Presbyterian Church, then across campus and downtown past City Hall, the fire station, and then into the old part of town.

We got slowed up between campus and downtown, where a lot of people were out walking. It was nice weather and dusk is a pretty time to walk in Arborville. And then we hit red lights on Liberty, Washington, and Huron. By the time we got to Aaron's neighborhood, it had gotten dark. But there was a nice full moon out. And Aaron's street was bathed in moonlight.

I pointed out the old stone Underground Railroad house to Kim.

"I bet you didn't have anything like that in Birmingham."

"I don't think so."

"There's Aaron's house."

"Where?"

"The little white one with the fence in front."

"What's that noise?"

"What noise?"

"Don't you hear it?"

"No. Yes. I do now."

It was a muffled *thump, thump, thump*. Then a long pause. And then *thump, thump, thump*. It seemed to be coming from behind Aaron's house. There was something familiar about it. Like I'd heard it before. And then it hit me. I knew exactly what it was. I grinned.

"You know what it is?" she asked.

"Yep. It's Aaron. We'll sneak up on him and surprise him. Let's be quiet."

"What's he doing?"

"You'll see in a second," I whispered. "Be quiet."

I unlatched the front gate with the WEL-COME. THE MACK HENRYS. hanging from it. We walked our bikes in and then I held my finger to my lips. I laid my bike down gently, noiselessly. Kim did the same.

Lights were on in the house. As we crept along the side of the house and got closer to the back-yard, the thumps sounded larger. They were in series of threes. Three thumps. Nothing for a few seconds. Then three more thumps.

Kim looked really baffled. I restrained a laugh.

We tiptoed underneath their windows. There were rectangles of light on the ground. We sneaked around and between them, like doing a ski slalom.

In a few seconds we were standing next to one of the steel supports that held up the back porch. I heard a sharp intake of breath from Kim. There was Aaron in the moonlight firing baseballs at the mattress hanging from the shed.

He'd fire three pitches and then run and get the balls and come back and fire three more pitches. It was beautiful. The kind of thing sports legends are made of. How did Aaron Henry, winner of twenty games in his first season in the majors, become such a great pitcher?

Well, when Aaron Henry was a kid growing up in Arborville, Michigan, on moonlit evenings he used to pitch baseballs at a mattress his grandfather, the great Buck McHenry, had hung on a shed in their backyard. Over and over, hundreds of pitches, he would throw to a bull's-eye on the mattress.

"I owe everything I am today to my grampa," Aaron would tell the reporters.

I was making up a story, I knew, but it could

happen. I looked at Kim. Her eyes were shining. "He's great, Jason," she whispered.

"How about when I say three, we both yell: 'Strike three. You're out'?"

She laughed. "Okay." She was game for anything.

"One, two—" I stopped. Above us a door had opened, floorboards creaked. We looked at each other. We couldn't shout at Aaron now.

"We're right under their back porch," I whispered.

And then Mrs. Henry's voice sounded, inches above us, it felt like.

"You have to call him in and tell him, Mr. Henry," she said quietly.

Thump, thump, thump went the three balls.

"What's he going to think of me, Jessie?"

"Jessie's Mrs. Henry, his wife," I whispered to Kim.

"He'll think the same of you as what he thought before. But you've got to tell him. After that, we can figure out a plan of action about those others."

What was she talking about?

"There's nothing to figure," Mr. Henry said softly. "Your man made the biggest fool of himself that he could make with those kids and that TV camera."

Kim and I stared at each other. What was he talking about? He had been a wonderful coach in our little practice game. And he had given a great interview to her dad. He would be letting people all over Michigan know about the old Negro leagues.

"Telling those kids I played with Satchel Paige and Josh Gibson and Cool Papa Bell. I even told them what life was like in the leagues."

What was wrong with him telling us that?

"Did you tell them the truth, Mr. Henry?"

"The truth of what I've heard. Not what I've ever been."

I froze. *Thump, thump, thump* went my heart in rhythm with Aaron's pitches.

"And the thing of it was," Mr. Henry said, "I made it real. Real to them and real to me. So real there were moments I thought maybe I *was* Buck McHenry."

I grabbed onto one of the steel supports. I couldn't believe what I'd just heard. And then I thought, maybe I didn't hear it right. I looked at Kim. Her face was scared. It was the first time I'd seen her look scared. I'd heard it right.

"And that wasn't even the worst of it, Jessie. The worst of it came when I started tellin' the TV camera and the whole world how Buck McHenry got in trouble with the law. He asked me that, Mr. Chuck Axelrod did, and I answered. I went that far, Jessie."

"Well, did you know why he got in trouble with the law?"

"Of course I didn't know, woman," he said angrily. "I told them what happened to me once when I was pitching for that semipro team. How I wouldn't throw a game on purpose and how the sheriff chased us out of town. But Jessie, that happened to me. It didn't happen to the great Buck McHenry."

"It might've, Mr. Henry."

"Woman, the great Buck McHenry wasn't throwing games in cow towns. He was pitching in Yankee Stadium and the Polo Grounds. In the Negro leagues. Pitchin' for the Grays and the Crawfords. Pitching in front of big crowds. Jessie, I *saw* Buck McHenry pitch in Detroit. I *saw* Satchel Paige pitch. I *saw* Gibson and Judy Johnson and Cool Papa. I paid money and I sat in the bleachers and I *saw*. I saw and never was."

He started to cry. Right there inches over our heads, Mr. Henry started to sob. The sound of his sobs tore through the floor and into my heart. Kim put her hand on mine, tugging at me. I brushed her hand off. I thought she was trying to comfort me.

"Jason," she whispered, "we've got to get out of here."

Of course we had to get out of here, but how? They'd hear us if we took one single step. We were right underneath them. And if they discovered us hiding here, then what? That would be worse than anything. They'd know we'd overheard.

"Mr. Henry, you best hush now. The boy is coming."

Aaron had stopped throwing. He had the three balls and was running toward the house. Kim and I froze. Aaron would be coming within a few feet of us. He did. He ran past us and took the steps two at a time and disappeared. Then we heard the screen door at the top of the stairs open and shut.

"Grampa, what time's it?" Aaron asked.

Mr. Henry cleared his throat. "It's not show time yet, boy, if that's what you're after."

"You all right, Grampa?"

"Sure I am."

"You sound funny."

"I got something stuck in my throat."

"Aaron, where are you going now?" Mrs. Henry said.

"See if it's on, Grandma."

"You just heard your grampa say that—"

210

The inside house door shut. A second later the TV was turned on in the other room.

"He doesn't want to miss a second of it, does he?" Mr. Henry said. We heard him blow his nose.

"You've got to talk to him before it starts, Mr. Henry."

"I can't, Jessie."

"Jason." Kim tugged at my sleeve again.

I shook my head. We'd had our chance when Aaron was clomping up the steps. That noise would have covered us. Now we'd have to wait for more noise.

"It's going to be all right, Mr. Henry. You told the truth to that TV camera. Maybe it wasn't Buck McHenry's truth, but it was your truth."

"Jessie, truth is a lie when it comes from a liar's mouth."

"Mr. Henry, truth is truth no matter who says it. All you did was make up a story so you *could* tell the truth. Furthermore, Mr. Henry, you weren't alone in making up that story. You had help. Who was it first called you Buck McHenry?"

"Jason."

I winced.

"Yes, but who was it made it official? Me! It was me who told them you were Buck McHenry. And why did I do it? Because it was helping the boy. The boy's alive now. He's got friends. He's on a baseball team. And you're going to coach him. That's what's important, Mr. Henry. That's what you've got to keep your eye on."

"You don't understand, Jessie. There isn't any team. There's just three youngsters who think I'm Buck McHenry. And if there is a team, the boy isn't goin' to want me to coach him. When he finds out, he's going to be ashamed of me and he'll be right. I'm ashamed of myself. And this Axelrod fellow? What's goin' to happen to him when he goes on TV with this pack of lies? When the truth comes out, he'll probably get fired."

I hadn't even thought of that. I turned to look at Kim. My right elbow banged into one of the steel poles.

"Did you hear something outside, Mr. Henry?" Mrs. Henry asked.

My heart thumped so hard I thought they could also hear that. Kim was rigid.

Mr. Henry said, "People will be calling the TV station. People who knew Buck McHenry. Who might still know him. For all I know Buck McHenry himself'll call in. If he's still alive. That darn baseball card of Jason's. That's where it all started. If it wasn't for that card, none of this would've happened."

"Well, it's happened, Mr. Henry. And the worst possible thing would be for Aaron to hear about it from someone else. All you got to do now is . . ."

We lost her next words, because just then there was a blast of TV noise. The door had opened. Over the noise we heard Aaron say, "Grandma, can I get somethin' to eat?"

We took off then. Kim and me, running close to the house. We didn't avoid the rectangles of light. If they didn't hear us, they wouldn't look for us.

We ran to the front of the house, grabbed our bikes, and ran them to the front gate. Kim unlatched the gate and went through it. I latched it behind us. That was risky, but I hate leaving people's gates open. She waited for me. She didn't know how to get home.

"This way," I said, and those would be the only words either of us said until we reached Washtenaw and Devonshire.

We didn't talk because there was nothing to say. One moment you're sitting on top of the world, the next moment you're living in a nightmare.

20

We biked hard. Mostly because Kim was pushing it. I didn't know what the big rush was. What was going to happen was going to happen. Fate was in charge of us.

We biked past teenagers, college students, people getting in and out of cars, taxicabs. We biked past people waiting at bus stops, waiting to get into a theater. We biked past people eating ice-cream cones outside a fancy ice-cream store. We biked past people sitting on stone benches. It seemed like half of Arborville was hanging out that night. Which was okay since it meant they wouldn't be watching *Sportsline*.

When we came to the spot where Devonshire came into Washtenaw, I pointed it out to Kim just the way earlier today I'd pointed it out to Aaron. Although now that seemed like years ago.

"You live four houses up."

She nodded, and when there was a break in the traffic she bounced her bike over the curb and crossed Washtenaw, standing up, pedaling hard. I watched her for a moment and then I pedaled slowly home. I was running out of gas. I was exhausted.

When I got to our house, I put my bike in the garage. Then I went and sat on the steps to get some breath and calm inside my body. I must have sat on our front steps for five minutes before I felt calmer. Then I went inside the house.

The TV set was on. Mom and Dad were watching it.

"Has it started?" I asked, alarmed.

"Not yet. There's still a few minutes," Dad said. "Where are Kim and Aaron?"

"They're not coming."

"I thought you were going to watch the show together."

"We're not."

I sat down on the sofa. Not facing the TV. I didn't want to watch the TV.

"Are you all right, Jason?" Mom asked.

"Sure."

"What's the matter, Jason?" Dad asked. "What happened?"

You can never fool people who love you.

"Everything's the matter," I said. "Everything." And then I started to cry. Out of nowhere I started to cry.

Mom came and put her arms around me. "Jason, whatever it is, it's all right."

"It's not all right," I sobbed. "And it never will be."

I wept. Like a baby in his mother's arms. Finally, I forced myself to stop.

"Do you want to tell us what's going on?" Dad asked.

"No." I wiped my face on my Baer Machine shirt.

They didn't say anything. Just looked at me with concern.

"All right. I'll tell you."

And then, not looking at them, looking at the carpet at my feet, I told them that Mr. Henry wasn't really Buck McHenry. That he'd gone along with it because I wanted him to and because of Aaron. I told my folks about Aaron. And I told them how Kim and I heard Mr. Henry confess the truth on his back porch. And how he cried because he'd told these lies to the camera and how scared he was now that they would come out. He was scared too for Aaron to find out. What would Aaron think of him? What would everyone in Arborville think of him? What

216

would the Baer Machine kids who all went to Eberwoods School where he worked think of him? Because sooner or later the truth would come out. Wouldn't it, Dad? Wouldn't it, Mom? Wouldn't the truth come out? On TV, in the newspapers, everywhere?

They didn't say anything. Which meant it would.

I almost started to cry again. Mom got me a Kleenex.

"Blow your nose," she said.

"None of it would have happened if only I'd minded my own business. Thanks." I blew my nose.

"You made a mistake, Jason, that's all," Mom said. "It was a mistake of enthusiasm. You just wanted things to be a certain way."

"You wrote a scenario for real life," Dad said, "and real life came and bopped you on the nose."

"I wouldn't mind it if it was just my nose that got bopped."

Dad laughed. "You'll be all right, Jason. And your Mr. Henry will be all right too." He looked at his watch. "Come. There may still be time to do something about it."

"What can we do?"

Dad lead the way to the kitchen. "Call Chuck Axelrod and ask him to kill the story."

217

"It's too late."

"Maybe not. Maybe the story's late in the show. There are commercials to get through at the beginning of every show."

"Who're you calling?"

"Directory assistance for Channel 4."

"What are you going to say to him?"

"I'm not going to say anything. You are. You'll talk to him."

"What will I say?"

"Just what you told us. I'd like the phone number for Channel 4, Detroit, operator."

"Suppose he doesn't believe me?"

"Then you'll have done all you can do." Dad repeated the phone number out loud to himself and started dialing again.

"It's ringing." He handed me the phone. "I'll go upstairs and get on the phone in the hall."

The phone rang at Channel 4. Dad started down the back hall to the stairs.

"WDIV, Channel 4 Detroit . . ." a telephone voice began.

"It's starting," Mom called out.

"Can I help you?"

"No," I said.

I hung up the phone and went into the living room.

Chuck Axelrod was on the screen, smiling into the camera saying, "On this week's edition of *Sportsline* we have a unique, heartwarming baseball story for you. It's local too. So stay tuned for *Sportsline!*"

"Dad," I called, "it's too late."

"I see that," Dad said. He was in the room. He came and stood next to me. On the screen there appeared a rapid succession of sports shots. Great plays in basketball, football, baseball, hockey.

And then an announcer's voice said over them, "*Sportsline* with Chuck Axelrod is brought to you by . . ." There followed the list of sponsors. Beer, cars, airlines, automobile tires, riding lawn mowers . . .

"Both of you, sit down," Mom said.

Dad sat down. I didn't. I wanted to run upstairs and jump into bed and pull the covers over my head.

"Come on, Jason," Dad said. "Sit down."

I shook my head.

"Life is going to go on, Jason. It's going to be all right."

No, I thought, it wouldn't be all right. Not for Mr. Henry. Not for Aaron. Not for Chuck Axelrod. And not for me. The only thing that could save the four of us now was if a bolt of lightning hit the TV station, or an earthquake swallowed up Detroit.

On the TV the commercials went on and on and on. For once I wished they'd never end.

21

But end they did and once more Chuck Axelrod's face appeared on the screen.

"Before we get to tonight's feature story," he said, "we have highlights of this afternoon's Tiger victory over the California Angels."

That's what they always do to you on TV. Tell you something is coming up and you keep tuned and then something else comes. In this case, a highlights tape.

Usually I love highlights—the great catches, home runs, steals—but right now I wasn't seeing them. I was picturing in my mind Aaron in his living room with Mr. and Mrs. Henry watching their TV set. Had Mr. Henry told Aaron the truth yet? Probably. Was Aaron sore at his grampa? Was he ashamed of him the way Mr. Henry said he'd be? That would be awful. Was Aaron sore at me? My head felt like it would burst.

"Jason, go to the refrigerator and get yourself some juice," Mom said.

"I'm not thirsty."

Next I pictured Kim in her big empty living room watching and waiting for the axe to fall. On her father. Because when the show was over, people were going to start calling Channel 4 to say that Mr. Henry wasn't Buck McHenry at all and that Chuck Axelrod was full of hot air and wrong facts.

Maybe Buck McHenry's family would call. Maybe, like Mr. Henry said, Buck McHenry himself would call. Oh God, why couldn't I turn my mind off?

Finally the highlights were over.

"I guess I will get a glass of juice," I said.

But then there were more commercials so I didn't have to leave. Mom turned to Dad. "Dick, isn't there something else on TV we could watch?"

"Jean, we have to watch this. If for no other reason than to know what Mr. Henry is in for."

"And Chuck Axelrod," I said.

"Yes, and Chuck Axelrod too."

"And Aaron. Especially if they haven't told him."

"Jason, stop picking on yourself."

"Dad, I started it all."

"You may have started it, but Mr. Henry picked up the ball and ran with it. He didn't have to go along with it, you know."

"He did though." My voice was getting hysterical. "For Aaron's sake."

"Jason, it's no one's fault. It's just something that happened," Mom said.

"It wouldn't have happened if I'd kept my big mouth shut and not tried to write scenarios, as Dad said."

"Shsh," Dad said.

The commercials ended. For a second the screen was blank and then—I gasped. There, larger than life, was my Buck McHenry card.

"Today's feature story," Chuck Axelrod's voice said as we looked at the card, "begins with a very unusual baseball card. A card of a famous pitcher in the old Negro leagues, the only organized baseball leagues black men could play in till Jackie Robinson broke the color barrier.

"This man's name was Buck McHenry, and he was ranked along with the great Satchel Paige as one of the great right-handed pitchers in the old Negro leagues."

There now flashed on the screen a series of old black-and-white pictures of stars from the old Negro leagues. Between the time he left Sampson Park and the show went on the air,

Chuck Axelrod had done research, got pictures, facts. No wonder he was famous. He worked hard. I felt so sorry for what was going to happen to him.

"McHenry pitched against immortals like Cool Papa Bell, Josh Gibson, Martin Dihigo, Oscar Huddleston, Buck Leonard . . . the list could go on and on. Unlike many of these great black ballplayers, Buck McHenry had only a three-year career in the Negro leagues. But a tremendous three years they were. In each of those years, Buck McHenry won thirty games or more. And there were those who claimed his fastball was better than Satchel Paige's. Faster than Bob Feller's, who was the king of smoke in the major leagues."

The Buck McHenry card came back on the screen, only this time it was the stats side. You could just about read it.

"From the back of Buck McHenry's baseball card we learn that after he suddenly and inexplicably quit baseball, he took a job as a school custodian right here in our own state of Michigan."

Chuck Axelrod was back on camera. He had jumped right over the scrapes with the law. For a split second hope rose inside me. But then I remembered that Mr. Henry had covered that in the interview taped in the park.

"Dad, could Mr. Henry go to jail for pretending to be Buck McHenry?"

"No. Shsh."

"If he did, would you defend him?"

"Yes. Be quiet."

Well, that was something anyway.

On the screen Chuck Axelrod was saying, "Today, on a Little League baseball diamond . . ."

"I've got to go to the bathroom," I announced. I really did. I wasn't fooling. That sometimes happens when I'm scared.

The sound of the TV followed me all the way to the toilet off the kitchen.

". . . in Arborville we *thought* we had rediscovered Buck McHenry."

I got as far as the bathroom door when I heard "we *thought* we had rediscovered." He had stressed "thought," not we.

I ran back into the living room. "Did you hear what he said? He said that—"

I stopped and stared. There we all were. On TV. The Baer Machine guys—Kevin and Cal and Tim and Tug and Art and Greg and Pete— and there I was and there were Aaron and Kim and then the camera zoomed in on Mr. Henry, who was talking to us.

"Jason, you're catching," he was saying. "Get

225

your gear on, boy. Aaron, you're pitching. Young lady, you're going to have to play everywhere else. You just play each . . ."

Chuck Axelrod's voice came back over Mr. Henry's.

"*Sportsline* had received a tip that Buck McHenry had changed his name to Mack Henry and was the custodian at Eberwoods School in Arborville. And further, that he was going to coach a new team in the Arborville eleven-year-old league called The Grandstand.

"This tip came from an Arborville youngster who collected baseball cards, who discovered the Buck McHenry card and decided Mr. Mack Henry was Buck McHenry . . ."

My heart pounded.

"There you are, Jason," Mom said. She wasn't even listening. She was just waiting to see me on TV.

And there I was, warming up Aaron.

"This *Sportsline* feature story belongs to that youngster who collected the Buck McHenry card as well as to two others. Two young people new to Arborville, one a girl named Kim Axelrod, my daughter . . ."

There was a shot of Kim smacking her fist in her glove.

". . . and a boy named Aaron Henry who for-

226

merly played Little League baseball in Tennessee. Aaron Henry was recovering from a family tragedy."

How did he find out about that? How did he learn that maybe Mr. Henry wasn't— And then it hit me. Why Kim had wanted to get away from Mr. Henry's house so fast. And why she had pedaled so hard to her house. She was a hundred steps ahead of me.

"Aaron had lost his father and mother and older brother in an automobile accident and had moved up to Michigan to live with his grandparents and start a new life up here. Our third youngster is our card collector, Jason Ross."

I thought I would faint. Blood rushed to my temples. There was a close-up of me catching. I was glad I had my mask on.

"Earlier that day Jason Ross had been cut from another team . . ."

Why did he have to mention that?

". . . in fact, the very team the newly formed Grandstand team was having a practice game against this afternoon. Unfortunately The Grandstand only had three players. But they did have the great Buck McHenry coaching them—or so we thought at the time."

A hundred steps ahead of me? A thousand. Light-years.

"However, life doesn't always have a storybook happy ending—or does it?" Chuck Axelrod went on. "Just before we went on the air I learned from a close source"—very close, I thought—"that Mr. Mack Henry wasn't the great Buck McHenry after all. Yes, he was a school custodian in Arborville. Yes, he had played baseball in the South before integration. But never in the Negro leagues. Mack Henry was one of those hundreds of young black ballplayers who traveled from town to town in old cars, old busses, trying to pick up a dollar or two playing local teams, and playing under all kinds of circumstances, on all kinds of fields, in front of all kinds of spectators. Often taking all kinds of abuse. You see, folks, the history of the black baseball player in America is more than a history of the Negro leagues and its great stars—the Satchel Paiges, the Josh Gibsons, the Cool Papa Bells, the Buck McHenrys. It's also the story and history of those who received no glory, who received no pay, who played in bumpy cow pastures in town after town, challenging the local teams, playing because they loved to play baseball. Today perhaps these men would be called journeyman players in the major leagues, .250 hitters in the major leagues. But they'd be up there, make no mistake about that. Not stars.

Not Hank Aarons, Ricky Hendersons, Willie Mays, but firmly placed in the constellation of all those who contributed to America's national pastime. They never had a chance to get their names and statistics onto the bubble gum baseball cards that America's youth collect today with such knowledgeability. But these men belong there. They played, lived, and died believing that America's national game was theirs too. And, as it turned out, it was."

"He would have made a fantastic trial lawyer," Dad said softly.

"No, Mack Henry, custodian at Eberwoods School, wasn't the legendary Buck McHenry that young Jason Ross thought he was. He was, if anything, something more. For today on a Little League diamond in Arborville, Michigan"— Chuck Axelrod broke into a wide grin—"Mr. Mack Henry, an old semipro ballplayer from the South, did something we suspect the great Buck McHenry never did."

"What was that?" Mom asked.

"Shsh," Dad said. The picture on the screen changed.

x

229

22

The game had started. Aaron was pitching. Kevin was taking strike after strike. And Chuck Axelrod was saying, "What Mr. Mack Henry did today was take three kids and coach them to victory over nine. Three players beat nine."

There was a shot of Kim getting on base. And then of Aaron hitting his home run. And Aaron striking out player after player and then shots of all of us shaking hands, and Tug saying simply, "You're good, man."

And then as the handshaking went on, a shot of Mr. Henry smiling as he watched everyone shake hands. "We don't know where the real Buck McHenry is today," Chuck Axelrod said quietly. "We hope he's alive, well, and happy. We do know where the real Mack Henry is.

"He's coaching a team called The Grandstand in the Arborville eleven-year-old league. And

230

it's a team looking for more players."

Now Chuck Axelrod was back on camera and in the studio.

"So we end a rather unusual *Sportsline* feature story with an appeal: If there are any eleven-year-old youngsters in Arborville watching this show right now who are not presently on a team and want to play for The Grandstand and be coached by Mr. Mack Henry, you are hereby asked to call Jason Ross at . . ."

And then he gave our number. Right there on TV. It was even shown!

Dad groaned. Mom laughed. My heart thumped with each digit. Then he repeated our phone number again and my heart thumped some more.

After that, commercials came on and Dad turned off the set. Then he looked at me. His face was somber. "Well, Jason, you did it. Thanks to you, our home phone number was broadcast to the whole world."

"Just southeast Michigan, Dick," Mom said.

And with that Dad started to laugh. And I laughed with him. "Wasn't it great what he did, Dad? He never mentioned what happened at all. Mr. Henry making that speech. He never showed it. You know, it's too bad in a way, be-

231

cause it was a great speech Mr. Henry made to us about a game he played in a long time ago."

"Jason, if I know Chuck Axelrod, and I think I do after tonight's show, the way he could make a story out of a nonstory, he'll use Mr. Henry's speech some other place, some other time."

"He made something out of nothing, didn't he? Just the way the old black ballplayers did. Chuck Axelrod's a genius. Don't you think he's a genius, Mom?"

"Yes. Certainly. But how did he find out—"

"It had to be Kim. I'm going to call her right now. She's a genius too."

I ran to the phone. Just as I got there it rang. I picked it up. "Kim," I said, "you did it!"

"Is this Jason Ross?" A strange voice asked.

"Uh . . . yeah."

"My name's Jerry Kelly. I'm eleven years old and I used to be a first baseman in Ohio. We just moved here last week. I was watching *Sportsline*. I'd like to try out for The Grandstand team. The one that was on TV just now. We live in Arborville. On Arborview Boulevard."

"That's . . . great. I better write your name and phone number down. Could you hold on?"

I put my hand over the phone.

232

"It's a kid who wants to be on our team," I shouted.

"Now it starts," Dad said.

I got a pencil and wrote down Jerry Kelly's name and phone number and told him that Mr. Henry or I would call him back.

"He sounds like a great coach," Jerry Kelly said.

"He is," I said.

No sooner did I hang up when the phone rang again. And it was another new kid in town who'd seen *Sportsline* and was eleven years old and wanted to play on The Grandstand team. I took his name and number too.

That was just the beginning. For no sooner did I hang up on his call when the phone rang again. And it was still another kid. And after him, still another. The phone started ringing off the hook. Kid after kid after kid called.

Who would have believed there were that many new eleven-year-old kids in town? And then, wouldn't you know it, I started getting calls from some of the kids we had tried to recruit earlier today and couldn't. Andy van Gasse called. And Victor Perles. And two more kids who'd said they didn't want to play but now had changed their minds. All in all before the phone stopped ringing, I had taken down fifteen names and phone numbers.

"Mom, Dad," I yelled, "we've got a team. A full team and then some."

"From all those calls I think you could start a separate league," Dad said. "Come here and tell us about it."

The phone rang again. Here we go again, I thought.

"Hello."

"Hello," a familiar voice said.

I was so startled I forgot I had been going to call her.

"Kim," I said, "you did it. You really did it. It was you, wasn't it, who called your dad?"

"Yeah."

"I didn't even think of it, I was so scared."

"I was scared too."

"And your dad was so great. He's a genius."

"He's okay. Did you get calls?"

"Are you kidding? As soon as the show ended kids started calling. New kids in town. And some of the kids who turned us down before. Kim, I've got fifteen names, and some of the new kids sound good."

"Did you tell Mr. Henry and Aaron?"

"No."

234

"You better, Jason. I hope he still wants to coach us."

"Why wouldn't he?"

"Come on, Jason. We heard him say he was Buck McHenry. Maybe he won't want to face us."

She was right. I hadn't even thought of that. And worse, I thought, how was Mr. Henry going to face the Baer Machine kids at Eberwoods School on Monday? And suppose Aaron was ashamed and didn't want to play?

"You still there, Jason?"

"Yeah."

"Are you going to call Mr. Henry and Aaron?"

"Would you do it for me, Kim?"

"Come on, Jason. You're captain. You've also got the names of the new kids. We've got to have a practice tomorrow."

She was right. We had to have a practice tomorrow. We were behind enough as it was. This would be a very hard phone call to make, but I had to grit my teeth and call and find out if Mr. Henry was still willing to coach us and if Aaron was still willing to be on the team.

"Okay, I'll call."

"And call me back," she said.

"Come on in here, Jason," Dad called out.

"I've got one more call to make."

"Who are you going to call now?"

"Mr. Henry. Kim said I had to. She's right."

"Can't you call him tomorrow?" Mom said. "It's getting late."

"It'll be too late tomorrow, Mom. We've got to have a practice tomorrow."

"He better call Mr. Henry," Dad said. "But Jason, make this the last one. Okay?"

"Okay."

The phone rang only once in the Henry house when Mrs. Henry answered it. She must have been sitting on it. Guarding him. People must have been calling them already, I thought dismally.

"Mrs. Henry, it's me. Jason Ross."

Silence. I couldn't tell whether it was a hostile silence or what. Nervously, I filled it.

"Mrs. Henry, did you . . . uh . . . see . . . uh?"

More silence.

"Mrs. Henry, I . . . didn't mean . . . to, uh, make trouble for Mr. Henry."

She hates me, I thought. I don't blame her.

"Who is it this time, Jessie?" I heard Mr. Henry's voice in the background.

"Jason Ross."

Pause. Then, "I want to talk to him."

236

Now I was in for it. Even his footsteps coming to the phone sounded angry. Kim should have called him. He'd have a harder time being angry at her.

"Jason?"

"Mr. Henry, what I was, uh, calling about is, uh." I stopped. Breathed in. "Did you see the *Sportsline* show, Mr. Henry?" This was awful. I wasn't handling this very well.

"Yes, boy. I saw it. Did you?"

I gulped. "Yes, sir. I thought, uh, it was a, uh, good show."

Silence. "Did you?" I couldn't tell what he was thinking.

Change the subject, I thought. "Mr. Henry, I got fifteen calls from kids who want to play on our team. I got all their names and phone numbers and Kim thinks we should have a practice tomorrow at Sampson Park if it's, uh, okay with you. . . ." My voice died.

More silence. This was it. We either had a coach or we didn't.

"You mean you kids still want me to coach you?"

"Oh, Mr. Henry." My eyes suddenly felt wet again. "Mr. Henry, you're a great coach."

"I'm not Buck McHenry, Jason."

"I'm glad you're not, Mr. Henry."

He laughed. And a load flew off my back on the wings of his laughter. To hear that familiar laugh. It was music.

"Boy, I was telling stories."

"It was my fault, Mr. Henry. I insisted that you were Buck McHenry."

"How did Chuck Axelrod find out, Jason?"

He asked it so fast I wasn't prepared. It was like being fast pitched. I didn't know what to say. I couldn't tell him that Kim and I were trapped below his porch and heard his confession and, worse, heard him cry. This was just terrible.

My silence went on and on. Finally he broke it. "Maybe someday I'll ask the man himself," he said. Then he laughed. "And then again, maybe I won't. It doesn't always pay to inquire too closely into things. Especially when they come out all right in the end. Jason, those kids who called. You tell them to be at Sampson Park tomorrow."

"What time?" I tried to keep the elation out of my voice. I tried to sound matter-of-fact.

"Let's make it one thirty."

"I'll call them right away. How's, uh . . . how's Aaron?"

"He's right here. You want to talk with him?"

"Could I?"

"Aaron, you want to talk with Jason?"

238

⁜"Yeah," I heard Aaron say.

Mr. Henry said to him, "Jason got fifteen more players for our team."

I didn't hear Aaron's response to that, but a second later he was on the phone.

"Jason," he said.

"How're you doing, man?" I was trying to sound cool.

"Okay. How you doing?"

"Okay." I took a deep breath. "You see the show?"

"Yep. My grampa isn't Buck McHenry."

"I know. It's okay though, isn't it?"

"Wait a second. Grampa, what're you standing round here for?"

I didn't hear what Mr. Henry said. But Aaron then said, "Because I want to talk private with Jason, Grampa. That's why."

Mrs. Henry's voice sounded in the background sharp and clear. "Let them talk privately, Mr. Henry."

Silence. Then I guess Aaron was alone with the phone. "You still there, Jason?"

"Yeah."

"I saw you."

For a moment I didn't understand what he said. He said it so fast.

"What'd you say?"

239

"We saw you. Me and my grandma."

"What're you talking about, man?"

"Me and my grandma saw you and Kim."

"On TV, you mean?"

I was getting goose bumps. I didn't think he was talking about the TV show at all.

"No. Before then. Grampa heard someone moving around outside the house. He checked the back. Grandma and I checked the front. We saw you and Kim running with your bikes out front."

My knees felt weak. I sat down on a kitchen stool.

"You still there, Jason?"

Barely, I thought. "I'm still here."

"You found out about my grampa then, didn't you?"

"Yes."

"And that's how come Mr. Axelrod found out, isn't it?"

"Yes. Kim called him."

"That's what Grandma and I figured. Grampa doesn't know how he found out."

I said nothing.

"You still there, Jason?"

"Yeah."

"Chuck Axelrod was good on TV, wasn't he?"

A flood of relief came over me. Aaron wasn't

240

sore. He wasn't sore at me. He wasn't sore at Kim. And most important of all, he didn't sound sore at his grandfather.

"He was great."

"Jason?"

"Yeah."

"My grandma says Grampa made all that stuff up on account of me."

"And me. Aaron?"

"What?"

"I was scared you'd be sore at your grampa."

"Oh, I never believed that stuff anyway."

He wasn't telling the truth. He'd believed just the way I'd believed it, and Kim and her dad and the Baer Machine kids had believed it. We'd all believed. But it was all right. It didn't matter now.

"Did your grampa tell you about the practice tomorrow?" I asked him.

"No."

"Well, we got one. At Sampson Park at one thirty. I've got to say good-bye now. I've got to call fifteen kids. Hey, would you like to call some, Aaron?"

"Sure."

"You could call five kids. I could call five. And Kim could call five. How does that sound?"

"Sounds good. Lemme get a pencil."

And that's what happened. Aaron called five kids. I called up Kim and told her what happened and she agreed to call five kids.

After that I started calling my five kids. I had just started on the first one when Dad came into the kitchen and stared at me. "Jason, you promised."

"Almost all through," I said cheerfully. "Hello, is this Jerry Kelly? Jerry, this is Jason Ross, captain of The Grandstand team. You called me earlier. Well, good news, man, we're going to have a team. Mr. Henry's called a practice for one thirty tomorrow at Sampson Park. Can you make it? Great. Let me tell you how to get there. . . ."

23

We had a great practice the next day. And after that, for game after game after game, we had a great season.

We wound up in third place behind the Bank and Baer Machine. Aaron pitched shutout ball every time out, but the rules are that no kid can pitch more than four innings a game and we didn't have anyone that good after him.

Kim turned out to be one of the best second basemen, excuse me, base persons, in the league. She and Aaron made the all-star team. I didn't. But I got my share of hits and believe it or not some were leg hits, ground balls that I beat out to first. One ground ball I hit against the Bank team I can still hear Mr. Henry shouting, "Hot coals, boy. Hot coals." Reminding me not to look where I hit the ball. Just pick up my feet and run. Which I did. That lesson in the school corridor seemed a long time ago.

Jim Davis wasn't able to get away from the store for any of our games except our first game against Baer Machine. And that was when he met Mr. Henry for the first time.

Jim had a camera around his neck. He stuck out his hand and said to Mr. Henry, "So you're the one Jason insisted was Buck McHenry?"

I almost died. But Mr. Henry chuckled and said, "Not only Jason. I insisted on it too . . . for a while."

Jim thought he was kidding. He laughed. So did Mr. Henry. I sort of smiled weakly.

That game against Baer Machine was the game I worried about most. It wasn't just the game that I worried about. School hadn't yet ended and I worried that the Baer Machine kids had told everyone who went to Eberwoods School about Mr. Henry pretending to be Buck McHenry.

But they hadn't. Aaron told me his grampa said no kid at Eberwoods ever said a thing to him about the Buck McHenry business. Maybe Mr. Borker had something to do with it. He didn't turn out to be such a bad guy after all. Aaron said his grampa told him the kids were respectful to him the rest of the school year.

But would they be respectful in a game situation when it looked like they might lose? Would there be some nasty bench jockeying by them? There wasn't. I think it was mostly because of Aaron's fastball. They knew it wouldn't pay to get Aaron mad. He threw hard enough when he was being friendly. We beat them on their own diamond at Eberwoods, 5–2. They got two runs off Jerry Kelly, who relieved Aaron in the fifth inning. Incidentally, they never called us "bubble gum ballplayers" either, which I was sure they would from the way they used to tease me about my baseball cards. I think they laid off because we were a good team. You never want to rile up a good team.

That game, as I said, was the only one Jim Davis saw, and at that I'm not sure he saw much of it. He spent most of the game taking pictures of everyone. Including Mr. Henry.

Later, we found out why.

About a week after the season ended, Jim gave a team party down at The Grandstand. It was a Sunday afternoon and Jim closed The Grandstand early, which was something since Sunday's his biggest day after Saturday. We had the party in the middle of the main room, smack in the middle of baseball cards, posters, pennants, T-shirts, all the stuff. Jim had ice cream, pizza, pop. Halfway through the party he made a little speech.

"I want to thank all the players who made this such a fantastic season. The Grandstand team didn't exist before the season started and we came in among the top teams. I never had the time to take you kids for pizzas or Dairy Queens. So I'm trying to make up for it now. Also I have a little present for each of you."

Jim then gave each of us a baseball card of ourself. In color. In our Grandstand uniform, batting or running or fielding or throwing. They were made from the pictures he'd taken during the Baer Machine game.

On top of each card our position was listed and so was the name of The Grandstand and its address. Jim's always the businessman.

On the back side, the stats side, it told how we batted and threw and there was inside scoop on each of us.

About me, it said,

JASON ROSS, 11, catcher, bats right, throws right, captain of team, and among those responsible for The Grandstand team being formed.

About Aaron, it said:

AARON HENRY, 11, pitcher, throws right, bats right, voted MVP in Arborville eleven-year-old league, and among those responsible for The Grandstand team being formed. All-Star.

And about Kim, it said:

KIM AXELROD, 11, second base, bats right, throws right, tough, feisty ballplayer, good hitter, fastest runner on team, among those responsible for The Grandstand team being formed. All-Star.

Jim also had a card for Mr. Henry. When he gave it to him, there was applause and everyone crowded round to have a look at it. Mr. Henry read it, chuckled, and passed it around.

It was a picture of him coaching during the Baer Machine game. On the stats side it said:

MACK HENRY, former pitcher in semipro leagues in the South, was winning coach in his first year in Arborville eleven-year-old league. Also responsible for The Grandstand team being formed.

It was a swell card, and it linked him and me and Aaron and Kim. Which was as it should be.

Jim also took a lot of kidding about The Grandstand being mentioned so many times. It was a great party.

One Saturday afternoon in the fall Kim and I biked over to Aaron's house with our baseball cards. Mr. Henry was there. Kim's cards were every bit as good as I expected. I brought my best and showed them. My 1955 Mays, my Diamond Stars. Kim showed her incredibly expensive 1952 Mantle. And before you knew it we were back in the discussion about why Mantle's cards were always worth more than Mays's, even for the same years when Mays had the better stats.

I told them what Jim had said about the market determining the price of a card and how it was mostly white kids who collected.

Aaron was very quiet. Mr. Henry, who had been listening, said, "I think Mr. Davis is right. Question is, is he always going to be right?"

I looked up at Mr. Henry. The three of us were seated on the floor. "You mean will more black kids start collecting?"

"I mean more than that, boy. I'm asking if folks'll ever collect baseball cards without noticing what the color of the man's skin on the card is."

None of us had the answer to that.

That evening I repeated Mr. Henry's question to Dad. Would folks ever collect baseball cards without noticing what the color of the man's skin on the card is?

"Jason, I don't have any idea," Dad said.

"Da-ad," I insisted.

Dad looked at me. He was silent for a while, and then he said, "Jason, I think people will only become color-blind about cards when they become color-blind about people."

248

"When will people become color-blind about people?"

Dad shook his head ruefully. "And I used to think collecting baseball cards was a mindless hobby. Jason, I don't know if people will ever be decent to each other."

"I think someday they will."

"Do you? Well, maybe your generation will have better luck making it happen than ours did."

"We will," I said.

"I hope so," Dad said.

Aaron has started collecting baseball cards. Only his collection is getting smaller instead of getting bigger. He started with two cards besides his own, and now he's down to one.

The first card was the Buck McHenry card — the card that started me off on my search for a legend.

The second card was the card Jim made up for his grampa, Mr. Henry.

So far so good. But then Aaron did a crazy thing. He glued the two cards together on their stats sides so that they made one card. I was shocked.

"What'd you do that for?" I asked him. You're never supposed to fool with baseball cards. You want to keep them in mint condition, if you can.

"They go together, Jason," he said.

"Maybe, but you've ruined the Buck McHenry card. Now you can't trade it or do anything with it."

"I don't want to do anything with it, Jason. I just want to look at it."

And look he did. And I looked with him. What else could you do with that card? We turned it over and over, from young powerful strong Buck McHenry to gray-haired old Mr. Henry back to Buck McHenry again. And after a while that card began to grow on me.

True, it wasn't really a baseball card anymore. It had no value. You couldn't trade it or sell it or do anything with it. All you could do was look at it.

I looked at it, and I remembered that day back in April when I set out to find Buck McHenry and found old Mr. Henry. The day I went looking for a legend and found a man.

"Aaron," I heard myself say, "I'll trade you for that card."

Aaron just laughed.